Sustaining Air

Modern and Contemporary Poetics

Series Editors
Charles Bernstein
Hank Lazer

Series Advisory Board
Maria Damon
Rachel Blau DuPlessis
Alan Golding
Susan Howe
Nathaniel Mackey
Jerome McGann
Harryette Mullen
Aldon Nielsen
Marjorie Perloff
Joan Retallack
Ron Silliman
Jerry Ward

Sustaining Air

THE LIFE OF
LARRY EIGNER

JENNIFER BARTLETT

THE UNIVERSITY OF ALABAMA PRESS
Tuscaloosa

The University of Alabama Press
Tuscaloosa, Alabama 35487-0380
uapress.ua.edu

Copyright © 2023 by the University of Alabama Press
All rights reserved.

Inquiries about reproducing material from this work should be addressed to the University of Alabama Press.

Typeface: Warnck Pro and Courier New

Cover images: Photographs of Larry Eigner; courtesy of the Larry Eigner Estate
Cover design: Danielle Guy

Cataloging-in-Publication data is available from the Library of Congress.
ISBN: 978-0-8173-6081-8
E-ISBN: 978-0-8173-9458-5

for larry

A Gloucester child grows up beside the sea.
The song of the surf is his first lullaby.
When he swings high on a swing, the sea is under his shoes.
—*Gloucester's Golden Age of Fishing*

Contents

Foreword: Getting Things Together   ix
by George Hart

Preface   xiii

Acknowledgments   xvii

Larry Eigner's Calendar   1
compiled by George Hart

1. The Eigners and the Polanskys   7
2. Laurence Joel Eigner   11
3. Robin Hood's Barn   15
4. The Idea of the "Boy Poet"   19
5. Ten Words a Minute!   23
6. This Is Poetry   29
7. Here We All Are   34
8. Olson   38
9. Camp Jened   42
10. The Little Magazines   49
11. The Glassed-In Porch   57
12. Black Mountain College   63
13. Hidden Form   68
14. A Beeaut-i-ful TV   84
15. On My Eyes   91

16. Nel Mezzo del Cammin   96
17. Another Time in Fragments   101
18. Denmark's a Prison   106
19. A Temporary Language   112
20. The Cornerstone House   118
21. McGee Avenue   125
22. Later Life   133

List of Abbreviations   137
Notes   139
Bibliography   163
Index   171

Photographs follow page 73.

Foreword

Getting Things Together

George Hart

I discovered Larry Eigner's poetry in a used bookstore on University Avenue in Palo Alto, when there were used bookstores on University Avenue in Palo Alto. It was toward the end of the last century, just as the Santa Clarita Valley was becoming Silicon Valley. I was beginning a dissertation on postmodern and neoromantic nature poetry, following the trajectory of postwar American poetics charted by my dissertation advisor, Albert Gelpi. The book was Eigner's *Waters / Places / A Time* (1983), edited by Robert Grenier, who had been a student of Al's at Harvard in the 1960s. Grenier had, around that time, concluded a ten-year stint as one of Eigner's caretakers and roommates in a household in Berkeley, just across the bay. Despite those few degrees of separation, no one had ever mentioned Eigner to me.

I am sure I picked the book up because of the cover. The colorful, geometric Black Sparrow Press design was familiar—I liked other poets published by that press. Then, like many other readers in their first experience seeing an Eigner poem, I was impressed by and intrigued with such spare, immediate, visually exact use of language on the page. It didn't take long to figure out that Eigner was the postmodern nature poet that I was looking for. *Waters / Places / A Time* itself provided some information. Beyond the poems themselves—so many great ones in this collection—the book includes a prime example of a Eigner specialty, the author's note. It tells us when he was born (1927) and where ("north of Boston, south of Gloucester," locating him as a New England poet between Robert Frost and Charles Olson), and says that he had cerebral palsy and had moved from the East Coast to the West Coast in 1978. It also comments on how meaning is (possibly) made and what the scope of a poet's interests (near or far) may entail. What else did one need to know?

Jennifer Bartlett's *Sustaining Air* tells us, filling in this bare outline of Eigner's background, life, and poetics. In his note, Eigner himself wonders what facts like birth dates, locations, and cerebral palsy have to do with one another: "how much things (can be got to) go together (work) is some mystery." Bartlett gets these things together, and we see how a child of immigrant and first-generation parents, who had significant disabilities, discovered and joined a company of poetic innovators. Location was a determining factor; as we learn in Bartlett's account of Eigner's childhood and schooling, proximity to Boston's teaching hospitals and research institutes provided access to early forms of disability services and special education.

Eigner's home in Swampscott, Massachusetts, also meant access to New England's cultural institutions based in Boston, primarily, but not exclusively, through radio and television. Cid Corman's radio program connected Eigner with another listener, Robert Creeley, and from there Eigner's contacts among postmodern Anglo-American poets grew. There is a persistent impression among readers that Eigner's life in the Swampscott years was one of isolation and immobility, but Bartlett opens a window into this time that shows us a very different scene. Although he preferred to socialize with other poets once he considered himself a writer, his family encouraged him to attend camps for young people with disabilities, took him on trips to Boston and New York City, and brought him to family events such as bar mitzvahs. The central person in his life in Swampscott was his mother, Bessie. Had Eigner been under the influence of another New England tradition, confessional poetry, we might have a portrait of Bessie and the Eigner clan in the mold of Robert Lowell's *Life Studies* (1959), shaped by childhood impressions and colored by memory. Eigner rarely wrote autobiographically, however, so the value of a biography is to provide such information as best it can. Bartlett has brought Bessie Eigner to life in what details can be gleaned from Eigner's vast correspondence and a few family heirlooms and recollections. Bessie Eigner's efforts to make sure her firstborn son could do whatever his abilities and interests let him do decades before the Americans with Disabilities Act are remarkable. Bartlett does not make her out to be a saint, to be sure, and the clashes between her and her equally strong-willed son, about everything from loud televisions to overflowing bookshelves to the family budget, portray the domestic scene we do not see directly in the poems.

We also get a better sense of what it meant for Eigner to join the company of postmodern poets as a person with disabilities. Bartlett tracks Eigner's efforts to publish collections of his work, beginning with Jargon Society's *On My Eyes* (1960). Because of his disabilities, Eigner required the assistance of an editor to select, arrange, and submit his poems to publishers. Along with Corman and Creeley, the New American poets, including Charles Olson, Denise Levertov, and Robert Duncan, were the first to help Eigner publish his work. Despite their, at times, ableist ideas about Eigner's embodiment, these poets' interest in reconnecting poetry to the body led to their support for his work. By the late 1960s, Eigner was actively seeking not only publication venues for his poetry but also a local community of writers with whom to share it. Bartlett introduces readers to Sam Borash, Eigner's poetry-loving, house painter friend, who took him to local writing workshops and poetry readings in the late 1960s and early 1970s. During this time, Eigner was discovered by the next generation of writers, Language poets such as Robert Grenier and Barrett Watten, who published his poems in their little magazines, included him in poetry readings, and invited him to visit their classes when they had academic appointments.

Language writing emerged in two distinct strains, one on the East Coast and one on the West Coast, so when it was determined that Eigner would move to the San Francisco Bay Area to be close to his brother Richard, there was a ready-made poetic community waiting for him. The move west is one of the most significant turning points in Eigner's life, and Bartlett's account of his experience in the independent living movement—first residing in a group home for people with disabilities, and then for ten years living with Grenier and Kathleen Frumkin, roommates and caretakers—demonstrates how rich and varied Eigner's experiences were in his new location. In his final years, Jack Foley, like Borash back in Swampscott, was Eigner's local buddy, who took him to readings, lectures, bookstores, and museums.

Larry Eigner's poetry continues to attract readers over two decades after his death. They come to his work not only for its precise use of language beautifully scored on the page, but also for its phenomenological richness, its commentary on poetry, society, ecology, and world events, its voice, its humor, and its humanity. Getting together the facts of Eigner's life, Jennifer Bartlett's *Sustaining Air* is the first complete portrait of one of the twentieth century's true poetic innovators.

Preface

I started reading biographies at a young age, beginning in middle school, when my father sent me a stack of books about the royal family. As a girl, I was obsessed with Lady Diana. The reason I love biographies is that I have always been interested in how other people live and move through the world. I am the kind of person who will glance into people's windows as I walk through the city.

My father, Lee Bartlett, is a poet, writer, and professor. When I was in high school, he published a biography of the poet Brother Antonius (William Everson). In addition to my own passion for reading about the lives of other people, his project had an influence on me. In graduate school, I wrote my dissertation on Muriel Rukeyser. What I found compelling about Rukeyser is how she redefined the word *poet*. While Rukeyser was certainly a poet and a great one at that, she also wrote biographies and novels. She was involved in direct action activism, was bisexual, and was a mother and a Communist. She had an FBI file. She also shared something with Larry Eigner: her work never has gotten enough recognition.

When I considered embarking on a biography, I considered writing about Rukeyser. However, in 2010, when Robert Grenier and Curtis Faville published the four-volume edition of Eigner's poems, my interest in the latter poet was renewed. My friend, the poet Charles Bernstein, facilitated a meeting between Grenier and me in October 2011. Grenier was Eigner's caregiver and housemate for ten years, his editor, and an unwavering supporter of his work. It quickly became apparent that the stars were aligned, and I had the support of Bernstein, Grenier, and the Eigner family, as well as my own. A project was born. Larry Eigner and I have three things in common: We are poets, we have cerebral palsy, and we have an unwavering passion for Charles Olson. Although my life has played out much differently than Eigner's, these commonalities make it possible for a particular insight and connection.

Eigner corresponded with many poets from North America working in the mid-twentieth century, as well as many from Europe and South America. He wrote to and received letters from everyone from Gerard Malanga, with a return address of Andy Warhol's Factory, to Margaret Randall during her time in Mexico. His archives hold letters from Louis Zukofsky, Larry Goodell, Daphne Marlatt, Hayden Carruth, Kenneth Irby, Jackson Mac Low, Jack Spicer, and Rosmarie Waldrop. He corresponded with editors such as Lawrence Ferlinghetti, Amiri Baraka, John Martin, James Weil, and, of course, Jonathan Williams. He also corresponded with many people not involved in the poetry world. Eigner had a lengthy correspondence with Arthur McFarland, a boatbuilder who lived in Friendship, Maine. Late in life, the poet had a robust correspondence with a physical therapist, Vance Morgan, who reached out to the poet to ask him questions about his poetry and disability. Even later in life, when he lived in Berkeley and had difficulty writing, he would correspond with whomever approached him. Given the depth of Eigner's correspondence, which also extended to family members, I have chosen to build his life directly out of his own words and those of the people who wrote to him. I had to choose a few poetic relationships to focus on, specifically Cid Corman, Robert Creeley, Denise Levertov, Jonathan Williams, Charles Olson, and Robert Duncan. It is important to note that, largely due to the circumstance of the time, Eigner's correspondence was nearly exclusively with white men. I also want to clarify that although Eigner and Olson have less than one handful of letters, it is apparent to me through following Eigner's thought processes, reading lists, and writing that Olson is the poet who influenced him the most.

Throughout the biography, I have used Eigner's poetry in many ways. Given that his poems were grounded in moments of time, I begin each chapter with a quote from a poem. Throughout the book, poems also function as part of the narrative. Finally, I provide a brief analysis of a few poems. Note that Eigner's poems have complex spacing and line breaks. The poems embedded within the text are printed in Courier font to replicate the monotype of Eigner's typewriter. The spacing of the poems is approximate. I have also attempted to replicate passages from Eigner's letters as close to the original.

Sustaining Air is written with disability justice in mind, and I use contemporary language when possible. According to the social justice model of disability, it is the environment that disables people, not our bodies. At times, I use the word *impairment* to describe Eigner's physicality. According to the social model, the word *impairment* is used to describe how an individual's circumstances make daily life difficult. The biography also means to clarify the myths that have surrounded Eigner's life and disability: *He couldn't walk.* He could. *He couldn't write by hand.* He did. *He didn't have any kind of formal education or leave his house until he moved to Berkeley in the late 1970s.* In our research, my dear friend and colleague George Hart and I found these myths to be untrue. I was also surprised to find that Eigner's first public reading was years before I thought, and that, once again, Charles Olson was his greatest influence, not Cid Corman. Corman was fundamental to Eigner's life in poetry, along with the support of Eigner's mother, Bessie; his brothers, Richard and Joseph; and Robert Grenier. Eigner would not have built a life as a poet in the way that he did without Corman. Corman was the first editor of Eigner's poetry, and he introduced Eigner to nearly every poet the latter corresponded with. Corman also had insight into Eigner's relationship with Bessie, his family life, and disability in a way that no other poet did. However, in the long run, Eigner took the most poetically from Olson, whom he referred to as *Dear Pro*. To help clarify Eigner's social life, I came up with the idea of creating a calendar. Hart quickly embarked on compiling the calendar, and the biography begins with it. In writing this book, I realized that Hart was *my* Cid Corman, and this would be a very different book without him.

As I was writing the final pages of Eigner's biography, one of my favorite writers, Paul Auster, released a long biography on Stephen Crane. I began to ruthlessly second-guess myself. How could I spend ten years writing a biography that is barely two hundred pages long? What was I leaving out? What did I miss? Although there are certainly many things I omitted, at the end of the day, this biography was written by a poet and therefore is not a typical, comprehensive biography. Rather, it is one poet speaking about another. *Sustaining Air* is meant to be a starting point, not an ending.

           Portland, Oregon, 2010—Laugarvatn, Iceland, 2020

Acknowledgments

Many people have supported this project in various ways over the twelve years it took me to complete it. Larry Eigner's biography could not have been possible without the support of the Eigner family, particularly Larry's brother Richard and his sister-in-law Beverly. The Eigners welcomed me into their home and gave me access to primary sources including photographs, letters, and books Eigner owned. I also want to thank Eigner's brother Joseph, his sister-in-law Janet, and his cousin Edwin, as well as Jon Polansky.

The biography could not have been possible without the support and help of Lee Bartlett and Anne Foltz, Charles Bernstein and Susan Bee, Hank Lazer, James Yeary, Roxann and Michael Foley, Eric Rydin, and Robert Grenier. I also want to thank wonderful people at the University of Alabama Press: Dan Waterman, Sara Hardy, Jessica Hinds-Bond, Blanche Sarratt, and Kelly Finefrock.

Throughout the process, I had editorial help from many people. I would like to thank Sue Landers, Natasha Dwyer, and Caroline Henze-Gongola and Francesca Capote.

I want to thank the wonderful librarians who were crucial to the project: Melissa Watterworth Batt at the Thomas J. Dodd Research Center at the University of Connecticut, James Maynard at the University of Buffalo, the librarians at the New York Public Library Berg Collection, and Carolyn Waters at the New York Society Library.

As I did not have institutional funding for the project, many people made financial donations to support this work. These include Samuel Ace, Royal Alvis, Shelly Andrews, Andrea Baker, Michael Bergelson, Jeff Bergman, Anselm Berrigan, Jay and Piley Bianchi, Nicholas Birns, Sheila Black, John Bloomberg-Rissman, Lary Bremmer, Ava Capote, Sean Carey,

Margaret Carson, Kate Colby, Norma Cole, CA Conrad, Kyle Dacuyan, Maria Damon, Alexis Danzig, Michael Davidson, Ian Demsky, Steve Dickison, Michael Eskin, Caiden Feldmiller, Jim Ferris, Gloria Frym, Knar Gavin, Lawrence Giffin, Jackie Goldenberg, Arnold Goldman, Anthony Green, Lynn Heginian, Owen Hill, Laura Hinton, Bob Holman, Janet Holmes, Jeff Hoover, Erica Hunt, Porter James, Lisa Jarnot, Pierre Joris, Joel Lewis, Peter Littlefield, Sam Lohman, Jessica Lewis Luck, Jo Mariner, Daphne Marlett, Gregory McDonald, Vance Morgan, Jessica Murray, Marc Nasdor, Michael Northen, Tara O'Connor, Scott Pound, Virginia Ravenscroft, Jamie Reid, Evelyn Reilly, Rise and Resist, Kit Robinson, Lou Rowan, Ann, Harold, and Simone Rubin, Linda Russo, Beth Seetch, Prageeta Sharma, Charles Smith, Marie and John Stewart, Adam Stutz, Steve Tills, Susan Timmons, Connie Voisine, Travis Wade, Karen Weiser, Nancy, Travis, and Roswell Wendel, and James Yeary.

I would like to thank the Lower Manhattan Cultural Council and the Thomas J. Dodd Research Center at the University of Connecticut for fellowships, Henry Ferrini and the Gloucester Writers Center, and Jón and Alda at Gullkistan in Laugarvatn, Iceland.

The photographs in this book are printed courtesy of the Larry Eigner Estate. Permission to use excerpts of Robert Creeley's letters has been granted by the Permissions Company, LLC, on behalf of Penelope Creeley. Excerpts of Cid Corman's letters are used by permission of Bob Arnold, literary executor for Cid Corman. Permission to use excerpts of Jonathan Williams's letters has been granted by Thomas Meyer, executor of Jonathan Williams's estate.

I would like to thank my dear friend, scholar George Hart, for the years of work and thousands of emails as we went through this journey together. George has always been a true friend to me and is always willing to share ideas. Finally, I am most grateful to my husband, Jim Stewart, our son, Jeffrey, and our many pets throughout the years.

Sustaining Air

Larry Eigner's Calendar

Compiled by George Hart

August 7, 1927 Larry Eigner is born.[1]

July 7, 1929 Brother Richard is born.

December 13, 1933 Brother Joseph is born.

February 1939–June 1941 Attends Massachusetts Hospital School in Canton.

August 1940 Has bar mitzvah at 23 Bates Road, Swampscott, Massachusetts; receives Royal manual typewriter as gift.

1952 Attends William Carlos Williams reading at Brandeis University in Waltham, Massachusetts.

Early May 1953 Takes a trip to New York City; acquires copies of literary journals and Williams's *Paterson* from the Gotham Book Mart; visits the Museum of Modern Art and Radio City Music Hall.[2]

July–August 1953 Attends Camp Jened, "which is equipped for handicaps," in Hunter, New York, for two weeks.[3]

May 2, 1954 Visits with Cid Corman and Vincent Ferrini in Gloucester, Massachusetts.[4]

July–August 1954 Attends Camp Jened for the second time.[5]

September 12, 1954 Visits with Charles Olson and Cid Corman at Vincent Ferrini's house; father Israel drives him there.[6]

September or October 1955 Attends Boston Art Festival for the second time.[7]

June 1957   Attends Creative Arts Festival at Brandeis University and hears William Carlos Williams and Karl Shapiro read.[8]

Mid-May 1958   Visits Charles Olson in Gloucester.[9]

Early September 1958   Is visited by Denise Levertov while he is working on *On My Eyes*.[10]

July 1959   Visits Charles Olson at Fort Square apartment in Gloucester.[11]

Late August 1959   Visits Arthur McFarland, Mitch Goodman, and Denise Levertov in Friendship, Maine.[12]

Spring 1960   Visited by Charles Olson and Jonathan Williams at 23 Bates Road.[13]

April 1960   Attends reading by Denise Levertov in Cambridge, sponsored by the *Harvard Advocate* (Olson also present); is introduced by Levertov to Robert Lowell.[14]

September 20, 1960   Has an operation "to get that ball-bearing out of my behind" in Massachusetts General Baker Memorial Hospital; comes home October 6.[15]

January 23, 1961   Has "2nd operatn" for same condition as in 1960.[16]

April 1961   Attends reading by Kenneth Rexroth in Cambridge, sponsored by the *Harvard Advocate*.[17]

September 21, 1962   Receives cryosurgery on thalamus to tame "wild" left side; in hospital for about two weeks.[18]

August 1963   Visits the Museum of Science in Boston.[19]

October 1964   Takes first airplane flight, to Saint Louis to visit Joseph and sister-in-law Janet Eigner, "wk before Halloween."[20]

June 26–August 22, 1966   Visits brother Richard and sister-in-law Beverly in San Francisco; visits Saint Louis on the way home. During time in San Francisco: rides cable car with Beverly; visits Muir Woods in Marin; encounters Allen Ginsberg and Lawrence Ferlinghetti outside City Lights Bookstore, invited by Ginsberg to a reading of "Wichita Vortex Sutra" the following evening; at reading "G. followed by 'a surprise poet,' R. Creeley, in f[a]ct"; date of arrival in San Francisco (June 26) begins new numbering system for his poems, starting at number one.[21]

1968   Is visited by Allen Ginsberg, Gregory Corso, and other poets at 23 Bates Road.[22]

September 1968   Visits cousin Ruth Polansky Bloom in New Jersey.[23]

June 6, 1970   Participates in reading at Marblehead, Massachusetts, bookstore with Vincent Ferrini, Judy Steinbergh, and others; "with a kid reading stuff of mine," "1st time any of mine read in public or to others."[24]

July–August 1970   Visits brother Richard in San Francisco and brother Joe's family in Saint Louis; visits Golden Gate Park with Richard and Robert Duncan.[25]

September 1970   Attends cousin's son's bar mitzvah at Marblehead temple.[26]

October 24–25, 1970   Attends readings by Vincent Ferrini at Marblehead bookstore.[27]

November 1970   Begins participating in a writing workshop sponsored by the Water Field Free School.[28]

June 1971   Louis and Stephanie Rowan, publishers of *Friendly Local Press*, take Eigner to Cézanne exhibit at the Boston Museum of Fine Arts.[29]

June 11–13, 1971   Eigner's parents attend father Israel's fifty-fifth-anniversary class reunion, Eigner's attendant for the three days is Sam Borash's wife; Borash hosts Eigner for the Independence Day holiday the following month.[30]

July 30–August 9, 1971   Visits brother Joe and family in Saint Louis.[31]

September 12, 1971   Visits home of Sam Borash and reads poems with other local poets.[32]

October 17, 1971   Reads at YMCA in Lynn, Massachusetts, as part of National Poetry Day celebration.[33]

March 26, 1972   Attends meeting of New Hampshire Poetry Society in Concord, New Hampshire; friend Sam Borash drives there and back.[34]

May 11, 1972   Reads to Robert Grenier's class at Franconia College, New Hampshire; Sam Borash drives there and back.[35]

Late May or June 1972   Attends performance of *Marat/Sade* at Marblehead High School with mother Bessie and cousin.[36]

Late July 1972   Visits Vincent Ferrini with Sam Borash.[37]

October 4–18, 1972   Visits brother Joe's family in Saint Louis; on October 11, reads to a class at the University of Missouri.[38]

November 19, 1972   Attends event at Brandeis, Cid Corman's brother reading Corman's work in relation to exhibit of Origin Press publications.[39]

March 25, 1973   Reads with Vincent Ferrini at Cambridge Artists' Cooperative; Robert Grenier is at the reading with a few students from Franconia College; Bob Teague reads some of Eigner's poems; Eigner reads as well, and his poems are projected from slides.[40]

April 12, 1973   Visited by Allen Ginsberg and Peter Orlovsky at 23 Bates Road during Salem State College Kerouac celebration; attends reading by Ginsberg, Orlovsky, and Gregory Corso the previous evening.[41]

August 7, 1973   Is visited by Bruce Andrews and David and Maria Gitin at 23 Bates Road; two days later, visits Vincent Ferrini in Gloucester with Sam Borash.[42]

August 25, 1973   Two screenings of *Getting It Together: A Film on Larry Eigner, Poet* take place at Salem State College student union.[43]

November 11–December 14, 1973   Visits brother Joe and family in Saint Louis; attends Diane Wakoski reading at the Mary Institute.[44]

May 15, 1974   Attends a "read-in" at local Swampscott bookstore.[45]

July 1974   Eigner's parents receive Sony color TV from Richard and Joe for fiftieth anniversary; old TV is moved into Eigner's room.[46]

August 14, 1974   Is visited by George Butterick at 23 Bates Road, in search of letters from Charles Olson.[47]

October 6, 1974   Asked to be a reader for George Franklin's thesis at Franconia College.[48]

December 5–7, 1974   Visits Franconia College as guest of Robert Grenier; George Franklin and another student drive there and back.[49]

January 30, 1975   Attends reading of novelist (from nearby Beach Bluff neighborhood) in Cambridge bookstore.[50]

November 6–8, 1975   Visits Franconia College as guest of Robert Grenier; Barrett Watten drives there and back.[51]

June 1–8, 1978   Visits brother Joe in Saint Louis with mother for nephew's and niece's bar (bat) mitzvahs; brother Richard and his family also present.[52]

March 19, 1978   Father Israel dies; Eigner gives date as March 19 in letter to Jonathan Williams.[53]

August 1978 Moves to California, first residing in group home for people with disabilities.

December 8, 1978 Attends "An Evening with Louis Zukofsky for a Sharing of the Out-Takes" at San Francisco Art Institute; Robert Duncan also present.[54]

Early July 1979 Visits Angel Island in San Francisco Bay with Robert Grenier, Kathleen Frumkin, and her son, Ezra.[55]

November 28, 1979 Attends reading by Robert Duncan and Jerome Rothenberg with Lyn Hejinian and Geoff Young.[56]

December 1979 Moves to 2338 McGee Avenue in Berkeley with Robert Grenier and Kathleen Frumkin.[57]

December 27–30, 1979 Attends Modern Language Association (MLA) Annual Convention in San Francisco with brother Richard; hears panel discussions on Robert Creeley, Robert Duncan, and Warren Tallman; with Kathleen Frumkin, attends reading by Gary Snyder, Philip Whalen, Robert Bly, Richard Brautigan, and Lucien Stryk.[58]

Late December 1979–early January 1980 Is visited by Robert and Penelope Creeley, who stay at McGee Avenue during and after MLA Convention.[59]

February 1980 Is visited by mother Bessie for over two weeks.[60]

April 1980 Selects Citizens Party affiliation when registering to vote; attends readings by Alice Notley, among others; takes a whale-watching boat tour; attends a wheelchair basketball game.[61]

May 12, 1980 Reads at Tassajara Zen Mountain Center, invited by Norman Fischer.[62]

August 1980 Is visited by Anselm Hollo, who stays at McGee Avenue the first week of the month.[63]

August 19–22, 1980 Takes a camping trip in Kings Canyon National Park with Robert Grenier and Kathleen Frumkin.[64]

November 1980 Attends Robert Duncan lecture on Shakespeare with Robert Grenier; attends reading by Joanne Kyger and Michael Palmer at Julia Morgan Center in Berkeley.[65]

November 1981 Is visited by Tom Raworth at McGee Avenue after the latter attends a reading in Berkeley; attends Ronald Johnson reading; hears Allen Ginsberg read at New College of California.

December 18, 1981   Attends reading by Philip Whalen at the University of California Alumni Center in Berkeley.[66]

January 30, 1982   Reads with Barrett Watten at Julia Morgan Center in Berkeley.[67]

April 1982   Participates in "Wilderness Project" for adults with disabilities; travels to Calistoga, California, and takes a twenty-minute ride on a glider.[68]

May 14–15, 1982   Visits Yosemite National Park with the "Wilderness Project."[69]

March 1983   Reads with Robert Grenier at St. Mark's Church in-the-Bowery, New York City.[70]

January 9, 1985   Breaks five ribs in van returning from University of California gym.[71]

December 1985   Attends performance of Handel's *Messiah* at St. Joseph the Workman, Berkeley.[72]

March 10, 1986   Reads at Larry Blake's in Berkeley, arranged by Jack Foley.[73]

October 14–23, 1988   Attends events that are part of National Poetry Week II in San Francisco with Jack Foley; hears Anne Waldman read.[74]

October 1, 1989   Robert Grenier relocates to Bolinas, California, breaking up the household at McGee Avenue.[75]

June–July 1990   Travels to Massachusetts with brother Richard for their mother's birthday celebration.[76]

January 23, 1993   Mother Bessie dies.

June 15–October 15, 1993   Eigner's poem "Again dawn" is inscribed on exterior of University Art Museum in Berkeley.[77]

September or October 1995   Is visited by Bob Holman at McGee Avenue.[78]

November 17, 1995   Makes last public appearance, at New College of California tribute to Gertrude Stein, organized by Lyn Hejinian; reads a selection from Stein's *Three Lives*.[79]

February 3, 1996   Dies at age sixty-eight.

1

The Eigners and the Polanskys

We stumble
beyond the impossible cyclone and woods
into familiar streets by the coast.
—"D e L i m i t s" (*CP*, 1:75)

The poet Laurence Joel Eigner lived for the first fifty-one years of his life in Swampscott, Massachusetts, on Boston's North Shore. In the early 1900s, Swampscott was a fishing village that hosted a large commercial fleet. The primary industries of the town mirrored those of its neighbors: Gloucester was the center of the US fishing industry, and nearby Lynn was known for its shoe factories. Although Eigner would spend his life pursuing a career as a man of letters amid this culture of industry, this environment—or what the Gloucester poet Charles Olson referred to as "polis"—was central to Eigner's life and work.[1]

As with any area where fishing is central to the economy and lifestyle, weather was a preoccupation, and the community and often the lives of fishermen depended on the moods of it. The drama of weather captivated Eigner at an early age. On September 21, 1938, shortly after his eleventh birthday, New England experienced one of its most deadly hurricanes. The Great New England Hurricane, as it was known, was particularly devastating.[2] There was no real warning of the strength of the storm, and communities did not have time to prepare. The hurricane formed out of a cyclone in the eastern Atlantic, near the Cape Verde Islands. Nearly a week later, it hit Puerto Rico, and a freighter alerted the US Weather Bureau (now the National Weather Service). But the bureau vastly underestimated the storm's reach, and nine states and Canada were affected. The hurricane resulted in over six hundred deaths (including ninety-nine lives lost to flooding in western Massachusetts), and it devastated forests across the Northeast; over two billion trees in New England and New York were damaged.

Although Eigner was away at a residential middle school when the storm happened, its effect on the community stayed with him. He later alluded to it in the poem "This":

```
the weather surrounding us, even blue
from our nostrils   even
walls of storm, soft or

                     horizontal sea³
```

The hurricane's path nearly reached the Eigner family home, 23 Bates Road. Despite the house's proximity to the ocean, a winding trail through skunk cabbage would have been difficult for Eigner's mother, Bessie, to navigate with him as a small child. He wrote, "every so often mother remarked too bad I'd got so heavy she couldn't any longer take me, pushing the old small sagging straw carriage the shortcut five minutes through the woods or the other way up the hill and along the sea road."[4] Although his trips to the beach were infrequent, the coast and the weather it brought with it would become a central theme in his poetry.

The North Shore was developed along the Atlantic Ocean coast, connecting a series of small towns. Fifteen miles from Boston, Swampscott was originally a resort town as it bordered Revere Beach, the first public beach in the United States.[5] By the time of Eigner's birth in 1927, all its big hotels, such as the Ocean House, where Henry James once stayed, had burned down or flooded. The possibility of getting to Boston by car transformed Swampscott into a commuter town, and its population became divided between affluent residents who lived along the coastal strip and the working-class families in the northern part of town.

In 1927, the year of Eigner's birth, mostly working-class Italian families inhabited the short road where Eigner and his family lived.[6] Although many Jewish families lived on the North Shore, the Eigner family was the only one in this particular neighborhood. As he grew up, he watched the small street become gentrified as access to nearby Boston increased and white-collar workers moved into the area.

The Eigner family, however, had been settled along the New England coast for some time.[7] Born in 1871, Eigner's paternal grandfather, Joseph, immigrated to the United States from the Austro-Hungarian Empire when he was a teenager. Joseph was part of the large influx of Jews from eastern and southern Europe between 1885 and 1915. Polish and Russian Jews were the largest single group to settle on the North Shore. Many were cobblers, giving Lynn its nickname, "Shoe City." Most likely, people immigrated to Lynn because of nearby ports of arrival in New York and Boston. In 1913, the small town had four Jewish congregations and three synagogues. Initially, Joseph Eigner went into shoe manufacturing, like many settlers in Lynn. The business was successful, and eventually he sold it and used the money to invest in real estate. He built a mansion on a hill in Lynn, where he and his wife, Celia, raised eight children: three girls and five boys. Israel, born in 1894, would become Larry Eigner's father.

After the 1929 stock market crash, Joseph went bankrupt, and he died shortly thereafter, in 1932. Although the exact circumstances of Joseph's death were unknown, the damage due to a life spent striving for financial success made a lasting impression on his grandson. Eigner later wrote,

"Keep at it," they say when they see L.
    reading, then disappear down the front steps
    and plenty die, playing the black market
    a heart attack in middle age[8]

Despite the loss of Joseph Eigner's fortune, the real estate in Swampscott was listed in Celia's name, so the properties remained in the family. One property, 23 Bates Road, was the two-family house where Eigner and his brothers, Richard and Joseph, would grow up.

Bessie Polansky, Eigner's mother, was born in Lithuania, which was then part of Poland. The family immigrated before World War I. Eigner wrote, "30-odd yrs ago ma thght aloud a few times how her family and/or the town must be going up in Nazi smoke."[9] He later recalled, "an aunt of my mother's, cd read Polish," and "grandma cd speak it."[10] He mused that it was puzzling how his mother's family came to have a Polish last name as Jews were not allowed Polish citizenship. Eigner later noted, "some ancestor bck there was a . . . relative of some king of Poland or something."[11]

The Polanskys settled in Salem, Massachusetts, in a house opposite the mansion where Nathaniel Hawthorne's novel *The House of the Seven Gables* (1851) was set.[12] Like most Jewish immigrants from eastern Europe, Bessie's parents were Orthodox and kept kosher. Bessie's mother, Tamara, listed in the 1940 US census as "Thelma," spoke Yiddish as her native language and never learned to speak English. "Brochen English" was often spoken at the dinner table, which Eigner would later say contributed to his "fascination with unusual or hybrid locutions."[13]

As a young woman, Bessie was a star pupil at Salem High School.[14]

Bookish, she absorbed the New England puritan work ethic and valued literary culture. After graduation, she intended to go to Bates College, a liberal arts school in Maine known for its progressive values (it was the first coed college in New England). However, the women in her family dissuaded her, and she took a stenography class that led to a brief career as a bookkeeper at a Boston bank. Her decision to leave her job, get married, and have children was significant; she would end up focusing her tremendous intellectual energy on educating and caring for her eldest son.

Bessie met her future husband at a party thrown by Israel's sister Annie. After a short courtship, Eigner's parents were married on the Fourth of July 1924, in New York City. Once married, Bessie gave up the Orthodoxy her family practiced and joined her husband's Conservative temple, Beth El in Lynn. Eigner later described the way the family loosely celebrated the Sabbath:

```
remember the sabbath
                the sabbath
the candles opposite the ice-box
  are twin
            the booming air the
            tv
light blazes away
downtown   in the kitchen   arm[15]
```

Although the Eigners were mostly secular and generally did not attend temple, rituals were important to them. In fact, Eigner's coming-of-age ritual, his bar mitzvah, would be the most significant event in his life as a poet. Not merely a metaphor for the beginning of "manhood," the ceremony would culminate in a life-changing event. Eigner would be given a typewriter.

2

Laurence Joel Eigner

a baby's first snow carries
little idea
—"a baby's first snow carries . . ." (*CP*, 2:293)

Laurence Joel Eigner was born on August 7, 1927, at Lynn Hospital on Boston's North Shore. He later described the event of his birth. Eigner wrote, "the doctor, Richard Williams, Mother says, apologized for not measuring her right. If he had, she's said, I would have been delivered in the Cesarean way. The doctor told my folks they could sue him for malpractice, but considering the thing an accident or something . . . they let it go. . . . Either my mother was too small or I was too big."[1]

During Eigner's birth, the doctor used forceps to help guide his body; this resulted in significant brain trauma, which caused Eigner's cerebral palsy. Historically, doctors and midwives used forceps or "vacuum extractors" to assist in difficult deliveries like Eigner's. Cerebral palsy is a neuromuscular condition caused by traumatic brain injury in utero, during birth, or in the first few years of life.[2] "Cerebral" refers to the brain, and "palsy" refers to the spasticity that accompanies the condition. The disability manifests itself in a number of ways. It can affect a person's speech, making it sound slurred; this is sometimes referred to as a "CP accent." People with no experience of the disability often mistake it for drunkenness, deafness, or a cognitive disability. Some people with cerebral palsy are nonverbal or have a speech impediment, making them unintelligible to strangers, while others have no impediment at all. Despite years of therapy, Eigner's speech remained heavily affected throughout his life.

The disability can also affect balance and movement, to the extent that someone with cerebral palsy does not have the strength, equilibrium, or motor skills to walk unassisted. People with cerebral palsy tend to have a specific gait if they are able to walk. Some use wheelchairs, while others use assistive devices, such as a walker or crutches, which Eigner used at different points in his life. In some cases, lack of muscle control is so severe that people are unable to care for themselves in mundane ways, such as eating or bathing. Eventually, the Eigners would find that their son's impairments were pronounced in all these areas.

While some people with cerebral palsy do have cognitive or learning disabilities, it is a misconception that the condition causes these intellectual disabilities. In some cases, a person with cerebral palsy may experience additional brain trauma that causes other disabilities, and people with cerebral palsy may also have other disabilities such as epilepsy. The intelligence of people with cerebral palsy is difficult to assess because intelligence tests often include a motor skills component, which people with cerebral palsy would not be able to master. Despite this, Eigner was found to have a high IQ when tested in middle school.[3]

Often, cerebral palsy is not diagnosed until after the baby's first year. It is unclear whether the Eigners immediately knew their son had the condition, although his mother most likely suspected it. Upon her son's birth, Bessie began recording his development in "Baby's Year Book," a gift from cousins Bee and Barney Cohen.[4] On September 26, 1927, she noted in her "impeccable handwriting" that the "baby began to follow voices." He "cooed . . . on his second month's birthday and during the week he started to try to raise himself in a sitting posture."

Bessie's notes describe typical milestones in her infant's development. She recorded his first smile, first laugh, and first word: "wawa" for water. She described him beginning to "creep" at just over a year old. Eigner's infancy was fairly typical, and his mother wrote of ordinary events. "Baby had a very lovely birthday, Mother made a cake. Daddy bought him a teddy bear and he liked it. . . . First tooth May 6, 1928." At eight months, he "held up his head and observed colors (full of smiles)."

The timing of his bris, the traditional Jewish circumcision ceremony, was delayed, but Bessie did not record the reason. For Orthodox Jews, the ceremony takes place eight days after birth; the timing is so strict that if the infant's eighth day falls on Yom Kippur, the holiest holiday, the ceremony will still be performed. Eigner's circumcision, however, took place three weeks after his birth. A delay of this length suggests that the newborn baby's health was poor. He may have spent his first few weeks in the hospital. Bessie also recorded that the family had a pidyon haben, or "redemption of the firstborn." The ceremony marks the birth of the firstborn son, who is celebrated for "opening up" the womb.

On July 7, 1929, Bessie gave birth to her second child, Richard. Another son, Joseph, would follow four years later, on December 13, 1933. Bessie recorded both sons' births and developmental stages in the book alongside their brother's. While there are notations under "Baby's First Steps" for his two brothers, Richard at thirteen months and Joseph at nine, there is no such entry for Larry.

By the time he was three, Bessie knew for certain that her oldest son had a disability. She kept records of his intellectual and physical development, "Larry talks not very plainly but well enough to be understood . . . he seems to have a very good memory. He knows quite a number of nursery rhymes." He "began to sit without back support," but there seemed to be "little improvement in his left side." By elementary school age, his impairments were clear. His speech was significantly labored and difficult to understand. He learned to walk with much difficulty but not independently. The left side of his body—which he referred to as his "wild" left side—continued to be particularly difficult to control; he had almost no muscle control in his left arm and hand.[5]

When Eigner was a toddler, the family moved from an apartment on Pine Street in Lynn to the house at 23 Bates Road in Swampscott.[6] It was a traditional New England two-family home, with apartments on the ground and second floors. When Larry and Richard were small children, the family lived on the second floor and rented out the first floor as an additional source of income. Once they were expecting their third son, Joseph, the Eigners switched apartments and moved downstairs to the larger space. Larry and Richard shared a bedroom throughout their childhood, beginning a bond that would last throughout their lives. As Richard remembered, "before Larry began his high school years . . . the front sunroom was converted to a bedroom for Larry's brother Joe . . . and the front porch, now glass-enclosed, became Larry's working space."[7]

Due to the gap in their ages, Joseph was not as close to either of his brothers when they were children, although he became closer to Eigner later in his life. While Eigner was very close to his mother and brother Richard, his father was a somewhat distant figure. Israel Eigner had a law degree but spent most of his career as an accountant. Both Richard and Joseph described their father as hardworking, quiet, and reserved. Eigner thought of his father as absent-minded and frequently lost in his own thoughts. According to Eigner, Israel's temperament left him ill-equipped to play with his children. He wrote, "My father wasn't up to playing anything at all much, playing cards or records or anything. You'd ask him to play a record and he'd dive into the phonograph sitting atop the record cabinet in our bedroom at the back of the house. . . . Before we learned to read we'd ask and ask till he got to reading us the funnies, comics . . . but in a minute or two he'd stop and we'd have to nag him all over again."[8]

Richard recalled that their mother was the "stronger parent."[9] While Israel financially supported the family, Bessie was in charge of the household. The Jewish adage "God could not be everywhere, so He created mothers," definitely applied to Bessie Eigner. She insisted that taking care of Larry was her responsibility. Most profoundly, his mother instilled in him the belief that he should avoid being a burden as much as possible and, as he put it, "help people help me."[10]

Bessie was not against challenging religious norms when it came to her son's treatment. When one doctor suggested eating bacon to help lessen his impairments, Eigner's previously kosher mother, trusting of the medical profession, served bacon with breakfast. As Eigner later wrote, "Mother had it in life or death matters any of the old injunctions were off."[11]

3

Robin Hood's Barn

I have felt it as they've said
there is nothing to say

there is everything to speak of
but the words are words
—"T h e C r i p p l e s" (*CP*, 1:99)

In the early 1900s, housing people with physical and intellectual disabilities in institutions became the norm.[1] It was common for children with disabilities to be "sent away," particularly if their families did not have the financial means to have them live at home. Those who were cared for by their families had limited, if any, access to education. Widespread institutionalization coincided with the height of social Darwinism and the eugenics movement in the United States. At the time of Larry Eigner's birth, eugenics was widely accepted in academia, and it was taught in many universities throughout the United States.

The practice of forced sterilization, an extension of the eugenics movement, was legitimized by the case of *Buck v. Bell*, in which the US Supreme Court ruled for the sterilization of Carrie Buck, who was found to be "feebleminded." In 1927, the year Eigner was born, Justice Oliver Wendell Holmes Jr. wrote in the majority opinion that "three generations of imbeciles are enough."[2] Although Buck's intellectual capacity is irrelevant, she was later found to have typical intelligence.[3] The error in her case highlights the fact that the practice targeted not only people with disabilities, but also poor women, "promiscuous" women, and women of color.

Over the course of Eigner's early childhood, so-called social reformers argued for segregation, forced sterilization, and bans on marriage for people with disabilities. Meanwhile, conditions in institutions where people with disabilities lived began to deteriorate. Places like Willowbrook State School on Staten Island in New York City functioned as warehouses for people with physical and cognitive disabilities as well as those with mental illness.[4] Until Willowbrook closed in 1987, residents were kept in dangerous, unsanitary conditions, and there were numerous, well-documented instances of residents being neglected and abused. In a study at the institution that ran from 1956 to 1970, patients were fed the hepatitis virus without their knowledge as part of an experiment on the disease.[5] When the abuse at Willowbrook was exposed, it was shocking to the public, which considered institutions the norm. Despite documented abuse, it still took over a decade for Willowbrook to be closed. It is fortuitous that the Eigners had both the financial resources and the commitment to take care of their son at home rather than having him institutionalized.

When children were diagnosed with cerebral palsy, it was believed that they could not be educated intellectually. Any of the few treatments at the time for people with disabilities were focused on the condition as a medical problem. Many children, of course, were kept at home and not given any treatment at all. Bessie believed that her son could have a normal, if not rigorous, education. From the beginning of Eigner's life, Bessie used all available resources to help him.

In the 1930s, when Eigner was of elementary school age, treatment for children with cerebral palsy was still limited but beginning to make headway. There were a few schools and summer camps that supported disabled children and their parents; they focused primarily on physical or vocational therapy rather than on intellectual development. It is lucky that the family lived in Massachusetts, one of the most progressive states for educating disabled children. Whether through Bessie's ingenuity or mere luck of location, starting around age six, Eigner was treated in the first pediatric neurology program in the United States, "Ward Nine" in Children's Hospital Boston, founded by Dr. Bronson Crothers in 1929. Eigner was an inpatient at the hospital for a number of months.[6]

In 1937, a colleague of Dr. Crothers, Elizabeth Evans Lord, published *Children Handicapped by Cerebral Palsy*, a book based on studies conducted at the hospital, with a medical explanation by Dr. Crothers.[7] Eigner was a nine-year-old patient at the hospital when the studies were done, and it is likely that he was one of their subjects. The author did not work to change the language around disability, which years later would be considered offensive. Lord referred to the children as "feebleminded," "crippled," and "defective," however, the studies did make the point, perhaps for the first time, of distinguishing between the physical and intellectual impairments of children with cerebral palsy. The book also provides insight into techniques that may have been used to treat Eigner. Specifically, as muscle tightness and spasticity are the most pronounced impairments for people with cerebral palsy, treatment at the hospital focused on exercises to relax and strengthen muscles.

Eigner and his mother visited the hospital at least three times a week. He later recalled riding in the front seat beside his mother, "behind the wheel of our Model T."[8] Staring out the car window, he read the billboards all the way to Boston:

```
They went and
lit for the country
around:
                    Sunday
a big sign
edgewise    in the back
over good roads
and fields of weeds
hotdog stands
gathered cider
                 the coast
where drivers en familie
were not blatant
                 and
   farmers
          look
               northward from haying
EAT AT CHILD'S
    in the distance⁹
```

Eigner hated therapy and later wrote, "reading, the beach and everything else was like vacation compared to physiotherapy, which was tough, scholarship was something to look forward to."[10] Through therapy, however, he learned how to walk with assistance. He described walking as "real scary, like mountain climbing on a seesaw."[11] Later, he wrote in an autobiographical piece, "the other person closing just behind, lift to step forward, now curve to go back, but left knee and hip jumpy, and there was an edge, ankle his shoe hurt unlikely to go down, heel in the air, everybody helping out right except him."[12]

In addition to undergoing treatment at the hospital, Eigner attended summer camp at Robin Hood's Barn in Vermont. Robin Hood's Barn was founded by Gladys Gage Rogers and Leah Coleman Thomas, who described running the camp in the 1935 book *New Pathways for Children with Cerebral Palsy*. Rogers and Thomas referred to children with cerebral palsy as "spastic." At the time, this was considered a neutral, medical term used to describe movement. Like many "neutral" terms around disability, "spastic" or "spaz" would later become an insult. The program was a response to the idea that fear was "too great a part in [the] life" for children with cerebral palsy—the fear of feeling physical discomfort due to spastic muscles or falls as well as the fear of being misunderstood because of their speech or mannerisms. Rogers and Thomas believed that "the spastic child must have [the] world adapted to [them]."[13] The camp's primary goal was to create an environment in which campers felt safe—or perhaps, at least, what Eigner considered a world at "proper arm's-length / for a spastic."[14] This language gives a glimpse into the poet's attitude toward people with disabilities and the way he distinguished himself from others.

The counselors at the camp encouraged relaxation over the rigorous muscle training that the hospital programs provided and used play, music, and poetry as therapeutic tools. One of the camp's goals was to give "the child with speech defects time enough to express himself," without pressure or impatience from adults.[15] This opportunity was crucial for Eigner, whose speech impediment was pronounced. It was also perfect for a budding poet who loved literature. The camp was based around the story of Robin Hood, and the children were encouraged to pick a character and act out the story. It was play coupled with literature and physical activity. All this made the environment incredibly progressive. Most, if not all, of the other treatment programs at the time focused exclusively on physical therapy rather than intellectual education.

Altering the environment to suit the children's needs allowed the camp enough time to "go through the daily activities of the normal child at a slower rate of speed."[16] The idea was that the children would be able to participate in all camp activities and be socially and physically active in a way that wasn't available to them in the typical world. A photograph of Eigner taken at the camp shows him as a young boy on the top of a jungle gym. His position looks precarious, and there is no adult in the photograph. Being away from the watchful eye of his mother must have been both terrifying and liberating. At the camp, he was beginning to experience the physical and intellectual world in new ways.

4

The Idea of the "Boy Poet"

> *the flowers*
> *and stars*
> *have opposite names*
> —"HAIKU" (*CP*, 2:291)

From an early age, Larry Eigner was a prolific reader; he found books to be "reassuring," a "respite" from what he called the "inexorable adventure of physical therapy and medical treatments."[1] He later reflected, "in order to relax at all I *had* to keep my attention partly away from myself, *had* to seek a home, coziness in the world."[2] In a poem written in 1951, he described being able to focus on "the book in his lap" only after learning to ignore the distractions caused by his body:

```
himselfhimself, his limbs and his mind
and so much sooner his tract, but he couldn't help that:
often as not he must live excitedly
And what happened to others would finally happen to him
--which self was wild now? A waste Well, he
laid it aside and held the book in his lap.³
```

Eigner's first experience with poetry came through his mother. Bessie was a dedicated reader who passed her love of books on to her children. His favorite book was *A Child's Garden of Verses* (1885) by Robert Louis Stevenson, and Stevenson's poems were the ones that influenced Eigner as he began to write. With his mother's encouragement, he began to compose his own poetry as early as the age of seven, writing what he later called "childish and crude" rhymes.[4]

In these early poems, Eigner was restricted both by his physical limitations—given that he hadn't learned how to type or handwrite—and by what he had been taught were the norms of poetry. Rhyme, for example, was a technique he used to keep poems in his mind until someone else could write for him. He often dictated his poems to his mother or his brother. Richard recalled how Larry "would wake saying 'I've got a poem!'"[5] While Eigner did not consider himself especially adept at rhyming, he later remembered his own keen ability to retain information: "I added, subtracted, multiplied, and even did some long division in my head—there was no other place to, I guess . . . and while I did visualize words all right when it came to spelling them, and at Boston's Children's Hospital where I was found to have a high IQ or somewhere else it was said I had a 'photographic memory.'"[6]

Prolific and ambitious from the beginning, he looked to Henry Wadsworth Longfellow as the poet to "match or outdo by equaling a good part of his output."[7] He "took to . . . the idea of being a Boy Poet" or someone who sold "ballads or whatever in the streets (ah, Newsboy!)."[8] For a time, it was his ever-practical parents' hope that he form a career out of it; they thought he might "make part of a living sometime in the future" by writing "Holiday-greeting-card verse."[9] His earliest poems reflect this interest in occasional writing. In May 1939, at age twelve, he wrote a poem for Bessie on Mother's Day:

```
Of all the pleasant times in May
Is set aside the fourteenth day,
When everyone has a chance to show
His gratefulness the best he knows,
To his Mother, who from the very start,
Taught him wisdom from her heart.
Each has his own and separate way
Of greeting Mother on her day.
And though it may be somewhat rough,
I hope this poem is enough.[10]
```

In 1937, Eigner's mother assisted him in typing and submitting work for what would be his first publication, in *Child Life* magazine. *Child Life* was a typical children's publication at the time and included contributions from readers; in the Hobby Club section, for example, children described pet lambs, rock collections, and books they had recently read.[11] A common advertisement showed Santa pointing to a Royal typewriter with the message "Next Christmas? Why not now?" It's possible that such ads inspired Bessie to later ask a relative to buy her son a typewriter for his bar mitzvah—a defining event for Eigner that also signaled Bessie's considerable influence on his life as a poet. At age nine, Eigner submitted his poem "When All Sleep" and won the magazine's Pen and Pencil contest:

```
When the sun is sinking
And the moon comes out,
All the little fairies
Go hopping all about

When the moon is shining
When in bed I stay;
All the fairies show themselves
And all at once they say,

"Let us dance together
And let us play a tune
Beneath the little twinkling star
Beneath the silvery moon."12
```

Eigner's subscription to the magazine was the beginning of his lifelong habit of getting reading material through the mail. In response to the magazine's call for writing on what it meant to be a "good citizen," when Eigner was about ten, he wrote a letter about the importance of safety on Halloween. "Halloween is a time for fun, but I don't think this means not being a good citizen. We don't have to go around scratching up store windows and ringing doorbells. There are other things to do. Maybe there's a Halloween parade in your neighborhood. If there's something around the house that would give you a comical or ghostly appearance, put it on and enter the parade. Maybe a friend of yours is having a Halloween party. If not, there might be a public one. Or you could sit around and tell ghost stories."[13]

When Eigner was a child, Halloween was a time when children and teenagers were allowed to roam the streets at night and pranks frequently turned into vandalism. Eigner's advocacy for parades and parties is interesting, given that he could not move around outside by himself and would have been in the house on Halloween. His letter, the first of many letters to the editor, also suggests that a kind of fear of other children was instilled in him. Due to the fact that he did not go to school and his brothers often didn't have people over to the house, he had limited experience playing with children.

Entering into his teenage years, Eigner took pride in the fact that he was a published author. His speech impediment meant that others outside of the family circle might not take the time to listen and understand what he had to say. But, in his poetry, he could give voice to his thoughts and feelings. And in writing his letters to the editor, a habit he would continue throughout his life, he began to participate in the larger world.

5

Ten Words a Minute!

We rise and dress in the morning,
We are greeted by the sun.
Proceeding to school we like to fool,
We have a lot of fun.

Oh, now it's time to get along.
We're on our way to school.
We like to play, an easy way
To learn the Golden Rule.
  —"Schoolmates" (*CP*, 1:17)

In February 1939, when Larry Eigner was eleven years old, Bessie and Israel enrolled him in the sixth grade at the Massachusetts Hospital School in Canton, Massachusetts.[1] It was his first formal experience with school. The school was founded in 1907, and it was one of the first schools in the nation to provide treatment and education for physically disabled children who had typical cognitive abilities.[2] The school was residential, and the students shared dorm rooms. While it provided typical classes and physical therapy, it also had a vocational focus.

Adjusting to the school was difficult for Eigner, who had much less privacy than at home and was spending all his time in the company of disabled children—something he had never done before. His brother Richard remembered it as an unsettling place where students were transported around in wheelbarrows, a common practice as wheelchairs were relatively rare and expensive.[3] Richard recalled that while some students had cerebral palsy, the school served children with many kinds of disabilities. The dormitories were chaotic, with ten or fifteen beds "and a horde of merciless kids."[4] Eigner described his roommates as belligerent: "two minutes after coming into the ward, you are in a fight, because you've said something very innocent, but somebody has called you a 'wise-guy' for it."⁵

One of his occupational therapists, actually named Miss Trainer, put him in roller skates as a way to practice balance. He felt guilty if he didn't work hard at this ridiculous task, but he often just ended up "kicking her in the shins."⁶ Over time, he became acclimated to the school. Eventually, it seemed "smaller and less mysterious and less daunting," and as he became acquainted with people, he "learned to take their knocks and even to welcome them as fun."⁷

During the first year at the Massachusetts Hospital School, he received his first walker, a contraption he later described as "four swivel wheels and a seat in the back end of the frame." In addition to using the walker, when he returned to living on Bates Road, he began using a wheelchair with "metal sides and footboards with folding-up fabric seat, one of the first such wheelchairs to be manufactured."⁸ With his wheelchair, he was able to use his legs to scoot freely around the house, pushing himself with his feet. He also continued to practice walking, holding on to a bar his family built along the house outside, and dragging the chair behind him with one foot in case he needed to rest. For outside use, he had a manual wood-and-wicker carriage, which required someone to push him as his feet couldn't reach the ground. It was this vehicle that his family used to take him to the beach or to football games in Phillips Park behind their house:

```
At the time, this park was a livingroom, the people, trees,
and without leaving any roads between them
myself on the outskirts⁹
```

Eigner's friend Arnold Goldman, who also grew up in Swampscott, remembered him as a young man "parked in his wheelchair" watching the football games. He recalled, "I remember him because he gesticulated wildly. In our ignorance, my peers didn't know what to make of it. We didn't know anything about cerebral palsy."¹⁰ Goldman also remembered Eigner telling him about the schoolchildren walking down Bates Road mocking his mannerisms. He said that eventually they would grow used to him and lose interest, until another generation of children would come along. At the time, Eigner claimed to be more amused than hurt by the exchanges. Although he never complained about his cerebral palsy, he was socialized to ignore it in certain respects, and his response to the children may have been the best way of dealing with the situation.

In March 1941, Eigner briefly left school, six months before eighth-grade graduation, to undergo two brain operations to "freeze" part of his cerebral cortex. The details are unknown, but from Eigner's later writing, it is clear that these surgeries were risky. These were risks the family was willing to take in exchange for addressing Eigner's disability. It is not that his mother did not accept his disability, rather that she wanted to make him as comfortable as possible. This was a time with numerous experimental operations for people with disabilities. Eigner later wrote about the operations in brutal terms, describing them as "3 or 4 clunk scrapings," like the "crackling effervescent checkerboard squares." He guessed that "maybe the surgery did a little good, no one could quite tell."[11]

By freezing part of the cerebral cortex (and with the help of physical therapy), the doctor predicted that uncontrolled movements could be contained. The spasticity was pronounced in Eigner's case, making routine gestures difficult, if not impossible. The left half of his body was particularly hard for him to control, and he described himself as all "nosy in all directions, curious what with enough things beyond sight and/or hearing, out of reach."[12]

After recovering from the surgery, when he returned to school in June 1941, he put together his first poetry manuscript. The chapbook of twelve poems, *Poems by Laurence Joel Eigner*, was printed by students.[13] The Massachusetts Hospital School was mostly based on vocational training, and it had a printing press for aspiring printmakers. It was with this machine that a group of students produced his first chapbook. The short collection included poems one might expect from a fourteen-year-old boy who grew up reading Henry Wadsworth Longfellow and Robert Louis Stevenson; it also contained a poem about the rain, foreshadowing Eigner's preoccupation with weather, which would become so present in his later work:

```
Rain

The air is as dry as the desert,
And the sun beats down in the plain.
The earth is suffering greatly
And feels the need of rain.

But look! On the eastern horizon
A raincloud can be seen,
And the great sun ducks behind it
As the rain comes down in a stream.

The workman pauses a moment.
A smile breaks through his lips.
The flowers open their petals
To drink the rain in sips.[14]
```

In June 1941, Eigner graduated "at the top of his class" with a certificate noting he was "improved to attend high school."[15] He spent that summer preparing for his bar mitzvah. The rabbi made the (unusual) accommodation of coming to Bates Road to give him Hebrew lessons. The ceremony took place at the Eigner house the same month as Larry's thirteenth birthday, in the "sun-parlor facing the small audience . . . in the living room." He later described it as "hard up to do," and said that his body "felt out of control and wild as ever." This was his first public performance, and he "somehow got through . . . Isaiah chapter 40, not the whole chapter but maybe the first ten or twelve verses."[16] Although he had no trouble memorizing the passage—bragging at one point that he had a photographic memory—his vocal cords, affected by the cerebral palsy, made speaking tiring and his speech difficult to understand.

As difficult as the event was, Eigner received a gift that would come to define the rest of his life. Instead of his receiving the traditional bar mitzvah gift of a pen and pencil set, his mother asked a relative, possibly a cousin, to give him a Royal typewriter.[17] Although Eigner did learn to write longhand, and later included marginalia in most of his books, the process was labor intensive, and his handwriting was virtually impossible to decipher. The reasons for his mother's push for this gift were various. She intended to have him homeschooled throughout high school, so she was giving him a tool to continue his education. It also was clear that her son wanted to write poetry, and it would save her time typing for him. It would bring him some independence and, at the very least, keep him entertained. But it was impossible for anyone in the family to predict just how greatly the typewriter would shape the trajectory of his life.

It is unclear how long it took him to master the machine, and Bessie would still type his papers throughout high school and college. Eventually, he was able to type fast enough using the most ambulatory part of his right hand: his thumb and index finger. In his typical sense of humor, he later referred to his "typing skills" on a Guggenheim grant application, reporting that he was able to type "ten words a minute!"[18] He likened the typewriter to the family piano, at which he would sometimes stand, using it to prop up books and papers as he worked:

```
                    I
    I can only play one note at a time
    (and I've got ten fingers) This is the piano

    and I should think of something I have to
                  play
```

```
    and have to vary     without looking

        from        precision of simple things

bam

            with only that and
          the tune in my mind¹⁹
```

Although the Massachusetts Hospital School had added a high school program, Bessie chose not to send him back to school. Instead, she enrolled him in a homeschooling program through Swampscott High School. The town sent a public schoolteacher to his house to oversee his progress. He recollected that he "took all the subjects as attentively" as possible, and he "took to geometry especially." He "was out to learn . . . everything, so that in an emergency in case . . . could advise a companion how to fix a flat tire for example." He worked on math, practicing long division in his head because "there was no other place to" as he still hadn't learned to write by hand. His primary interests, however, remained reading and writing. He "[kept] an eye out for colorful phrases, lines" when he read a play or book and paid close attention to "how to begin a paragraph, say, and where to end it and begin the next, should there be a next."[20] During this time, he also had poems published in the Swampscott High School quarterly, the *Swampscotta*.

After Eigner graduated from high school, Bessie arranged for him to take correspondence classes through the University of Chicago; commuting to a college or university was not an option.[21] Despite the fact that he had learned to use the typewriter, his mother continued to type his papers, most likely to save time and minimize errors. Together, they completed seven correspondence classes. Among these courses were English Composition and Introduction to Poetry. The latter required students to buy the anthology *Approaches to Poetry* (1935), edited by Walter Blair and W. K. Chandler.[22] The anthology included few contemporary poets. Blair was known more as a Mark Twain scholar than a poetry anthologist, and the collection included predictable works: excerpts from Edmund Spenser's "The Faerie Queene" (1590), traditional ballads, sonnets, odes, pastoral elegies, and satires. At this time, Eigner was beginning to think about what free verse meant and how he could begin to write without the constraints of rhyme or meter. One correspondence course he chose was in versification. When he asked the instructor in one of his letters, "what there was really to 'free verse,'" the disappointing reply was simply that free verse was "just cut-up prose."[23]

When he started taking college courses in the 1940s—although modernist writers had been writing for some time—the closest he came to any contemporary form in literature was in John Steinbeck's novels, for which he immediately felt an affinity. He admired the author for his clarity and plainness of style and argued, "I think all types of readers like a simple word now and then, especially when the idea is simple."[24] He was attracted to writing that was direct and accessible. He commented on the poetic elements in Steinbeck's work in a college paper: "rhythm and sound are important—repetition is important and effective . . . very concrete because he wants to make the scene and the feelings vivid." Of Eigner's essays, his professor wrote, "I hope you will keep on. Sometimes—quite occasionally—I feel that you've overloaded your materials; but you are hammering out a method of expression that is your own."[25]

Eigner's interest in modernism and free verse, a bold step for any writer at that time, coincided with his self-described writer's block, the only one in his life, which came right after college. For the "boy poet" who had been published from an early age, this must have been particularly frustrating. He was discouraged by what he saw as the limitations of traditional poetry, and he was actively seeking out new ideas. He was on the cusp of joining a community of poets, brash unconventional young men (and a few women) who were devoted to expanding the ideas of the modernists and creating new ways of writing. In a short time, he would be immersed in this culture, which would radically change his writing and life.

6

This Is Poetry

and they say how
stars will collide
—"in the blackout . . ." (*CP*, 1:58)

In 1948, Larry Eigner's brother Richard left Swampscott to attend Dartmouth College.¹ The move was a big change for both brothers as they had shared a bedroom and were close throughout their childhood. Richard was, like their mother, a critical part of his brother's support system; although three years younger, he was attuned to his brother's interest in poetry, which was often inspired by programs on the box radio the two kept between their beds. Sometimes, Richard would transcribe his brother's poems before Eigner learned how to use the typewriter.² As Richard could attend college in person and his brother could not, it made sense that he would want to bring what he learned home with him and share it with his brother.

On his first vacation home, Richard stumbled across a radio program called *This Is Poetry*, which he immediately shared with his brother. The weekly broadcast, run by the poet Cid Corman, was the first radio program in the United States dedicated to poetry. The show was funded by Brandeis University and broadcast on WMEX in Boston. Corman described it as "usually a fifteen-minute reading of modern verse on Saturday evenings." In addition to reading poetry, he "[took] some liberties" reading "from *Moby Dick* and from stories by Dylan Thomas, Robert Creeley, and Joyce."³

Like Eigner, Corman was a native of Massachusetts; he was born in Roxbury and attended the prestigious Boston Latin School.⁴ Just two years older than Eigner, Corman had already experienced some success as a poet; he had won the Hopwood Award from the University of Michigan, and in addition to the radio show, he ran poetry programs in public libraries with a high school friend, the young writer Nat Hentoff.

Eigner was immediately taken with the show, and he first wrote to Corman in 1949, beginning a relationship that would last nearly forty years. He later described the event: "[A] couple of months after finishing up the last course [at the University of Chicago], I bumped into Cid Corman reading Yeats, on the radio, in his first program, I gather, from Boston. I disagreed with his non-declamatory way of reciting and wrote him so. This began a correspondence in which I got introduced to things and the ice broke considerably."[5]

Corman was in touch with the poets Charles Olson, Robert Duncan, and Robert Creeley. Through Corman, Olson (who would become Eigner's primary influence) was aware of his work early on. Corman wrote to Olson in June 1951, "Larry Eigner, as you may remember from previous talk, is the young fellow suffering (badly) from cerebral palsy." Although his description of Eigner's disability was off-putting (if of its time), he was taken with the work. Corman wrote to Olson, "I like his reactions because he tells exactly and helpfully, frank in his failures, and difficulties, etc."[6] The bond Corman, Eigner, and the others shared from the start was a disinterest in poetry that put the "self" at the poem's focal point. All descendants of the poet Ezra Pound, they were interested in writing work that was considered experimental. Corman encouraged his friend to get away from the idea of formal poetry that he grew up with and explore "blank verse." Slowly, Eigner began to step away from the poetry of his youth. His brother Richard considered the shift partly a rebellion against their mother.[7]

Corman quickly took on the role of mentor, a situation that Eigner readily accepted. In one of his first letters, in 1950, Corman wrote, "Your writing pleases me. It is very gratifying that you have not only taken criticism but persisted with it to the point of improvement. Now you can begin to write." He followed with, "You must teach yourself—and be patient with yourself. . . . Write. Write. Write. I'd like to publish something of yours someday. Don't disappoint me."[8]

Although, Corman could be boorish at times, Eigner took it in stride, and he learned to take advantage of it. He soon began sending Corman poems to get advice. One of the first poems Eigner sent Corman was "A Wintered Road," a poem of six quatrains narrating a scene of Swampscott in winter:

> Rain and the cold had made the street
> Clear, metallic; like a plate's
> Stems, animals, and incident
> Held abstract in one element –
>
> Except this was all around,
> Out the window, hedge, fence, ground,
> Rough reality within
> The supernatural discipline.
>
> Maples stood unassuming then,
> Frozen water budding them,
> Bud piled on bud   each opening
> Awake to this fierce whitening.
>
> Tall grass, weighed over, matted, lined,
> Was tangled in a quick design
> And a stringent thatch of frost
> Which let no spore, no seed be lost.
>
> Only the houses and telephone poles
> Were ample, wooden, free, almost
> Their spring, fall, summer selves. Black wires
> Spaced windless air with their firm layer
>
> And outdoor cripples, elbow-oared
> In the road lurched slowly homeward, towards
> Where they could witness this alone
> And ring up neighbors on the phone.[9]

Corman was interested in preciseness. Although he found the poem to be "observing and careful in tone and language," he pressed Eigner to "say exactly" what he meant and "keep the overtones, ambiguities, tied to . . . ideas. Pack words tight—and yet naturally."[10]

At this time, the metaphor of the "cripple" was widely used in poetry and probably something Eigner picked up from the poems he read in school, but Corman intuited Eigner's deliberate juxtaposition. Cripple, defective, and handicapped were words commonly used to describe people with physical disabilities. These words reflected the attitudes of society; disabled bodies were used as a popular metaphor in poems to express moral defects. Even though Eigner would not have access to terminology and ideas of disability empowerment until much later in his life, he had the intuition at a young age to use the metaphor in a new way. The "overtone" that Corman referred to might have been the presentation of the metaphor of weather "crippling" people, in contrast to the poet's disability and the way others in the neighborhood viewed him.

Corman emphasized the importance of reading when developing as a poet. He advised Eigner that it was "good to have books, around, including some you never read 'cover-to-cover' style." He noted that "poetry is rarely read through, except by a professional reviewer (and then usually very badly), in a short period of time. When you read poetry well you will find yourself reading as carefully as though you were writing."[11] Following Corman's suggestion, Eigner read poets like Marianne Moore and translations of Arthur Rimbaud's work. With the latter in mind, he took Corman's suggestion to learn French with a dictionary.[12] He would later use this "elementary French" in letters that he didn't want his mother reading.

Around the same time that Eigner began corresponding with Corman, Richard brought E. E. Cummings's poems home from school.[13] Cummings was the first innovative poet that Eigner read. Much of Cummings's content was traditional, but he employed idiosyncratic grammar, punctuation, and spacing. Although Ezra Pound, Gertrude Stein, and other modernists had been publishing for decades, none were taught in schools.[14] Cummings, on the other hand, was immensely popular in both academia and mainstream culture, despite his avant-garde leanings.

At first, Cummings was hard for Eigner to grasp. Corman encouraged him to stick with it, although somewhat brashly. He wrote that Cummings's "work is not at all difficult, although it seems to be—superficially." He argued that "in most cases, you can figure out exactly why he does the things he does with language. His ideas are clear, if sometimes not very enlightening. Because language is handled 'differently' you tend to read it badly. Give it some thought, and it should come through nicely."[15]

Eigner took Corman's advice to heart, and after reading Cummings, he began to consider how a poem need not be rigid, but rather could move organically, "extend itself, naturally, quietly, and be like taking a walk, light, in the earth."[16] Eigner felt that a line break could be like a typographical device, functioning much like a comma or colon in a sentence. He took the idea from Robert Frost, ironically a more traditional poet, that a poem could "take its own course" and that "maybe the most a poem can be is a realization of things to come to or that come together." He was beginning to realize that a poem could reflect a "process of thinking" with "no hierarchy."[17] He later reflected, "In writing poems I've managed to get the experience, once I hrd I didn't have to rhyme, use metre or even regular grammar, whch undoubtedly were too much for me to handle, except very briefly. . . . I got along by ellipsis." Having become "dissatisfied with pentameters," he realized he no longer wanted or needed to write like Frost.[18]

On Corman's recommendation, Eigner also began reading William Carlos Williams as an example of how to "say things freshly . . . simply, directly, cogently."[19] In 1944, in the introduction to his book of poems *The Wedge*, Williams described a poem as a "machine made of words." He attested that no individual part of the poem should be redundant and that a poem can be "pruned to a perfect economy."[20] Eigner considered it paradoxical that although Williams was a doctor, he relied on the metaphor of the poem as a machine rather than a natural (or human) organism. Corman also suggested that Eigner pay attention to Williams's "no ideas but in things," the idea that the poet could depict abstract concepts through concrete objects.[21]

As his work developed, Eigner would come to pick and choose from the ideas of the poets he read. Although he was resistant to Williams's work and his reliance on "no ideas but in things," Eigner would later embrace a similar concept derived from the poet Louis Zukofsky, who formulated the notion of "thinking with the things" versus thinking *about* things.[22] As Eigner's work developed, he resisted using the landscape—the birds, trees, weather, and so on—as abstractions or metaphors and avoided cluttering poems with adjectives or adverbs.

Within a year, Eigner would begin reading Charles Olson, who described writing as an organic process.[23] Olson's methodology, whereby poems extended from the poet's own breath and physical circumstance, resonated strongly with Eigner.[24] Later, he compared Olson's *The Maximus Poems* (1953) to Williams's *Paterson* (1946–58) and expressed a great preference for the former. He had difficulty with Williams's use of the vernacular and found that the work "didn't often get very far from everyday speech, normative grammar and all."[25] He argued that sometimes Williams's poems didn't depart that much from the writing in the *Saturday Evening Post*. Despite his mixed feelings, Williams happened to be the first poet he saw read in person.[26] As his work began to develop, he began writing to many poets, but he never had a direct correspondence with Williams. Corman suggested, instead, that Eigner reach out to the young poet Robert Creeley.

7

Here We All Are

I feel my life again the strangeness
it should be the same
   —"I feel my life again the strangeness" (*CP*, 3:890)

A few months after Larry Eigner began writing to Cid Corman, he started corresponding with another young poet, Robert Creeley. Like Eigner, Creeley had made Corman's acquaintance through *This Is Poetry*. Creeley gave his first public reading on the show, although the reason that he had traveled to Boston from the farm where he lived was to participate in a poultry fair.[1] In his first letter, Eigner asked for Creeley's "vital statistics," to which Creeley responded, "By way of other things, I'm 23 and have a wife and son, aged 2 and some, and here we all are, like they say."[2] "Here" was Rock Pool Farm in Littleton, New Hampshire. Creeley described it to Eigner: "The farm, or as much of a farm as it is, at this point, doesn't take much of my time. Just enough to keep me busy when I give up on the writing, etc. We are building up a breeding flock of several varieties of poultry, or Barred Rocks, Rhode Island Reds, Buff Leghorns, and Partridge Wyandottes in the big birds."[3]

The tone of Creeley's letters was different from what Eigner was used to in his correspondence with Corman. Creeley's writing was direct, challenging, and heavy on the four-letter words. In one letter, Creeley confessed, "The truth is: I smoke hashish & fuck a good many women other than my wife? The truth is: I read 24 hrs a day, sometimes more, & make extensive, exhaustive notes in what time's left me?"[4] Creeley's attitudes were particularly scandalous for the conservative 1950s, and his forthrightness must have surprised Eigner.

Although Eigner was just a year younger than Creeley, he perceived himself to be less educated. In his letters to Creeley, Eigner portrayed himself as intellectually lacking. He complained of lapses in his reading and difficulty "whenever I hit something that is unfamiliar, in a unique, say, or 'difficult' idiom, or whatever it is, I am, for 1 thing, very anxious, or at least eager, to break it down, assimilate it, get familiar with it." He told Creeley that he thought himself to be "not very much in yr. level or whatever it is."[5]

In reaction to Eigner's assertion that Corman and Creeley could intellectually "handle more stuff" than he himself could, Creeley responded that he could neither "understand nor see the point of this comment." He asked Eigner, "What do you know abt (1) what I read and (2) what do I know abt what you read (you've noted abt, say, 4 bks, and I'm not certain I've noted even as many as that). . . . Well, shit, I certainly can't speak for Cid here, and wish to hell you wdn't bracket us, since WHY?"

Creeley was not interested in intellectual distinctions, and he insisted that he wouldn't "talk down to anyone" as "that being one vice" he had "no use for." He resented that Eigner would even "suggest 'condescension' or anything of that sort" because it would be "hopeless to speak or to even try to speak once we have that to consider."[6] Still, he was more than willing to give Eigner advice on poems in his letters. Shortly after they started corresponding in 1950, Eigner sent Creeley the poem "Split in one point we were . . . ," which he wrote immediately after "A Wintered Road." At the time, to give each other feedback on poems, they typed and retyped poems in their letters, something that was very common among poets corresponding. While the poem was a step away from rhyme and meter, each line began on the left-hand margin:

```
Split in one point we were.

No pins. Not here, not there

But everywhere, at once. We think


It was, perhaps, the best way.

We phoenixes, unable to rise again.
```

Creeley suggested breaking the poem into less formal line breaks, spacing, and punctuation. He recopied a new version of the poem into a letter:

```
In one point were we.

No pins. Not here, not there

But everywhere, at once.
```

```
                           We think

     it was, perhaps, the best way.

     We phoenixes, unable to rise again
```

He urged Eigner to compare the two versions to "see which seems to make for the 'sound' sense/rhythm you are looking for." Creeley wanted to "shake it up," to show the "possible, infinite variations . . . in any line." He advised Eigner to use punctuation (or lack thereof) as a device—omitting the period so that the last line "simply . . . hangs there/ that 'idea.'"

Like Corman, Creeley asked for preciseness. He suggested that the poet "hit straight and hard" to get "line/words to pull FULL wt." He suggested that the poet "drop caps at the beginning of lines" or to be ready to justify "why . . . you have them there" rather than relying on "a hangover from a set method." He reassured Eigner that "these aren't tricks," but something that "each man works thru/ to his OWN logos/ method. For a good man: becomes his trademark, sign."[7]

Soon after, Eigner found himself resisting the tradition of starting each line in his poems with a capital letter—what he called "a big B"—as if each line were intended to mark "the Beginning of all speech." He also developed an "aversion more or less to going back to the left margin after beginning a poem." And he found that "the simplest and most immediate thing" was punctuation, given that the words were forceful enough to drive the energy in the poem.[8] He later noted, "I try to make the punctuation, including spacing, distancing as good as I can. Else I'm dissatisfied. If too many lines start same distance to left, it doesn't seem to move enough, it's flat . . . so each line has a quieter beginning."

He complained to Creeley that he "shd've concentrate" on memorizing his poems word for word instead of trying to organize them. He felt the need to "get to the typewriter, for every other little thing," and he wished for a "pocket size that cd stamp marginal scribbling in books. That way I cd use any number of pages too—without getting mixed-up and unwieldy, and without the chance of blowing down to the dirty floor." To Eigner, it felt like an endless struggle to get organized. He was worried that he hadn't "snapped out of a certain laziness" and felt a constant compulsion to be "to be weak-minded, scatterbrained, forget things, get excited, etc."[9]

Still, between the influences of Creeley and Corman, he was writing a nearly a poem a day, sending many letters a week, and reading constantly. He did not limit himself to reading other poets, but read novels, newspapers, popular magazines, and science and math books. As he was not able to obtain reading material on his own, he was at the mercy of items people sent in the mail, his parent's subscriptions, and books his brothers brought him. However, he read everything with equal attention, and ideas from what he read quickly began to come into his poetry. This immersion in poetry was a way to take attention away from his difficulties, and he rapidly began to move toward creating his own aesthetic.

8

Olson

> snow moves
> this morning
> from the cloud
> you can see there's wind
> the trees show it
> slightly where
> they stand
> the small clusters
> harboring
>
> —"get a / hand-out . . ." (*CP*, 3:936)

Although Larry Eigner developed significant relationships with Cid Corman and Robert Creeley, the poet who would come to influence him the most throughout his life was Charles Olson. Olson was sixteen years older than Eigner, almost an entire generation. Unlike Eigner, Olson was not interested in poetry in his youth; he did not start writing poetry until he was in his thirties.

Something Olson shared with Eigner was a significant tie to Boston's North Shore; his family began spending summers in Gloucester when he was five years old, and he returned to live there for long stretches throughout his life.[1] Influenced by his father, who was a postman in the area, Olson spent some summers working the town postal route; this experience would be foundational when he composed his major work, *The Maximus Poems* (1953), which centered on the history and culture of Gloucester.

As a young man, Olson attended Wesleyan University, where he began studying the work of Herman Melville. After graduating in 1933, he continued his work on Melville with the support of the university. He briefly taught at Clark University before entering Harvard as a doctoral student in the newly formed History of American Civilization program. Still following his passion for Melville, he left Harvard when he received the first of two Guggenheim grants to continue his work on the novelist. His thesis, "The Growth of Herman Melville, Prose Writer and Poetic Thinker," remains unpublished.

Throughout his twenties, before he began writing poetry, Olson was involved in politics. He moved to New York City, where he worked as the publicity director for the American Civil Liberties Union. He began a relationship with Constance Wilcock, who became his common-law wife, and they had a child named Katherine. After a few years they relocated to Washington, DC, where Olson worked for the Foreign Language Information Service.[2] A disciple of the New Deal, Olson was inspired by his hero, Franklin Delano Roosevelt. When Roosevelt died suddenly of a brain hemorrhage in 1945 and Harry Truman became acting president, Olson was devastated. It was then that he turned away from politics entirely—he never voted again—and, in his own words, decided to become a poet to "Write like forever!"[3] He wrote the poem "For K," a celebration of leaving politics, which was published with "A Lion upon the Floor" in *Harper's Bazaar* in 1946. One year later, he published a version of his thesis on Melville, *Call Me Ishmael*, and he went on to dedicate his life to writing poetry and poetics.

In 1949, shortly before commencing work on *The Maximus Poems*, Olson wrote a "manifesto" that he called "Projective Verse." He wanted to depart from the work of his modernist predecessors: he "realized that [Ezra] Pound and [William Carlos] Williams, and especially [T. S.] Eliot . . . would not suffice; he had to draw up his own *ars poetica*."[4] The essay was a call for contemporary poets to turn away from traditional form and toward what Olson called "composition by field," or a poetics based on the individual breath.[5] He was introducing an alternative to conventional poetry, which he believed "ignored the creative possibilities opened up by the modernist experimentation."[6] In October 1950, "Projective Verse" appeared in *Poetry New York*. Eigner received a copy of the magazine from Creeley, who wrote, "Am sending you a copy of POETRY NY. Because I want you to read Olson's article there. Nothing else in it."[7]

In "Projective Verse," Olson made a distinction between "closed" poetry, or poetry written in uniform meter and rhyme, and "'open' or 'projective' poetry, shaped by the individual poet's breath and physiology."[8] He urged poets to be "wary of similes, adjectives, and description" and to be "willing to break syntax open, since it imposed restrictive logical conventions on thought." Olson insisted that a poem derive from "certain laws and possibilities of the breath, of the breathing of the man who writes as well as of his listenings," rather than follow a predetermined form. He believed that when composing, the poet was able to "declare, at every moment, the line its metric and its ending—where its breathing, shall come to, termination."[9]

Given Eigner's search for a way to expand his poetry beyond traditional form, it is not surprising that he became absorbed in Olson's work after reading "Projective Verse." He noted that even before he read "Projective Verse," he understood how "immediacy and force have to take precedence over clarity in a poem."[10] To his mind, Olson wasn't presenting new ideas, but validating the ones he was already considering. Relying on what he had learned from Cid Corman and E. E. Cummings, Eigner had discovered that the "simplest and most immediate" tool in a poem could be punctuation; "once words were forceful enough," he could use "the distances between words" as powerfully as the words themselves.[11]

Eigner was invested in the poem's pattern of energy, in its "flow from writer to reader, speaker to listener, if not an exchange between them." The poet could create the rhythm of a poem through his breath; the reader would have to use intuition to follow the poem's progression rather than rely on typical grammar. For the sake of "immediacy and force" in the poems, it was important for Eigner to be "elliptical," leaving out any words that struck him as superfluous. This would mean forming a new syntax that departed from what he later called "everyday speech" in the work of William Carlos Williams.[12] He would use the words "immediacy and force" to describe his own poetry throughout his life.

Coincidentally, shortly after Eigner read "Projective Verse," Corman wrote to him advising him to find his "own language in his poems." Clearly under the influence of Olson, Corman argued that Eigner should pay close attention to his "way of talking (not merely in vocabulary, which is secondary) in phrasing and content."[13] Of course, given the poet's cerebral palsy, Eigner's "way of talking" was fragmented, another aspect that added to his use of the ellipsis when considering speech. Eigner's use of radical ellipsis is apparent in his poem "O p e n," written in 1952 and later published in Donald Allen's anthology *The New American Poetry* (1960):

```
They nod at me and I at stems
Yes, I agree   But I flower myself.
or can't change
```

```
    Yes, passes.         As I, pass on the air
    As i,    pause
    As i dream, sight
     I have been on all sides
           my face and my back
    Disappears   any time a world can
    Reality                             dissolve
              abstract, abstract, o little
                    seeing that word
    blue against the stack-
              o i walk i walk
    the pavements
    assume they are yellow

              the flowers seem to nod[14]
```

Although the poem begins with lines at the left-hand margin, as the poem continues it expands to use the rest of the page. In an unusual move, Eigner employs the "I" in the poem, but Eigner's "I" (sometimes capitalized, sometimes not) is not central; he is not "confessing" anything. Rather, the poem also shows how the body informs the poem and creates the form. It relies on Eigner's attention to spacing and the beginnings of his physical relationship to the typewriter.

Eigner wanted to walk without the assistance of devices or other people, but this was not possible. He could, however, achieve this kind of unconstrained movement in poetry, without the assistance of traditional forms, meter, and rhyme. Before reading "Projective Verse," Eigner had already progressed from writing in traditional rhyme and meter to employing a freer form. As Corman described it, "If you murder grammar all the way, it is fair enough—since you do it as it is done."[15]

For Eigner, the freedom to rely on his own breath when writing poetry was deeply compelling. In contrast to reductive interpretations that ignored Eigner's poetic agency by focusing on his cerebral palsy as autobiographical detail, the concept of breath embedded his disability in the construction and form of the poems themselves.

9

Camp Jened

The cripples are beyond religions
Although full of euphemisms
We all live better, nowadays
—"T h e C r i p p l e s" (*CP*, 1:99)

Larry Eigner's brothers, who both graduated from Dartmouth College, eventually moved across the country, leaving him at home with his mother, father, and extended family. After law school, Richard moved to the San Francisco Bay Area to set up a firm. Joseph moved to Ann Arbor, Michigan, where he was studying microbiology. While there, he married, and with his wife, Janet, he settled in Saint Louis, Missouri, where he taught at Washington University.

With her younger sons, and later grandchildren, in different parts of the country, Bessie wanted to visit their respective families. As Eigner entered his twenties, tension arose within the family as to how they should spend their summers. While he was still fully dependent on his mother, he was coming into adulthood and wanted to be part of deciding the trajectory of his own life, if not at least his own summers. However, Bessie also needed a rest from caregiving and wanted to take her yearly vacation to Saint Louis.

For many years, her oldest son went with her to visit family. She found traveling with him difficult. The passing of the Americans with Disabilities Act was still decades away (it wouldn't be passed until 1990), and boarding an airplane involved a journey across the tarmac and up a long flight of stairs. Although Eigner was able to make his way onto the airplane by himself, he still needed his brother's help once he got to his destination. He relayed to Cid Corman that his mother was "no doubt worrying abt brothers' backs" because they had to carry him off the airplane when they arrived. He reiterated that Bessie was "always on the lookout I shdnt burden the family or complain or be unappreciative."[1] As always, he felt pressure to help others help him, and he felt that his mother was overly concerned with him not burdening others.

Bessie believed that sending her son to a summer camp for people with disabilities was the only viable alternative. She did not trust his father to serve as caretaker, a somewhat logical conclusion, given that their son would be alone all day while Israel was at his job in Boston. Although they had the funds (the Eigner family did employ housekeepers), Bessie refused to have health-care attendants or other such help in the home. Sending Eigner to a summer camp did seem like a reasonable alternative to leaving him with his father. Bessie also wanted him to interact with people his own age and potentially bond with other young people with disabilities.

For his part, Eigner did not want to be around other disabled people.[2] He wrote to Robert Creeley that he was going to Camp Jened, "a camp in the Catskills for Cripples."[3] He made clear in the letter that his mother was "forcing" him to attend. Once he connected with Corman and began writing, he saw his identity as a poet, and he wanted to be in the company of other poets. Most importantly, at camp, he would have to adhere to a structure that prevented him from being at his typewriter twelve hours a day. He was to somehow gain access to a typewriter, most likely in the camp office. A handful of letters to his parents were typed on camp letterhead, and he wrote a play that the campers produced—or attempted to. He wrote to Corman, "I managed to write a little skit in a couple of hours for a Winter Theme Evening," though it didn't quite go as he expected: "cripples took up the whole cast, instead of some of the counsellors i had in mind, and they got out around 1/10th of it. That made it a real big deal. as far as i I wanted them to extemporize, what i put down was the way i had got the plot, etc; but they set abt memorizing lines -- and then, of course, they were better characters than they were actors.[4]"

Although Eigner was frustrated at being at the camp and referred to his fellow campers as "cripples," Jened was an extremely progressive environment. In the 1960s, ten years after Eigner attended, the early disability rights movement was born at the camp.[5] Judy Heumann and others who attended the camp formed relationships there that would prove pivotal years later when they created the disability civil rights movement in San Francisco, eventually leading to the passage of the Americans with Disabilities Act.

Something that was unusual about the camp, even when Eigner attended, was that it included campers of mixed ages; teenagers attended with adults. Jened's longtime director, Larry Allison, described it as a place where the relationships between camper and counselor were blurred. The camp was also integrated racially, so, for one of the few times in his life, Eigner interacted with people of color. With the exception of Amiri Baraka (LeRoi Jones), his poetry connections and social circle remained nearly exclusively white throughout his life (and until he began corresponding with Denise Levertov in the later 1950s, he also didn't have any female friends, poets or otherwise, outside of his family).

In the long run, Eigner's summer at Jened proved useful on many levels. He experienced independence from the watchful eye of his mother and her diligent schedules. At Jened, he was "free to circulate, in a sheer physical sense of acreage covered daily on foot . . . and in a rather mental sense, there being no goals or important schedules, as formerly there had been schooling or therapy."[6] Part of the camp's philosophy was to provide a space for the campers to be "regular adults," free from family and societal restraints as well as "the physical barriers of the outside world."[7] This was of particular importance to Eigner, who felt restricted by his mother's scheduling and the inaccessibility of Swampscott, which made it difficult for him to leave the house. At Jened, he wrote to his parents about wanting to try new activities: "Maybe this wk I'll try the boat ride, or maybe even swimming, and see if I can float hand holding to the crib rope and not touching bottom or whatever." He hilariously noted how the other campers "look like so many dying fishes etc, in the water. A lot of the small fry own life jackets."[8]

Dating and sexuality were also part of Jened's culture. Considering the social climate of the camp in the 1960s, Director Allison recalled:

> I remember very, very distinctly—and this is in adult camp—a couple who wanted to have sex, and the counselor came to me and said, "So-and-so and So-and-so want to have sex, and they can't do it themselves; they want me to help them." . . . As the director of the camp, I thought, "Oh, my God, I'm gonna get sued on this. I don't want the lawyers to even know about this."
>
> But it was—I mean, it was kind of like, "Man, you talk the talk; you better walk the walk." This was one of these moments of truth. You know, here are two adults. They are both severely physically disabled in terms of their range of motion, their ability, they were in love and ultimately got married and they wanted to have sex but needed the help of a surrogate. And so, the counselor was coming to me for instructions.[9]

In mainstream society, people with disabilities were seen as asexual. This misconception still exists, but at the time it was very much a taboo for anyone to discuss sexuality. Although the camp got more progressive in the decade after Eigner attended, romance among campers was present even in the early years. Soon after returning home, he wrote a novella, *Through, Plain*, that explored relationships at the camp.[10] *Through, Plain* had long passages of poetic descriptions of the place and a loose plot; it was based on the romantic drama of the camp, dramas that were also interwoven into the letters he wrote to his parents. At Jened, romance was "One of the things in the air!" He mentioned "a girl at the camp" to his mother, writing that he was "stumbling over her quite a bit." Yet he remained reluctant to become involved. As a teenager, he had had a crush on an "Irish neighbor girl." He remembered, "back in my teens" falling "out of propriety" and thinking he should tell his mother, but "I'd wiggle too much if I did."[11]

In *Through, Plain*, his narrator, a thinly veiled version of its author, fantasizes about what it would be like to have sex with a girl, "certain parts of her, prominently in the arm and her legs too, were usual, like connecting rods and what else; it seemed clear the way the bones were. He wondered, slightly, over a time, what lying down by her would be like, and as if it was a little unheard of, or how she felt. It was the first time he thought that specifically, though looking back, what would they have on, and when or just where would it be?"

Romance affected his friends at the camp directly. Part of *Through, Plain* focuses on someone he describes as a "heart-sick" roommate:

> One morning the week before Oscar had knocked and come in saying Christopher refused to get up. His roommate had strong arms and was a "Counselor-in-training," with certain jobs like running the movie-projector every other showing.
>
> . . .
>
> "He won't get up because Della wouldn't promise to marry him yesterday. When she was feeding him supper. She said she liked him very much but she also liked somebody else she said. So he says he won't get up till she takes it back."
>
> "He won't?" . . .
>
> "No. And it'll be time for breakfast in a minute. What shall we do?"
>
> "He won't starve," James said.
>
> "He doesn't want lunch either. He won't do anything. He's in a

tough position, you know," he said, clomping in a couple of circles, with his thumbs at his hips. "He's heart-sick."

"He'll get up," he said, jiggling when he'd put his shirt on.

Later, the two characters discuss the nature and possibility of romantic connection:

"Well, that's neither here nor there," he told him.

"D'you, d'you ever have fortune-telling, try to see the future, ascertain what it's going to be like?"

"Crystal ball?"

"Speculation, should be take care of."

"Oh, no telling.. exactly; things have been piling up badly. Why what do you think about the future?!"

"O, I don't know."

"Well, everything turning out, we'll live on a farm maybe, have'a couple of bambinos," picking his arms together up behind his head quickly enough, with the extreme shaking grin.

"Well, possibly, possibly."

"But I ima-gine you don't believe any 'a that."

"It's one problem, I suppose, you know I was in love once too."

"But the trouble is they keep talking. Things would be all right, only they talk so much. Jabber, jabber."

"What do you care if they talk? It's got nothing to do with you: they're having a good time."

"If you had an idea of what I'm going through, boy, you'd see what I'm doing."

"Look, you can't tell anything by me. I was in love myself once as a matter of fact."

He was looking at the clothes-rack. "You were? How old were you?"

"Started younger than you are. 14 till 18. It's got nothing to do with age."

"What did you do?"

"I didn't get up so much.st"

"Did you write letters?"

"No, lived on the same street"

"What did you think of it? It wasn't puppy love was it?"

"Oh . . ."

"There was a girl in school I was after year before last, or the year before that," he said. . . .

"She was Irish," he said. "All they know is a lot of talk. That's the only thing they care about!" He was sitting up.

"And if it isn't real in the world," he said, "then why do they write so many songs about it?"

"Oh THAT, that's Tin Pan Alley, Chrisst."[12]

Despite penning this confession about the Irish girl in the novella, Eigner wrote to Bessie that the possibility of having a girlfriend was one thing for which he never asked.

Although he rarely addressed sexuality directly in his poems, he did touch on it in work he was writing around the time he attended Jened. It is possible he wrote the following lines about the girl in camp who "had news" for him:[13]

```
Now I put her away, combustible beauty
with ideas of little use

    what did those goings-on amount to
at night    Was she there
Was she there,   always?

             hair and brown eyes
which I can hardly remember

 and the bent moments of her face
 I only saw glimpses of

            and have her mixed up with
     others from history
```
[14]

While at Jened, Eigner opened up about sexuality and romance in his letters to his mother in a way that he may have not felt comfortable doing in person, though he remained somewhat cagey about the subject. Although they had a tumultuous relationship, he also clearly regarded her as his confidant. In the 1950s, openness about sexuality was uncommon and would have been quickly silenced, particularly in the puritanical environment in which Eigner grew up. This is what made early Creeley letters so bold—his willingness to flaunt his affairs and drug use. Yet Eigner did not feel that he could return the confidence, and instead he shared these feelings with his mother.

As much as he resisted going to the camp, it was mostly a positive experience. The fact that he was surrounded by disabled people being open about romance and sexuality had an effect on him. Although he would never come to have a sexual relationship himself and continued to believe that this wasn't a possibility for disabled people, the camp must have opened his mind. Just as he found a measure of freedom and independence in writing poetry, when faced with the need to express himself romantically, Eigner turned to writing.

10

The Little Magazines

from the sustaining air
fresh air
There is the clarity of a shore
And shadow, mostly, brilliance
summer
the billows of August
When, wandering, I look from my page
I say nothing
when asked
I am, finally, an incompetent, after all
—"from the sustaining air . . ." (*CP*, 1:87)

Through correspondence, Larry Eigner was quickly becoming part of a community of poets. As they worked outside the mainstream and generally did not publish in academic journals, poets like Cid Corman and Robert Creeley created networks of small presses; they published their own work and that of their friends, alongside the poems of older, more established modernist poets.

Soon after Eigner began corresponding with Creeley in 1950, the poet asked him for poems to include in his budding journal, the *Lititz Review*. Creeley started the magazine with the printer Jacob Leed, who had access to a George Washington handpress.[1] For the project, Creeley solicited the work of poets he admired. Creeley wrote to William Carlos Williams, John Berryman, Wallace Stevens, and Marianne Moore asking for submissions.[2] He solicited work from Gloucester poet Vincent Ferrini, who forwarded a pair of Charles Olson's poems with his own.[3] He also wrote to Ezra Pound, who had been arrested for treason. In response, Creeley received a rejection letter that claimed that Pound was unable to engage in any correspondence:

> E.P. is, emphatically, not writing. You cannot expect a man to carry on an argument from a mad house. But you are very lucky to have got hold of a press and there is plenty to do with it if you are so disposed. . . . There are some forty volumes of E.P. out of print and none of you (?) young men appear to make any effort to get them into print, or to deal with the mass of stuff he has written during the past twenty years. . . . If you are at all interested in the first two paragraphs above, I will be glad to continue the above correspondence.[4]

The letter was signed "D. Pound," who turned out to be "Dorothy Pound, Mrs. Pound." Creeley was angry at what he took as a dismissal, complaining to Leed, "They lack, altogether, the energy that their illustrious chalice once 'contained.' . . . I expect this annoys, etc., at least gets them to the idea that I am not of their camp—which, god knows, I am not." Ultimately, he found it "better, much better, for my own part, to make [William Carlos] Williams the patron saint." He also received a "promise from Marianne Moore to submit whatever work she has in the next year, and after that some of the fables, La Fontaine, etc., she's been working on."[5]

As the first issue was coming to fruition, Leed broke his right wrist in a car accident. He had already typeset and printed a practice run with a pamphlet of three of Creeley's poems: "Columbus, Etc." on one side, "The Proposal" and "La Passante" on the reverse. But the practice run was not enough to get the machine in working order, and Leed considered the "one good run [to be] a fluke."[6]

After Leed's accident, Creeley traveled from Littleton, New Hampshire, to Lititz, Pennsylvania—a "long drive, which he could scarcely afford." As Leed later recounted, the two attempted to continue the printing "three-handed," but "by the end of the afternoon it was obvious that it was hopeless. We got beer at the country bar at the top of the road. . . . Creeley went back to New Hampshire to send out letters of distress, hoping as a last chance to find somebody willing to put $350 into the magazine."[7] Despite the fact that Creeley did get a backer, the *Lititz Review* folded before its first issue.

Corman wrote to Eigner that he was considering taking over the project, but funding was a concern. He told Eigner his first objective was "to find people with artistic interest who have money to invest in a cause that can give them no financial returns and only vicarious satisfaction."[8] Eigner sympathized. He wrote, "What you say abt the state of the little mag (and which I am sure coming to agree with) makes it a ticklish problem what's WORTH printing." Eigner wrote that while one didn't necessarily "write for the ages . . . you do, in a sense, EDIT for the ages."⁹

Over time, Corman's plans turned into *Origin*, which had its first issue in 1951.¹⁰ The journal was largely inspired by his correspondence with Charles Olson. Olson urged Corman to resist accepting money from academia, in this case Brandeis University, which funded his radio program. He feared that if Corman took money from the academy, "the magazine would become another academic arbiter of taste run by a committee of editors." Olson counseled Corman that the guiding principle should be "not taste but ENERGY."¹¹

Corman wanted to focus each issue on one poet, or a small group of poets, "on the principle that the mag ought to be read cover to cover as a single effect."¹² Although he worried that this would earn him a reputation of building a poetic school or clique, Olson urged him that it was a good idea, and ultimately, he did dedicate each issue to a single writer or small group of writers. On an envelope dated March 1, 1951, Olson wrote to Corman, "'O my sone, rise from thy bed . . . work what is wise.'"¹³ Corman chose this for the magazine's epigraph, securing Olson's hand in the venture, and the first issue was largely dedicated to Olson's work.

Corman did not include Eigner's work in *Origin* until its ninth issue, and, notably, he chose not to publish Eigner's poetry until much later. Instead, in 1953, he published two of Eigner's prose pieces: "Act" in the ninth issue, and "Quiet" in the tenth issue.¹⁴ Corman and Eigner did not share the same kind of relationship that Corman had with Olson. While their connection was more intimate in some ways, it remained a mentor/student relationship as opposed to the peer relationship Corman had developed with Olson. Corman pressed Eigner to continue writing fiction, and later a play, and published two more of his short stories in issues twelve and nineteen of *Origin*.¹⁵ Corman's reasoning for excluding Eigner's poetry in the early issues of *Origin* and focusing largely on his prose is unclear. At this point, Eigner was equally invested in writing prose as much as he was poetry and very keen to get published. Corman's decision to privilege one form over the other did not bother him. Still, it was a strange decision on Corman's part, given how carefully he nurtured Eigner's poetry.

Although Eigner aligned himself with Corman and Creeley, he still thought of himself as an apprentice. Despite their continuing support of his work, neither was the first to publish his poetry as an adult. That honor went to Harvey Schwartz, a bookstore owner on the West Coast who published "in the blackout" in his journal *Goad* in summer 1952:

```
    in the blackout
    waiting for death, wanting sleep
    and the walls had nothing more to reflect
        world
                the sea
    a shock wave
      and fliers a mile away
    were planes of another country

    Afterwards the sun came round

    and they say how
    two stars will collide[16]
```

Despite not being able to publish Eigner in his first attempt, Creeley remained interested in his work, and the two continued to correspond. After moving to Mallorca, Spain, with his wife, Ann, and their children in 1953, Creeley made a second attempt at building a literary press.[17] Inspired by Robert Graves and Laura Riding Jackson's Seizen Press, the couple attempted to collaborate with a friend who had encouraged them to move to the island, Martin Seymour-Smith. It became apparent, though, that it wasn't going to work, and Creeley began his own project, Divers Press.

Eigner decided to send Creeley a pile of poems, with the assumption that Creeley would shape them into a manuscript and publish it. Angry and startled, Creeley wrote back, "I literally can't print a book for you— no matter what I think of it, and I can hardly accept it sight unseen, even, damn honestly, from you." He was upset with Eigner's presumption and apologized for not having made himself "all clear long ago, to save us both this embarrassment."[18]

Eventually, however, Creeley had a change of heart and agreed to put together a small manuscript for Eigner and publish it.[19] In July 1953, Divers Press published Eigner's chapbook *From the Sustaining Air*, in an edition of 250. Creeley chose the poems, arranged them, and picked the title, a line from the final poem. As Eigner published more books over the course of his lifetime, this way of working—where his publisher pulled together a manuscript from a loose selection of Eigner's poems—would become the norm for him.[20] Although Eigner allowed Creeley to arrange the manuscript, there was still quite a bit of back-and-forth. They strongly disagreed about the ending of the title poem. Eigner's original version ended with the line "(how should I record this weather?)." Creeley insisted that the line be removed, so that the poem would end, "I am, finally, an incompetent, after all." Creeley felt that Eigner's last line created too much of "a bright neat solution." He continued, "For me it makes more of a bug re the tone involved. . . . I only bring this one back because I have this nagging damn preference for the poem sans this parenthetical last."[21] Creeley did have a point; the original last line had a more direct tone than the rest of the poem and gave the feeling of a summary. Eigner most likely wanted to include this line for just this reason; it brought both the poet and the reader back to the "billows of August" after the poet has lost his train of thought while "wandering" from the page. It also distracted from the line "I am, finally, an incompetent, after all." Although most likely a reference to the poet's inability to capture nature through words, the line could be read as pertaining to Eigner's disability, a topic he wanted to avoid. Eigner claimed that he had lost his copy of the poem and attempted to "reconstruct" a new version.[22] In this new version, he included the line "(how should I record the weather?)" but crossed it out in pencil, signifying that he agreed to Creeley's suggestion.

Once the chapbook was published, in 1953, Creeley sent a copy of it to William Carlos Williams. Williams responded, "Eigner's book is charming. I haven't got such a relaxed feeling from anything in years. It comes from the competence of the writer, his relaxation in the face of the world—of which indeed he seems scarcely conscious that it exists. There is no tension whatever but a feeling of eternity. It is hard to say how he has achieved this in the world today."[23]

Creeley retyped Williams's note in a letter to Eigner. When Eigner showed it to his parents, they were thrilled, and he wrote to Corman that he was surprised his "folks didnt suggest trying to get WCW's comment in local honor roll and Ch of Commerce sheet (I mean NEWSPAPER). . . . They often quote the principle, a little publicity never hurt anybody." Although Israel felt the "bk shd be $1.00, list price shdnt be 50¢."[24] Corman wrote from France, where he was studying at the Sorbonne on a Fulbright, that he had "been hearing left and right about WCW's reaction to yours/Truly amazin, huh?" He agreed it would do "some real good, if he could get his boost printed somewhere."[25]

Conversely, Eigner took offense to the letter. He felt that Williams was connecting the style of his poetry too directly to the palsy. He relayed to Corman, "Creeley forwarded a letter from Wms. citing my 'infectious' relaxation, and says I'm scarcely aware of the world's existence." He felt Williams was presenting him as "one of these tales"—the figure of a miracle, a disabled person overcoming all odds.[26] When his first full-length book, *On My Eyes*, was published by Jargon Press in 1960, his editor, Jonathan Williams, reprinted the letter but excluded that particular line.

As Eigner's style was developing, confessional poetry, which relied on the poet's experience of personal trauma, was beginning to gain prominence.[27] In 1946, Robert Lowell's second book, *Lord Weary's Castle*, was well received. Later that year, another Harvard poet, Elizabeth Bishop, published her first book, *North & South* (with Houghton Mifflin), which was republished with additional poems nine years later and won the Pulitzer Prize in 1956. In 1960, Lowell's fourth book, *Life Studies*, would win the National Book Award and be considered one of the first books of what would soon be called confessional poetry.

When a cousin visited the Eigners in February 1954, Eigner wrote to Creeley that he was from "up at U of Iowa . . . peddling (eagerly?) (seriously) AIR" to Lowell. His cousin was studying with the poet at the Iowa Writers' Workshop and evidently shared *From the Sustaining Air* with Lowell. The poet was critical of the work, and Eigner wrote to Creeley that Lowell claimed it too bad that this was the "maximum reached by young poets" because few working in "this style ever get any farther." Eigner called Lowell's opinion "the academic touch."[28]

Although Eigner would later meet Lowell, the poet's criticism of his work probably helped solidify his rejection of both confessional and academic poetry. Eigner didn't want to follow the lead of the confessional poets and make his personal experience central to his work. If he had taken this path, he would have written directly about his cerebral palsy, like the poets Vassar Miller or Christy Brown. When he did write about disability, especially in his early work, he typically wrote about it as the experience of the Other. Except for what he called the "hospital poems," written when he was in Massachusetts General Baker Memorial Hospital recovering from surgery in the early 1960s, he rarely wrote about disability from a personal perspective in his poetry. When he did, though, he portrayed it in a negative light, such as in the poem "THE CARICATURE":

```
man,as if   out
 of a painting

in a blazer pushing a chair
in which is another,     lolling
cripple

            ( and the Epileptic is wild for a moment
             (like a machine    thin
             especially in the arms

                    and some times afterward
```

```
            scarcely, yet  one of the office
         I take it for what she is
         or is quite likely to be
      yet with that happened face, her
   biggest keeping thing

   and the legs
                I sometimes imagine myself
   movements, men²⁹
```

Aptly named, the poem describes a doctor figure, "in a blazer" no less, pushing a "lolling / cripple" in a wheelchair. The term "cripple" harks back to the early poem "A Wintered Road," one of the first poems he sent to Corman, in which he used the term as a metaphor. Here, he uses it quite literally, possibly to describe something he saw on television or from one of his stays in the hospital. The fact that the poem is named "THE CARICATURE" is supposed to press back against the norms of how people with disabilities were regarded, and the description of the "Epileptic is wild for a moment / . . . / especially in the arms" could be a description of Eigner's own "wild" left side. Interestingly, he refers to the body as a machine, a reference to William Carlos Williams's idea of the poem as a machine composed of words, and Eigner's own idea of the body as a machine made for walking.

Around the time that Eigner was beginning to write, there were other emerging writers with cerebral palsy as severe as his own.[30] In 1954, Christy Brown published *My Left Foot*, an autobiographical novel that detailed his experience growing up as a child with cerebral palsy in Dublin in an impoverished family. In a brief review of the book, an education journal described Brown as "a Dublin boy crippled by cerebral palsy [who] describes his remarkable battle for self-expression and belonging."[31] This was an especially odd description given that when the book was published Brown was a man in his thirties and an alcoholic.

Although Eigner did not mention *My Left Foot* in his letters, he certainly was aware of Brown's success. Later in life, when he was approached about being the subject of a documentary in which the director wanted to highlight his disability, he wrote to Corman that he didn't want his life to be portrayed as a story of "overcoming" like that of "palsied Dublin novelist Christy Brown."[32] It made sense that he would want to identify as simply a poet rather than a disabled person or a poet with a disability, given the horrific ways cerebral palsy was portrayed in the public. There was simply no information about disability justice, identity, or positive ways to think about disabilities at the time.

Like many people with cerebral palsy or other congenital disabilities, Eigner never mentioned that he wished he were able-bodied. In letters, when he wrote about struggles with his health or hospitalizations, he mentioned these things matter-of-factly, with no judgment. Neither he nor anyone in his immediate family spoke about his disability as a misfortune. Rather, it was just the reality of the situation. Bessie, in particular, viewed it with the puritan resolve that they would make do. Years later, when an interviewer asked Eigner whether it ever bothered him that his life had been more difficult than others, his response was just the difficulties themselves, the things that externally got in his way.

Still, because of the era in which he grew up, and his family dynamic, Eigner could not avoid having some internalized ableism or prejudice against people with disabilities. Part of the way he dealt with this was by distancing himself from other disabled people. He fought against his mother's wishes to put him in any situation where he would have to interact with them. It is predictable that Eigner would reject Lowell's work, not only because of the narrative form, but because of the poet's reliance on his personal struggles with mental illness for content. For Eigner, who described himself as having an "aversion" to the left margin, Lowell's work represented everything he was resisting in his own poetry. Instead, he continued to work toward the concepts in Olson's "Projective Verse," focusing on the poet's breath instead of conventional form as the grounding for the poem.

11

The Glassed-In Porch

Today my brothers were here;
now at night there is you
myself under the sheets
But I grow old
because I was too much a child
—"after all the singing faces, you" (*CP*, 1:211)

After spending time at Camp Jened, returning to home life was a significant shift. Although Larry Eigner strongly resisted attending summer camp, he clearly got a lot out of Jened. When he returned home, at the end of summer 1953, he felt depressed and sluggish. It must have been a letdown from the activity of the camp and the company of people his own age. He described the scene at home to Cid Corman: "Miserable day today—raining all day, though yesterday was balmy. We're back to 3 people in the house now, very dead and empty prospect.... Maybe it would be worse if mother didn't keep thinking aloud abt housework, etc; or if we could get up what i really considered lively talk. Empty space with two people in the room or something."[1]

With both brothers attending college while he himself lived alone with his mother and father, the latter of whom was often in Boston for work, Eigner felt isolated. In a long poem titled "M o r e," which he wrote in 1952, he described the environment:

```
It is a quietness like snow
Light numbness of the mouth
            filling the window
```

```
but there are no tiny sharps
However, do not be deceived
the world isn't empty

        ( I am more idle than this morass

    street where maples cross²
```

Around the time Eigner started high school, his parents carved out a space for him to work. They transformed the glass-enclosed porch, which had been Joseph's bedroom, into an office for the poet.[3] It had a large desk, shelving, and a bar for him to practice walking. The space had a wide view of the yard, street, and neighborhood. Bates Road was still a quiet, dead-end street that abutted a large park, Phillips, with a football field. Beyond that was the wooded area that led to the ocean. Eigner often recalled that although there was no easy way to get through the forest to the beach, he was always aware of the ocean's presence.

His office space was such that he was surrounded by nature at one end and the living room at the other. It positioned him in the crux between the outdoors and the indoors. This was important in that it gave him a window—literally and figuratively—to the natural world. It was a place to watch the comings and goings of the neighbors and closely observe the weather that was always present in his poetry. That said, although it provided him with a space to work, he lacked any kind of real privacy. He complained about his mother coming in to clean, moving things around, and commenting on his ever-growing piles of papers. In the other room, the radio, and later the television, was omnipresent. The family kept it on even when people were not focused on it. He also often complained about being distracted by his mother's lengthy telephone conversations. When relatives or neighbors stopped by to visit—although he wasn't expected, or even invited, to participate—he would become annoyed with the distraction.

This situation made the environment oppressive in some ways. One factor was his complicated relationship with Bessie. While she was responsible for his education and gave him the tools to become a poet, she was also overprotective, and she strongly resisted letting him be independent. He had never been taught to have typical conversations and was effectively discouraged from doing so. In his mother's opinion, remaining quiet was a form of politeness. He wrote to his friend Sam Charters that Bessie told him, "The only decent conversationalist is the one who talks abt what the other lady's interested in." She believed that "before Larry can be good at anything (except highbrow writing) he must listen well and learn . . . and not ask foolish questions."[4]

However, he was able to meet periodically with poets in person. In spring 1954, he went to visit Vincent Ferrini and Cid Corman in Gloucester.[5] Even though Gloucester was barely one town away, it took a lot of effort for Bessie to drive him places. She had to hoist him in and out of the car along with his wheelchair. The distance to Gloucester was short, only about twenty-three miles, it was at least a forty-five-minute drive. Ferrini ran a frame shop in Gloucester, which gave Bessie a practical reason to go there. The shop happened to be a local hangout for poets—a happy accident for her son. This was one of the few times that Corman and Eigner met in person. Soon after, Corman would receive a Fulbright, taking him to Europe. In the following years, he would relocate to Japan, where he would settle permanently.

Eigner longed for conversation so much, particularly conversation that focused on poetry, that when he was with other people he would launch into a monologue. The poet Robert Grenier, who would become Eigner's friend and later his caregiver, described his own version of how he felt the poet was taught to communicate. He noted that Eigner "had an on-and-off button; he was either 'allowed to speak' or told to remain quiet. If he was allowed to speak, he would go on nonstop until he was told to be quiet again. Growing up this way, he didn't necessarily experience it as dominating the conversation; he experienced it as his own method of communication—you talked a blue streak until the visitor left."[6] Although this description is likely exaggerated, Eigner's letters *did* reflect this sort of stream of consciousness, and his way of communicating became a challenge for him later in life. Eigner lamented that personal relationships often seemed "kind of beyond reach or to begin with, scanty, unbalanced, more bruising."[7] In the poem "Company," he expressed how he felt those around him perceived him:

```
He saw things without thinking     they
didn't let him look,    they
included him
so much    That his eyes hung like moss
they were vivid   Surprising
time locked in the air
  like startling type
He came through and
killed a few himself[8]
```

Eigner wrote to Corman that he felt forced "to jump at the bidding of the old folks" and adhere to what he sarcastically referred to as their "adamantly reasonable routine."[9] His schedule—when to sleep, bathe, and eat—was wholly decided by his mother. Bessie got him out of bed, bathed, and dressed him.[10] She cooked all the meals, did the laundry, and cleaned. With the exception of teaching him how to type, Bessie didn't press him to learn to care for himself; she mostly discouraged it. Meanwhile, his father, Israel, was working full-time and commuting to Boston daily, which left the household and caretaking concerns to Bessie.

Although he was extremely grateful for her help, Eigner felt demoralized about not having the basic freedoms of adulthood. While his mother had the best intentions, her son felt she would never give him space and was always "nearby" with "glorious superior wisdom and practical knowledge, advice." His perspective was that Bessie was constantly "pulling the rug out from under" him in conversation and treating him as a "young thing all right."[11] She put enormous pressure on him to be compliant with her rules. He sarcastically wrote to Corman that everything his mother said or did was supposed to be for his benefit.[12] From Bessie's point of view, the schedules and rules were necessary to make the situation work.

Bessie pressed him to be compliant and, as she put it, help others help him. This was a concept that he internalized and that would stay with him his entire life. Frustratingly, he only had minimal input in his daily routines, even "after yrs of fights for some say-so in everyday matters."[13] Although he did not often include relationships directly in his poems, he addressed the tension between them, his need to be independent, and his desire to do things for her:

```
every day afterwards I sat at the table with her
and said the same thing
                        no, I don't need any help
                        I can get the food by myself
                        or I'll wait, I
                        was never hungry,   for food
I never dreamed    that moment

on my birthday she bakes a cake
         I wish I could do one for her from under my feet
```
[14]

Arnold Goldman, a local friend, visited often and later recalled their complex dynamic: "Clearly, he owed [Bessie] an enormous amount in discovering him and that he was educable. On the other hand, he was short with her and dismissive, and he didn't want me to be too polite [to her]. I would be very polite and would say, 'Your mother said this or that to me,' and he would sort of gesture, 'put that aside, we have literature to talk about, poetry to talk about, and writing to talk about.' He was short and was not best pleased, I thought, about any conversation concerning Bessie or his father."[15]

Eigner wrote to Charles Olson that while "a lot of people have been encouraging" about his poetry, his parents "would prefer me to write greeting cards and tv things," although "really their greatest preference is for me to keep them company . . . and be congruent with their mature selves."[16] Despite his mother's strictness, she made him feel like she was "too lenient" with him, and because of his interest in poetry, she viewed him as "a brat, intellectual."[17] Writing permitted Eigner to escape the limitations created by his individual circumstances and geographic isolation. His situation may have been different if he had lived in the city—even nearby Gloucester would have placed him in better proximity to Olson and Vincent Ferrini. As his number of correspondents grew, he turned his intellectual energy to writing letters, sometimes several a day. A major event was the arrival of the mailman, who would bring a steady stream of letters, magazines, and books:

```
A   P r i m e

Until the wave of his hand
  his letters looked like gloves

striding        (Parallel
(the hedge      the street

I know, eventually, he'll
come around

            to
    deliver something[18]
```

That letters, rather than spoken conversations, were his primary form of communication was not unique to Eigner. At the time, it was common for poets to write to one another numerous times a week, if not daily. Poets were scattered across the country, and events like readings were few and far between. With the exception of the Iowa Writers' Workshop, founded in 1936, the development of creative writing programs was many years away. Still, Eigner was influenced by his parents' opinion that the only way to have a valid so-called career was to be rewarded with a regular paycheck. At various points in his life, he explored the idea of getting a job; he wrote to Corman about wanting to be a manuscript reader ("at least—if my father will someday remember to get the addresses out of the Boston phone book"). But, as correspondence and poetry became central to his life, he felt more and more that he "should take [his] . . . brother's advice to become just a 'man of letters.'"[19]

12

Black Mountain College

a bird
depending on the weather
—"the bird / of wire like a nest . . ." (*CP*, 2:370)

In the mid-1950s Larry Eigner's primary influence, Charles Olson, began teaching at a school in Asheville, North Carolina: Black Mountain College.[1] Black Mountain College predated the Iowa Writers' Workshop by three years, but it was formed under a very different education model. Founded in 1933 by educator John Andrew Rice and novelist Edward Dahlberg, Black Mountain was based on the educational philosophy of John Dewey. Dewey's theory was that for education to be effective it must include a social element, and students could learn best through experience, which is how Rice set up the groundwork for the college. It was Rice's idea that the school be multidisciplinary, although the arts—including dance, painting, music, and poetry—would be at the center of the curriculum. Originally, the founders intended the college to function as a self-sustaining commune with a working farm for income, but that idea never panned out.

In its short, twenty-three-year history, the college was successful at bringing in well-known artists and writers. Experimental musicians John Cage and Lou Harrison taught classes. The school hired Josef and Anni Albers (neither of whom spoke English) from Germany to teach painting, along with Franz Kline, Willem de Kooning, and Jacob Lawrence. Cy Twombly, Elaine de Kooning, and Robert Rauschenberg all were students at one point. Buckminster Fuller designed the first geodesic dome during his time there, and Merce Cunningham was the college's dance teacher.

The founder of the publishing house New Directions, James Laughlin, arranged for Olson to come to Black Mountain. Olson began his career at the college in summer 1948, when Rice invited him to teach a class. The following year, Olson replaced Dahlberg as a permanent lecturer. Five years later, Olson moved to Black Mountain full-time to become its rector, a position he held until the college closed in 1956. Through Olson, Robert Creeley, Denise Levertov, and Robert Duncan (all of whom Eigner would have close connections with) were involved with the college. The poets Ed Dorn, John Wieners, and Jonathan Williams were all Olson's students. It was with Olson's encouragement that Williams started his Jargon Society Press, which would eventually publish Eigner's first full-length collection of poems.

After he started lecturing at the college, while he was still living part-time in Gloucester, Olson began composing what would become his major work, *The Maximus Poems* (1953). Olson saw *Maximus* in sharp contrast to two major modernist works available at the time: William Carlos Williams's *Paterson* (1946–58) and Ezra Pound's book-length poem *The Cantos*, whose earliest version was published in 1925. Olson found both to be lacking. In a letter to Cid Corman, he described Pound and Williams as poets informed by what he saw as two extremes—Pound's ego versus Williams's naive pastoral view of the city of Paterson.[2] Olson aimed to expand beyond what he saw as these poets' limitations. Like with *Paterson*, however, he intended *The Maximus Poems* to be based on historical documents of a city. Through Gloucester, he would explore the idea of civilization, the "great man," and the "polis" or ideal community. He based the book's primary subject on the Greek rhetorician and philosopher Maximus of Tyre.

By the time Olson began *The Maximus Poems*, he had rejected Ezra Pound as a mentor. In 1945, when Pound was extradited to the United States, after being accused of treason for his radio programs supporting Benito Mussolini, Olson covered the trial for Dorothy Norman's literary journal *Twice a Year*. Through the support of the literary community, Ezra Pound avoided criminal prosecution; he was committed to Saint Elizabeths Hospital in Washington, DC, until he was "fit" to stand trial. After some time, it was clear that he would not be able to do that, and he remained in the hospital until 1958. After visiting Pound a number of times at the hospital, Olson became disgusted with his anti-Semitic rantings. Not long after, Olson left for the Yucatán, and he began studying Maya culture as part of a rejection of the European history that Pound's work signified to him.

The first segment of *The Maximus Poems* appeared in Corman's *Origin*, and Jonathan Williams printed the first book-length edition of the poem: *Maximus 1–10*.³ Eigner read this first publication of *Maximus* and immediately connected with Olson's poetry. Technically, Eigner was Olson's first critic. He wrote a detailed letter to Corman comparing *The Maximus Poems* to *Paterson*.⁴ Although Olson himself probably would have resisted being compared with Williams, a poet he was attempting to negate in some ways, Eigner saw similarities in the two works. Eigner was intrigued by both poets' use and description of place as a "character."

Eigner looked toward primary sources, as both Olson and Williams had, to examine both poems more deeply. As he told Creeley in their early correspondence, when he encountered something unfamiliar and difficult, he was "very anxious, or at least eager, to break it down, assimilate it, get familiar with it."⁵ He wrote to Corman to discuss an article about the town of Paterson. Never having been to New Jersey, he assumed that "Paterson must be the metropole" for US industry after seeing "an ad in the NY Times for the PATERSON INDUSTRIAL COMMISSION."⁶ To further his study of *Maximus*, he read *The Port of Gloucester* (1940), a history book by "one James B Connelly." He also obtained a map of the Cape Ann Trail from the Gloucester Chamber of Commerce during an "unexpected ride" to the town. That same day he had intended to visit Olson but missed him.⁷

Although Eigner was definitely engaged with *The Maximus Poems*' use of geography and history, his primary interest was in Olson's use of language and the way it differed from William Carlos Williams's diction in *Paterson*. Eigner was particularly drawn to the "organic movement" in Olson's work; to Eigner, it flowed "natural, as natural as prose," in contrast to the writing of Pound, who had "classical roots in form."⁸ And unlike Williams's work, which Eigner believed didn't "get very far from everyday speech, normative grammar and all," Olson's text was "wilder and more freewheeling . . . a flow from writer to reader, speaker to listener."⁹ Eigner observed that the "chattiness [of Maximus] was more out of hand, less controlled." He also appreciated what he called Olson's "forwardmannerisms."¹⁰

In a sense, his descriptions of Olson's poetry were what he felt in his own body. Due to pronounced spasticity of his left side, he still referred to it as his "wild" left side. He described himself as "chatty all over the place . . . forward mannerisms . . . freewheeling."¹¹ When he wrote to Olson directly about *Maximus*, he confessed that "the main mystery" in writing poetry was how to "make up the mind while still being un-doctrinaire . . . where to draw a line between spinning out and pulling in and closing."¹²

The two poets got together in person in spring 1958, when Eigner's brother Richard drove him to visit Olson at his apartment in Gloucester,

28 Fort Square.[13] Olson picked Eigner up and carried him to his apartment, on the second floor overlooking the harbor. He then proceeded to retype one of Eigner's poems on his own typewriter—a process he called "stone cutting all the way." Creeley relayed to Eigner in a letter that Olson had been delighted to meet him. He wrote, "I've been getting belated reports on the gig at Gloucester—it seems to have been a goddamn Milestone, yet. Very wild. Olson particularly was very excited at meeting you. . . . 'So direct and witty and delightful. . . . Christ, I was taken! He's beautiful . . .' Wow."[14]

Olson became the rector of Black Mountain College in 1954. Eigner felt so passionately about the poet's work that he seriously explored the possibility of attending the college to study with him. In his imagination, the college would be like the summer camps he went to as a child and young adult, an idea that was not too far off from the truth. In 1956, he wrote to Olson: "too bad I'm dropping just you a line and not the registar as well." Eigner told him that despite being "ill in abt 3 ways," he "wdnt starve" as he had learned to "shovel ample food" into himself. He went on to say he "bet" he could "make it" despite suffering from skin problems and mobility issues. He specifically asked about the "facilities, heights of commons, bed, etc."[15]

Olson didn't address Eigner's request directly, but answered shortly after, "Thanks for the delight of yr card—please write more often, & don't mind that I am slow (this place occupies what time I have beyond my 'studies')."[16] Eigner continued to write Olson after this short exchange, but Olson never replied. Eigner was not aware that Black Mountain was struggling with significant financial problems and would close that very summer.

Throughout the rest of his life, Eigner's experience with Black Mountain and "Projective Verse" would guide him, and his poems would eventually become the exemplar of Olson's philosophy. Despite their differences, both Olson and Eigner enacted the breath as a guide for composing a poem. Olson's height—six feet, seven inches—technically qualified him as a giant, and he had a personality to match. He experienced his own medical concerns: emphysema, alcoholism, and health issues related to his thyroid. In contrast, Eigner's body and breath with his labored speech informed his writing, as did the conditions of the household: the television or radio, his mother's phone calls or visitors, and her schedule, none of which were under his control. It was through their conditions that both poets used their bodies as poetic tools to create new forms.

Once Olson left Black Mountain and returned to live in Gloucester, he focused on writing *The Maximus Poems*. Olson had daily visitors to his apartment, but he didn't keep up with much correspondence as he preferred to focus his writing energy on the poems. The one exception was the long-term correspondence he had with Robert Creeley, whom he referred to in the *Maximus Poems* as "the Figure of Outward."[17] If Eigner had been able to make the twenty-three-mile journey from Swampscott to Gloucester on a regular basis, the two may have been closer, as Olson considered visitors to be part of his writing process. Olson's silence, however, left Eigner completely undaunted, and he remained passionately engaged with Olson's work. Although Olson did not keep up the correspondence, he later mentioned Eigner in *The Maximus Poems*:

>   as Larry Eigner the one day yet, so many years ago I
>   read in Gloucester—to half a dozen people still—
>   asked me
>
>   why, meaning my poetry doesn't
>   help anybody.

Unable to go to Black Mountain while Olson was still teaching there, Eigner reached out to John Wieners, who gave Eigner his notes on Olson's lecture "A Special View of History."[18] Eigner believed that "A Special View of History" was the key to *Maximus*. Olson regarded both the imagination and research as necessary to understanding history, a concept he developed throughout *Maximus*, using the history of Gloucester and its fishing industry as a source.

The idea of the "great man," or the male archetype, was central to Olson's teaching. According to Creeley, Olson believed that "if you could locate what . . . qualif[ied] as a 'Great Man' in a particular social environment, you then had effectively the whole vocabulary for acts and perceptions."[19] Olson's dependence on the masculine ideal was compelling to Eigner, whose own circumstances prevented him from playing out this archetype. With his impairments and dependence on his family, he was unable to achieve the same sort of masculine persona that was pervasive throughout the poetry community.[20]

13

Hidden Form

just because I forget
to perch different ways
the fish
go monotonous

the
sudden bulk of the trees
in a glorious summer
—"LETTER FOR DUNCAN" (*CP*, 2:327)

Through his connection with Cid Corman, Larry Eigner was able to build the literary circle that he could not obtain in Swampscott. As the 1950s progressed, he had two main correspondents: Cid Corman and Robert Creeley. During this time, he also became involved with two more poets who would come to greatly influence his work: Robert Duncan and Denise Levertov.

Denise Levertov had an unusual childhood. Born and raised in England in an upper-middle-class family, she was homeschooled.[1] Her father, Paul Levertoff, was a Russian Jew who had been under house arrest during World War I. He immigrated to the United Kingdom and left his religion to become an Anglican priest—changing his name to Levertov.

Levertov shared a few life experiences with Eigner. In addition to being homeschooled, she also began writing poetry very young, at the age of five. When she was twelve, she sent a poem to T. S. Eliot, and she published her first collection, *The Double Image* (1946), at age twenty-three. In 1948, she immigrated to the United States, after marrying the writer and activist Mitchell Goodman. Through Goodman, she met Corman and became part of the circle that included Creeley, Charles Olson, and Eigner. Of this group of poets, however, Levertov was closest to Robert Duncan. The two began a nearly twenty-five-year friendship when Duncan reached out to her with a poem, "Letters for Denise Levertov: An AMuseMent."[2]

Unlike Levertov, who settled in New York City and Maine with Goodman, Duncan had significant ties to the West Coast; he lived in California nearly all his life. Duncan's mother died during his birth, and due to the fact that his father could not care for him, a couple, Edwin and Minnehaha Symmes, adopted him when he was a year old.[3] The Symmes were devoted Theosophists, and they chose to adopt the child after looking at his astrological chart and coming to the conclusion that he was a descendant from Atlantis. His parents changed his name to Robert Edward Symmes, which he later legally changed to Robert Duncan, after his biological father. The tenor of Duncan's childhood was one of the connections he had with Levertov, who was also interested in alternative religions and whose mother, Beatrice Spooner-Jones, descended from a Welsh mystic.

Duncan grew up in Bakersfield, an agricultural area in the lower Central Valley of California. After Duncan's adopted father's death, he went north to study at the University of California, Berkeley. After two years, he dropped out and spent some time as a student at Black Mountain College, where he would later briefly teach. He moved for a brief time to New York City, where he spent time with the writers Henry Miller and Anaïs Nin. In 1946, after being drafted and then (because of his homosexuality) discharged from the army, Duncan returned to San Francisco. By the mid-1950s, he had become a central figure in the San Francisco Renaissance, a group of emerging poets in the Bay Area.

Duncan began writing to Levertov about Eigner's work four years into their correspondence. He told Levertov that he was making his "first efforts to get at the rewards of Eigner's work,"[4] and that he was especially taken with the poem "Brink," a seventy-seven-line poem that begins:

```
the less I
take for granted

   the world going forward

      I am getting
      no younger

an illusion of this
     no, a

   death
```
[5]

Duncan felt passionate enough about "Brink" to write an essay titled "Three Poems in *Measure* One: An Open Letter," which featured a close reading of Eigner's poem, alongside critiques of poems by Edward Marshall and Edward Dorn. He counted the poem's syllables and deduced that the "sequence was built on three, four, five, six syllables," and that the "seven syllable lines again are turnings."[6] He believed that Eigner was "clearly [using] caesuras as elements in the count," but said that the reader could not "take the pattern for granted." Although the poem had its own internal rhythm, the syllabic pattern varied in what Duncan called the "hidden form." Relating the poem to Eigner's body, Duncan wrote that the poem's form was based on what "the nerves and unconscious system, which is all mathematics, apprehends, but which the intellect, mathematical struggler, cannot count."[7] He wrote to Levertov, "I thot isn't it a simpler process at work in his art—one only has to indicate that a close sequence in measure provides more subtle adjustments; and that—I do get that right—reestablishing himself (his line) in each line, he has the aesthetics of keeping syllable-count freely variable. No primitive or psychotic, he is secure (disciplined) in a voluntary movement (needs not, that is, have any schematic reiteration in order to achieve equilibrium)."[8]

Although Duncan believed that Eigner's disability influenced his form, his take on it was more complicated than simply causal. He wrote that what he called Eigner's "spastic disorder" might move him into "an unconscious cerebration" between "the mathematic and the chaos."[9] His assessment symbolized Eigner's balance between what seemed like "chaos" and diligent organization. In this, Duncan integrated disability into his interpretation of the poems without being reductive or condescending. Duncan's idea may have derived from the fact that he also had a disability; when he was three, he experienced an accident that affected his sight. Although he didn't identify as having a disability, Duncan wrote about how it affected his poetry.[10]

In contrast, Levertov's reaction to the work was more simplistic. She argued that there could be no preciseness in Eigner's poetry due to his impairments, or what she called his "deprivations." She wrote to Duncan, "I don't mean in any way to denigrate his work, but I think his illness plays a very large part in shaping it. As physically he shakes & jerks & has no coordinating power, & is deprived of many experiences, so in his poetry there are breaks, and incomplete apprehensions of physical objects or of the connexion between them, and irrelevancies or superficially apparent irrelevancies.... But what is miraculous and beautiful is that he makes his deprivations & disabilities into the very ground for his poetics."[11]

In her opinion, Eigner's line breaks did not add up to much more than typos. She believed that he did not have the muscular control to make a purposeful gesture while typing; his poetic form was the result of accident, not intention. By her own admission, similarly, she had difficulty understanding "Projective Verse." She later wrote in an introduction to Eigner's first full-length book that she "disliked the unclosed parenthesis" (a technique directly inherited from Olson) and thought of it "as a poor tool having no function that can't be better performed by other typographical means."[12] Later, she confessed that she "never really understood the breath theory that Olson talks about; but . . . line-breaks are determined not just by physiological breathing demands, but by the sequences of your perceptions."[13]

In addition to having difficulty with Eigner's poems, she found his letters to be "really chaotic," and she wrote to Duncan that she didn't believe that her inability to understand them derived from her own "rigid sense of order"; rather, they were truly "incoherent."[14] In a sense, she was accurate; in his letters Eigner would jump quickly from subject to subject without clear transitions. As an extension of his poetic form, and in order to save paper, he would use the entire sheet, writing notes in the margins in confusing directions. He also often used other people's letters, particularly rejection letters, for stationery. He adopted the habit of removing vowels from words—so that "could" for example would become "cld"—a practice that he picked up from Duncan or Creeley (who likely inherited it from Ezra Pound). This was in addition to his frequent typos.

Although in his letters to Levertov Duncan made fewer assumptions based on Eigner's disability, he avoided traveling to Swampscott to meet Eigner and his family. He wrote to Levertov, "I regret not having visited Eigner as you once urged me to; again I don't regret it, for I do not see his work then as I do now."[15] Duncan would only meet Eigner in person a handful of times, years later, when Eigner visited the San Francisco Bay Area. Levertov, on the other hand, spent quite a bit of time with him. They connected through another mutual friend, Arthur McFarland. Like Eigner, McFarland was a fan of Cid Corman's radio show, *This Is Poetry*, and after McFarland wrote to Corman, the latter put the two of them in touch. Coincidently, McFarland lived in the tiny town of Friendship, Maine, where Levertov and Goodman spent their summers. Levertov described McFarland to Duncan as "a Maine boatbuilder," someone who had been "progressively deaf since childhood," and a violinist who taught himself how to make the instrument and played in the local orchestra.[16] She felt a connection with him because, although he was not a poet, he was "tremendously well-read" and "god, the almost perfect *reader* we'd all like to have."[17]

McFarland and Eigner developed a relationship largely based on McFarland's interest in poetry. Eigner also felt comfortable writing to McFarland about ideas that he did not express elsewhere. As a working-class person, McFarland resisted the idea that poetry was just for academics. He wrote, "Ez Pound, in a moment of amiable contempt remarked there was no reason why an iceman shd not appreciate poetry any more than a plummer, I quote the sense, not the exact terms."[18] Later, as Eigner took an interest in environmentalism and overpopulation, he asked McFarland to explain birth control to him. It was wonderful for him to have a friend outside of the poetry circle in which he could confide.

Eigner asked Levertov and Goodman to drive him to Friendship, something Levertov resented. She wrote to Duncan sarcastically, "Larry expects to be driven up here." As their relationship developed, it came to replicate the one that Eigner had with his mother. As much as Eigner participated in the dynamic, Levertov fostered it with the infantile way she treated him, as well as her prejudices about his disability. She described him to Duncan as "shockingly crippled (yes, spastic). His body is all contorted, & his speech grotseq. and spitting, and it seems almost incredible that he has managed with his one usable hand, twisted as it is, & with the frequent typical jerking movements his body makes, to type out all those poems & stories."[19] Levertov, who also had a son, treated Eigner like a child. Eigner did not have any women other than Bessie in his life, so it was predictable that he would fall into the same sort of relationship with Levertov.

It is unclear how Eigner met Levertov, but he met Duncan through Cid Corman. Throughout the 1960s, Eigner continued writing the prose pieces that he started around the time of Camp Jened. Through the radio and television, he became interested in plays. He told Corman that he was delving into *The Playwright as Thinker* (1946) by Eric Bentley and in the same letter mentioned Jean-Paul Sartre and his take on the Electra myth.[20] In his typical fashion, he tried writing a play himself. *Murder Talk: The Reception* (1965) was based on a quirky household not unlike his own; the title was surely a reference to his mother's attitude toward politeness and silence. It also included stage directions.

In the hopes of getting *Murder Talk* produced or at least read to an audience, Eigner first sent it to the Poets' Theatre in Cambridge, which turned it down. Corman then suggested that he reach out to Duncan, who was then working at the newly formed Poetry Center at San Francisco State University. Corman felt that San Francisco was "the only place that it would probably be given a chance." He described the Poetry Center, and the Bay Area in general, as "open to anything offbeat."[21] The suggestion led to Eigner's first letter to Duncan.

Duncan reported back that the Poetry Center wasn't yet in a financial situation to produce plays.[22] Eigner was furious and even went so far as to accuse Duncan of not having read it.[23] In actuality, Duncan had read the play and suggested that Eigner send it on to Donald Allen, editor of the *Evergreen Review*. He wrote to Levertov that he was "working at Don Allen, an editor at Grove who is here for the summer, to get him to see Eigner." Allen was just beginning to work on the anthology that would become *The New American Poetry: 1945–1960* (1960), which would be foundational for the trajectory of American poetry in the latter half of the twentieth century. Duncan set his mind on having Eigner's work included, but he described his efforts to get Allen to like Eigner's work as fruitless. He continued, "Perhaps my rhetoric is to catch the eye of such? Sadly, enuf it does. And the beautiful straight thing excites only the poet."[24]

Eigner did send Allen poems, but Allen did not respond at first. When Allen did not write back in what Eigner considered to be a timely fashion, he demanded, "couldn't [you] decide whether to pass or not on the poems after six months?" Eigner wrote to Allen that he should say so if he didn't want any more submissions. Eigner considered the silence he received from editors in general to be "quite a factor in my restlessness, and the fragmentariness of my life." The letter was one of the few times that he mentioned his frustration with his disability. While he was being honest about his situation, his tone was also somewhat manipulative. He wrote: "a life-time of incoordination (palsy) is no joke. It means a constant struggle to keep getting around limitations mental as well as physical. . . . I guess it's just my restlessness. That makes me try to contribute to a few mags, sporadically, in any case. But the delays break things up further."[25] Allen eventually sent him a rejection letter with the excuse that he was not "quite ready for your poems," and a harsh assessment: "What bothers me, I guess, is that I never, or only rarely, feel you're really working with the language."[26] While he may have struggled with the work's fragmentariness, Allen may have been just as frustrated with Eigner's aggressive behavior.

These exchanges explain why Allen initially resisted including Eigner's work in *The New American Poetry*. Duncan, however, was insistent. To seal the deal with Allen, Duncan agreed to type clean copies of Eigner's poems. This commitment was a turning point for Duncan, who came to internalize Eigner's form, which would influence him throughout his poetic career. In a few years Duncan would go on to help Eigner assemble a full-length collection. Later, Duncan confessed, "Larry Eigner belongs not to my appreciations, but to my immediate concerns in living."[27]

Although being in the high-profile anthology didn't help Eigner gain immediate success, it solidified his relationship with Duncan. The experience also brought Allen around to an appreciation for his work. Most importantly, the inclusion situated Eigner where he wanted to be, alongside his peers.

The House of the Seven Gables

Larry (*left*) and Richard Eigner, Swampscott, Massachusetts, 1932

Israel Eigner with sons Larry (*center*),
Richard (*right*), and Joseph, 1938

Larry on top of a jungle gym, Robin Hood's Barn, summer camp for children with disabilities, Vermont, 1937

Eigner family, *left to right:* Israel, Richard, Larry, Bessie, Joseph, and unknown woman in the background, at 23 Bates Road, 1938

TO JOE ON HIS BAR MITZVAH
December 14, 1946.

Well, Joe, my brother, now, we say,
You are a man; and it is so.
But this is just a start--you know--
Another hour, another day.

For soon, like us, you will become
A judge of many questions, some
Too hard to be decided now;
Which you may learn to solve, somehow,
If, after seeking, you can find
Some eastern window in the mind
As yet unopened, still unknown.

But you'll not be the only one
Trying to overtake the sun.
So never think to feel alone,
Although your thoughts may be your own.

Larry.

Unpublished poem Larry Eigner wrote for his brother Joseph's bar mitzvah, 1946

Left to right: Larry, Joseph, and Richard, at 23 Bates Road, 1947

Eigner family, *left to right:* Richard, Israel, Bessie, and Joseph, with Larry sitting in front, 1949

Larry with unknown man at Camp Jened, 1953

Larry standing outside the house on Bates Road, 1962

Larry Eigner, 1964

Larry Eigner with Robert Duncan (*in the cape*) and others in Golden Gate Park, 1967

Larry Eigner with Robert Duncan (*in the cape*), Richard Eigner (*in sunglasses*), and others in Golden Gate Park, 1967

Larry Eigner, 1978

Larry with Beverly and Richard Eigner, date unknown

Larry Eigner in Berkeley, California, circa 1990

Larry Eigner, mid-1990s

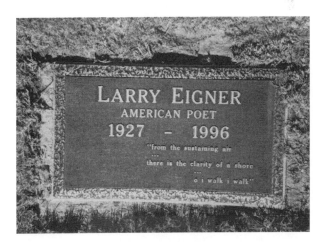

Larry Eigner's grave

14

A Beeaut-i-ful TV

Dress for the Mozart Serenade
I heard coughing out of the orchestra
—"Dress for the Mozart Serenade . . ." (*CP*, 1:101)

In April 1954, the Eigner household experienced a big change when the family purchased its first television. Eigner wrote to Robert Creeley, "Yesterday a beeaut-i-ful tv arrived." He described watching the new device: "like a rollercoaster it seems, maybe from the unfamiliarity."[1] He described the machine in the language of physical disability, calling it an "audiovisual prosthesis." Although the expression would be considered problematic in contemporary language, it was exact. The television did, quite literally, serve as an extension for Eigner's poetry and thinking. His glimpse into the outside world expanded considerably, and he was able to engage the arts, politics, and world events in a new way. He described the television, like the radio before it, as omnipresent. It remained on all day to keep his mother company as she did her housework, even though "none of us is watchin."[2]

Not interested in the distinction between so-called high and low culture, he watched everything from sports to news to art documentaries. When Eigner was young, he struggled with the question of "why Shakespeare should be of greater import, more relevant, than a ballgame."[3] Still, he found much of what was broadcast to be uninspiring: "singing commercials, news, sports, weather, and whodobeots and fame shows."[4]

In the mid-1950s, the networks primarily broadcast either soap operas or shows like *Candid Camera, Howdy Doody,* and *The Jack Benny Program*.[5] However, public broadcasting and network arts programming also created a "golden age" for the arts on television, bringing operas, plays, and classical music into homes and making them available to audiences who would not have otherwise had access to the arts. In his letters, the poet mentioned watching plays, classical music concerts, and tours of museums. After watching such a program, he wrote to Corman:

> Say, how do you participate when it comes to painting? Hardly seem like acting and identification. Metropolitan Museum on tv Saturday. 2 men stand on either side of a pictchoor and chat—2 full-grown men. ? Well . . Or going to a museum and just LOOKING.
> I did sure get a different view of thing prints of i got in a pocket-bk here. Like Vermeer's milkmaid, though i have it in color, on the back cover —the space, lighting too perhaps. Despite the poor reception.
> Just the size of the screen maybe.

In the same letter, he wrote about a trip with his family to see the circus in Boston. He wrote to Corman that the "greater part of the show" felt like "sleaziness enough—some of it positively nightmarish." The circus's aspect of morbidity reminded him of his recent reading of "The Theatre of Cruelty" by Antonin Artaud or "at least a perpetuation of the morbid, a relapse into it":

> trained but not housebroken before he did his trick the elephant did his
> flats
> among all the ~~sharps~~ and sharps
>
> yes, I ~~Saw~~ seen the elephant shit
> the circus was a tent
>
> the circus was a tent
> i saw the elephant
>
> (Which proves him an automaton and spray at the same time
> I wonder if he had to.

In addition to the television, his reading, and his occasional trips, the weather that enchanted Eigner as a child remained central in his poems, so much so that a reader could easily detect in what season they were written. In his poem "D e L I m i t s," he considered "how to make pictures of the weather / Nobody can tell." Sports on the television helped mark the change in seasons, when "as many as thirty games / in the middle of the year you dread the fall / waiting for what follows." And then, with the ending of the baseball season (the family being Red Sox fans), "what follows" is the time when "animals must retreat / and the winter must be got through."⁶ Winter, although certainly beautiful on the North Shore, created even more restrictions for movement outside the house.

The passage of time in general was very much a consideration in Eigner's work, and he often used it in the titles of his books. Like many people with disabilities, Eigner experienced time in a unique way. This concept would later come to be known "crip time," or the idea that disabled people have circumstances, from their own impairments and social conditions, that prohibit them from moving through the world at the same pace as able-bodied people.[7] Despite this, he also wrote at one point that "Time has never passed slowly." He described himself as someone who had "never known boredom."[8] The circumstances of Eigner's life created the possibility for deep observation and reflection, and time for him had a quality of fragmentation. He wrote in the poem "Again Dawn":

```
    the sky dropped
         its invisible whiteness
  we saw    pass out
                 nowhere

         empty the blue
             stars

     our summer
              on the ground

   like last night another
                       time

     in fragments[9]
```

Birds also were constantly present in his poems. With a few exceptions, he did not name the kind of bird, or any kind of object, in his poems. Harking back to William Carlos Williams, he stayed true to the idea of "things" for the sake of themselves, rather than as metaphors, leaving out unnecessary adjectives or other descriptors. It could be argued, however, that the birds that were ubiquitous in his poems represented a kind of freedom of movement that he could not experience. Again, he was aware of Williams's notion that a poem is a "machine made of words." Eigner's interest in the interconnectedness of nature and humanity (the machines of the television and radio) was reflected throughout his poems, not to mention in the "machines" needed for him to move through the world—first his walker, then his wheelchair.[10]

Although the lines in his poems were fragmented, they remained declarative; he didn't include commentary or give the reader guidelines for how to read the poem. Instead, he would invoke a scene, and like a wanderer, the reader would have to create their own interpretation. Instead of creating a kind of confessional or narrative poetry that guided one through a story or experience, Eigner observed that writing (and reading) a poem has "often enough been like discovering things."[11]

In this, the poems often took on aspects of nature walks without the walking. He considered the writing of poems to be like an "assay" to relay "things come upon" or "a stretch of thinking."[12] He came to believe that poems had their own organic shape—and motion—that was not entirely controlled by their author, who should be "willing enough to stop anytime," even though the poet might have the tendency to want to "live forever" in the poem. A poem could "extend itself, naturally, quietly," and it ought to have the same effect on a reader, who could stop or pause anywhere.[13] Later in life, when writing to Jack Lorts, a student who was interested in his work, he described spacing as "a piece of punctuation except possibly the indentations which i like to have pretty various for the sake of movement and getting off the page." He also noted that "a lot of [his] poems begin without capitals, for something risen out of the continuum of speech and thought, a node, rather than a big, formal proclamation or what have you."[14] He believed that if "too many lines start the same distance to the left, it doesn't seem to move enough, it's flat."[15] In this, the poems could become one continuous conversation. This may have also been one reason he chose to simply date many of his poems instead of giving them titles.

Throughout the 1960s, Eigner's poems combined these collages, including his reading, the television, and the view outside his office, which looked onto the short, dead-end street full of trees and birds. In some ways, he was unable to be proactive in his own education. He could order books and little magazines by mail, but he did not have access to bookstores or even the nearby Swampscott Public Library. Few public buildings in Swampscott were accessible. As his friend Robert Grenier noted, "Eigner was very skilled at making due with what he had; both in life and in the creating of his poetry."[16] The critic George Hart notes that Eigner "made" poems with "matter drawn from various sources (what he is reading, what he hears on the radio or in the neighborhood, what he sees on TV or out his window, what he 'sees' or 'hears' in his imagination or memory), emphasize interconnectedness."[17]

One of the poet's favorite shows was Leonard Bernstein's *Young People's Concerts*, broadcast from the newly built Lincoln Center in New York City.

Bernstein started the program in January 1958, just a few weeks after becoming music director of the New York Philharmonic. The program was designed to nurture an appreciation for classical music in children. Eigner was particularly interested in the segment on Beethoven.[18] In discussing the composer's work, Bernstein described the notion that "freedom must carry with it the meaning of freedom to limit oneself and one's material." It was a line that must have resonated with Eigner. Beethoven, of course, was another artist with a disability. Bernstein, in fact, described the composer's disability within the confines of that era's negative perception: miraculous and flawed. In Bernstein's opinion, the composer was "a homely human vessel, and a defective one at that," having "become deaf by the time he was thirty-two years old, [he] spoke a voice that was more than human."[19] This description probably didn't sit well with Eigner, who had a lot of anxiety about artists with disabilities being thought of as "special."

Still, he was compelled, not only by the music, but by the composer's life. After watching Bernstein's program, he read *Beethoven: His Spiritual Development* (1936). In it, J. W. N. Sullivan described Beethoven's death: "there had been a violent storm, and suddenly there was a lightning flash and a great crash of thunder. It seems to have aroused the dying man from his unconsciousness. He raised his clenched fist, opened his eyes, and looked upwards for several seconds with a 'very serious threatening expression.' As the hand dropped, he fell back dead."[20]

In response to Sullivan's book, taking almost word for word from the text, Eigner wrote the poem:

```
Beethoven's fist
   in the end at the thunder he imagined
      a chord  to go on something else
         as may have been   different

         fell back   words
   silent    no more remembered
         in those walls

            that succession a round
```
[21]

In a second poem, "A l o n g L i n e s O f," he moved beyond the text of the biography and combined the musical score with the "movement" outside his window. The "horns loping the / piano / in strength the / drums with history" combine with the man-made world of a "stalled car outside / the building," and the natural world of "shaded / nameless trees."[22]

With Eigner's passion for the natural world and weather, it makes sense that his interest would turn to ecology and preservation. In the 1960s, he began reading Rachel Carson's work. Carson, originally a marine biologist, was most famous for her book *Silent Spring*. Published in 1962, *Silent Spring*, which focused on the negative effect of pesticides, was largely responsible for the contemporary environmentalist movement. Although exactly when Eigner became aware of Carson's work is unclear, it definitely had a strong effect on him. He wrote to Corman that he was "getting into" Carson's *Under the Sea Wind* (1941). He wasn't entirely thrilled with Carson's writing style, which he described to Corman as "Disney-ish in spots . . . and hardly a gripping opus." The book reminded him of "scenes like displays" or dioramas at the natural history museum he visited with his parents.[23]

Despite his misgivings with the quality of the writing, what compelled him was Carson's explanation of the world's interconnectedness. It was this interconnectedness that Eigner brought to his poems and that would influence him as he became more and more invested in environmentalism. He used *Under the Sea Wind*, along with a copy of John James Audubon's *The Birds of America* (1827–38), to write his poem "the music, the rooms." He had been "roaming around in [*The Birds of America*] and coming back to it rather comfortably for a few wks." He mentioned that the color plates in the book were easier to "connect better than ever with fine art for all sorts of sundry reasons." He was interested in the "different powers of flight and migration distances and routes," both as a point of science ("aeronautics, physics, et al") but also as something mystical (bird flight that "satisfies a more spectacular, sensational *kind* of curiosity").[24] He brought this together: the weather, ecology, and birds (and idea of flight), as well as the television in the poem "the music, the rooms," in what Hart called Eigner's "interconnected in extremis."[25] In the long poem, he considers "how distance is to some bird / in the wind," "a malnutrition / Kenya," and simply "on the screen, / the swimming moon / enters eclipse / out the window, and other station / none of us is watching."

Beginning with Carson, Eigner came to link his environmental concerns to starvation and overpopulation. In the late 1960s, he read the bestseller *The Population Bomb* (1968) by Paul Ehrlich. Ehrlich addressed the link between overpopulation and problems with the environment. His book brought public attention to the negative impact of the world's growing population on the earth's resources, although it was criticized for being alarmist. Many people also felt that Ehrlich's ideas were too extreme, verging on science fiction, when he suggested that governments should use measures such as adding "temporary sterilants" to the water supply.[26] Some of Ehrlich's ideas reflected the culture of forced sterilization and eugenics that Eigner grew up with. Ehrlich believed in mass sterilization used historically against poor families, disabled people, and people of color.

The focus on overpopulation as an environmental issue was interesting given the fact that Eigner had no direct experience with sexual intercourse and only rudimentary knowledge of birth control. He didn't have an emotional experience with sex (beyond masturbation), so his ideas were purely academic. One news source the family relied on was the *Saturday Evening Post*, to which Eigner had once, hilariously, compared William Carlos Williams's poetry. In the *Post*, Eigner read an article by Dr. John Rock. Rock was a practicing Catholic and fertility specialist who supported the newly developed birth control pill, something that would have been unheard of in the church. Although Eigner had no information on the subject (he was neither Catholic nor sexually active), he felt passionate enough about Rock's article to write a letter to the editor in support of his position. Although the *Post* published a couple of letters in response to Rock's article, it did not accept Eigner's.[27]

He continued to pay attention to the news. He addressed the civil rights movement and news about political figures in letters. The 1960s brought the Bay of Pigs, John F. Kennedy's assassination, and the moon landing. Although Eigner was attuned to all these events and mentioned them in his letters and poetry, he was political in his own way, and diligently wrote letters to the editor, another habit he may have picked up from his mentor Charles Olson, who wrote to the *Gloucester Daily Times* on a regular basis.[28] But, in terms of the poetry, Eigner remained focused on form and projection, the importance of collage, and what he referred to as immediacy and force.

15

On My Eyes

> *when you search the*
> *spontaneous thing*
> *objects*
> *the belief*
> *shuts the air*
> —"The Fine Life" (*CP*, 1:263)

By Larry Eigner's thirtieth birthday, he had published in numerous magazines, and Robert Duncan was in the process of working with Donald Allen to get his work into *The New American Poetry* (1960). The journey to publish Eigner's first full-length book, however, was arduous and full of complications for all involved. Over the course of four years, Charles Olson, Jonathan Williams, and Denise Levertov all had a hand in the project. Although Eigner was diligent and persistent in the face of back-and-forth on all sides, the publication of *On My Eyes* saw numerous setbacks and almost did not come to fruition.

As early as 1953, Eigner began corresponding with Williams in the hopes of publishing a book with Jargon Society Press. Eigner understood it was important to build a relationship with Williams; small press publishers tended to publish poets with whom they shared social connections and relationships. Keeping up with Jargon's titles was the best way to do that, and throughout 1954 and 1955, Eigner paid close attention to its catalogs, ordering as many books as he could afford. It was also his way of participating in Black Mountain College, where the Jargon titles where published.

After a couple of years, he began to write to Williams specifically about his own work. He told Williams he had compiled a manuscript that he was submitting to Bern Porter Books, a press advertised in the back of the *Black Mountain Review*. Anticipating rejection, Eigner intended to "go down the list" of publishers who paid; he was frustrated that most presses not only did not give royalties, but also asked authors to help pay for printing costs. He complained about the "hordes of my reject slips." In the same letter, he asked Williams whether City Lights, a press in California, charged its authors, but he did not end up reaching out to its editor, Lawrence Ferlinghetti.[1]

When Williams and Olson came to visit him in Swampscott, Eigner got the impression that they wanted to publish a full-length book of his work.[2] There was a miscommunication, however, as their intention was merely to publish just *one* of Eigner's poems as a broadside. They raised the possibility that sales of the broadside might raise enough money to fund publication of a full-length book in the future. At first, Eigner was angry about the situation, but after the miscommunication was resolved, he wrote with excitement to Williams that he was "already wondering to who i shd distribute my allotment" of broadsides. He asked, jokingly, should the broadside go to "Big critics Old school teachers friends who are kind of broke Neighbors The postman ??"[3] He was still under the impression that Olson would eventually help him arrange a complete manuscript. He took a trip to Gloucester with his brother Richard and left a pile of poems on Olson's doorstep (with a note in Richard's handwriting).[4]

In the letter to Williams, Eigner continued to explain that he had heard from Vincent Ferrini that Olson claimed to be "drowned in 10,000 [of Eigner's] poems" and didn't know what he wanted.[5] From the beginning, Eigner never held back when pushing to get published, and he lost his temper with Olson, writing, "Well what I want is the ms of that book Jonathan means, as I take it, to publish, an intention for which I do have some evidence."[6] The "evidence" was a reference to their original meeting, in which the broadside was mentioned. Meanwhile, Eigner was doing his best to continue to help Jargon out financially. He wrote to Williams that he was trying "to round up subscriptions," perhaps as a way of making money for the press so that Williams would publish his manuscript.[7] In the same letter, he mentioned that his manuscript had reached seventy poems, and he was running out of places to submit it.

Between approximately 1956 and 1960, while holding out hope that Williams would publish his book, Eigner sent the manuscript to many publishers, including Fulcrum Press in England, LeRoi Jones's Totem Press, and Raymond Souster's Contact Press. Writing from Japan, Cid Corman deduced that "despite all the gab no one has done anything with your manuscript." Commiserating with Eigner's plight, he wrote, "As a writer whose destiny is to be unknown and disregarded (which is no complaint or lament, since it is better so), I can't offer much advice." He did, however, offer "to do something here, quickly, under ORIGIN PRESS provided your uncle or whoever is willing to invest if none of these enthusiasts has produced something DEFINITE (I don't mean a promise)."[8]

Corman's response, in addition to being a sincere expression of support for his friend's work, reflected a feeling of competition with Williams. He considered Jonathan Williams to be a dilettante who preferred to spend money on lavish dinners and alcohol rather than publishing books. He promised that if Eigner let *Origin* take over publishing the book, "unlike JW, things happen quickly or not at all. JW diddled with Zukofsky's 'A' a couple of years: I did it exactly on schedule."[9] For Eigner, sending copies to different publishers was an extremely complicated process. He did not have access to a mimeograph or copy machine, and while he owned carbon sheets to make copies, he rarely mentioned them in his correspondence, and they would have been impossible for him to maneuver. Retyping manuscripts took hours, especially with Eigner's eccentric spatial organization.

And so, when Williams asked Levertov to go to Swampscott to help type the manuscript, she boldly complained that "it wd be a form of Chinese torture to me to try to type someone else's poems, esp. poems like Larry's." She argued that hiring a real typist would "save weeks and months of trouble and heartbreak."[10] Eigner's parents would not give him the money to hire help. Still, he managed to make four copies and one table of contents, which he enlisted his father to type.

However, he was becoming more and more nervous about the lack of communication from Williams and Olson. He wrote to Williams that he was hesitant about sending them anything else "without hearing from either of you Carolinians as time goes by." He urged Williams to "send a wire, collect, or what. I dunno, but how abt answerin?"[11] Instead of returning the poems to Eigner, Williams mailed them to Olson, with a note that said, "PS / This, I think, is the last batch from Larry. I've begged him to stop."[12] A few months later, Olson returned the manuscript to its author. Eigner told Williams, "I wrote Olson last wk asking if i cd help in any way, etc. An hr ago his response came: he returns the all the mss, figuring he says, that I'm my own best editor."[13] Levertov chimed in, writing to Williams, "As far as editing is concerned, I don't see why Larry just because he is a spastic shd be treated like an idiot. He can edit his own book. He knows what he wd be willing to cut."[14]

Neither Williams nor Levertov understood how difficult it was for Eigner to edit his own work. Arranging the manuscript was a logistical problem; he simply didn't have the physical capability to lay the poems out or move the pages around. He told Williams the only way that he could work was "in bed with folders btwn my legs. And i have had ideas after all."[15] Still, he pressed Williams, "I want yr advice. And information of course : How many pages (Charles thinks 75) ? How many lines can go on each page ? What are the width exigencies?" He begged Williams, "Is there anythin else you cd tell me, fer god's sake. If so, plase do, fer god's sake."[16]

To pay for the publication, Williams asked Eigner to ask his parents to make a donation to Jargon. Bessie was especially resistant to giving the press any money. Both of his parents expressed a "good number of sour grapes . . . when it comes to printing at any expense."[17] Eigner wrote to Duncan insinuating that Bessie and Israel regarded his poetry as a hobby, suggesting that they said, "we havent got those big lots of money 'for spiritual things.'"[18] In addition, Williams was being cagey about how the money would be spent. Eigner wrote to Williams, "folks saw your letter, where you say, in type 'Cant do anything till $4,000 are paid up.'"[19] It was clear that Williams was planning on using the money to repay debt from previous publications, and there was a distinct possibility that the Eigner book might not surface at all. Eigner read an open letter from Jargon in the journal *Wake* declaring a moratorium on any forthcoming Jargon titles; he wrote to Williams asking for clarification.[20] Williams did not answer.

In another letter, Williams proposed that the Eigners contribute a lesser amount. Bessie "scoffed" at the idea of giving anything. Israel was sympathetic to his son, and a familial blowup ensued. Eigner wrote, "Next thing Mama i hrd exploding abt $1000 to Daddy, that he shd give or not but not say anything to her, etc., and when i went in for it she let fly, went down cellar, etc., . . . threatened to leave in th morning, etc." Bessie felt Israel was a pushover for wanting to fund the book. She accused her son of not having enough respect for her way of "handling" Williams.[21] Bessie's way of dealing with the situation was to throw away Williams's letters. Eigner resorted to writing to Williams in the "elementary French" that he had picked up by listening to the radio, and he was able to sneak letters to the mailbox with the assistance of the housekeeper.[22]

Meanwhile, he wrote to Levertov to ask what had become of Williams, who was not replying to Eigner's missives. She assured him that he had "every right to feel very mad at Jonathan" as "he's acted with unforgiveable irresponsibility towards you."[23] Although it remained unclear when, and if, the book would be published, Levertov spent many months writing an introduction for it. She shared her thoughts about the poems in detail in her letters to Duncan. Her letters attested to her belief that Eigner's work was the product of his impairments. She wrote, "whether from the special circumstances of his life or not, he sees the world from an unusual angle . . . for Eigner cannot get at the 'real' sea unless through the agency of others. . . . He has to do a lot of guesswork about living, as most people know it."[24] She expressed ambivalence about whether to mention Eigner's palsy in the introduction. She wrote that to name his disability in the introduction would "inevitably *seem* a special plea" to readers, who might approach the poems with pity.[25]

Amid the ongoing family arguments about whether funding the Jargon project was feasible, someone from the extended family (possibly an uncle) *did* pay for Eigner to self-publish a small collection of poems. *Look at the Park*, published in 1958, was a stapled mimeograph with nineteen poems published in an edition of approximately one hundred.[26] It's possible that the family funded the collection to distract Eigner from publishing with Jargon. *Look at the Park* garnered a small but important audience. Corman wrote that he had heard about the publication through the poet Theodore Enslin. He suggested that Eigner send copies to several poets and shared the addresses of Louis and Celia Zukofsky, Gary Snyder, John Ciardi, and Philip Whalen—all of whom would be "likely to read the work with fair attention."[27]

The publication of *Look at the Park* did nothing to quell Eigner's passion for getting *On My Eyes* into print. Around Easter 1960, his parents drove him to Cambridge to attend a reading Levertov gave in Harvard Yard. He attended the reading in part to find out the status of the book. He briefly met Robert Lowell, who was then teaching at Harvard, and he made fun of the poet in a letter to Corman. He described the reading and the reception ("Upstairs a couple editors we sd a few words") and remarked upon being introduced to Robert Lowell, "Robt Lowell she [Levertov] had say hello to me, etc. Big ponds." It was at this event that he also first met Gordon Cairnie, the proprietor of the Grolier Poetry Book Shop in Cambridge. Israel, eager to promote his son's work, "flashed into action" to share Jargon's listing in its catalog for the forthcoming *On My Eyes*.[28]

In his usual sarcastic manner, Eigner told Corman there was quite a bit of posturing among the poets at the event: "everybody was jawing away as if re stocks, bunds and dresses, ah, the jaws." He described his parents as proud but overprotective, "crowing over the allegation they were all crowded around me, blind to the fact, of crse, that when it wasnt Denise sitting next to me it was Olson."[29] A few months later, in September, Eigner wrote to Corman that finally, "The bk is in press and the proofs are done! . . . Jonathan expects to deliver in person our copies around October 11th, on his way up to Gloucester. I oughnt to get a flagpole and wave, I figure."[30] On Halloween 1960, the long-awaited copy of *On My Eyes* arrived on the doorstep of 23 Bates Road. Eigner was thrilled after the more than a year he had struggled to bring the book to life. Bessie must have been thrilled as well, if only to have the complication with Williams resolved.

16

Nel Mezzo del Cammin

Strange knees:
I bend one and step down
My hip rides over it . Another, leg,
is in full view and ends the flight.
I stand self, read(in a world I've been through before
—"Strange knees: . . ." (*CP*, 1:109)

In a letter to Cid Corman, Larry Eigner referred to turning thirty-five as "Nel Mezzo del Cammin," a reference to Dante's *Inferno*, "mid-way in life's journey."[1] This midway point was a difficult time for Eigner; he spent much of the early 1960s in the hospital.[2] In September 1960, he went into Massachusetts General Baker Memorial Hospital for an operation to treat his hemorrhoids. He was there for nearly a month. Two years later, in September 1962, when he was thirty-five years old, he went back in the hospital for a series of brain operations similar to those he experienced in middle school.[3]

The Eigners learned about the procedure he would undertake while attending an alumni event at the Massachusetts Hospital School, where their son had attended middle school; the director was recommending people who might benefit from the experimental procedure. A former classmate had undergone the surgery, and Eigner wrote to Corman that the doctors were "still observing her, sizing up results."[4] A nervous Corman wrote, "let me hear how whatever operation goes. You have me on tenderhooks," adding, "I hope you're not being used as a guinea pig."[5]

Cryosurgery was indeed dangerous and could even be considered brutal. Eigner described the process to Jonathan Williams as a "cooling [of] th[e] cortex inch on inch by blasts of freon gas reduces shake in palsy temporarily this allowing surgeon to locate points to be burnt out permanently."[6] The goal of the surgery was to partially paralyze his left side to cut down on unwanted spasticity; while his left side would not be entirely stilled, it would no longer be a constant distraction. A friend and poet, Jack Foley, noted, "Larry used to tell me that his whole left side was wild . . . the way he controlled it was not to think about it. But if he forgot it totally, it would go wild. But if he thought about it too much, it would go wild. So, he had to maintain a balance between not thinking about it but thinking about it just enough to control it."[7] Often when Eigner mentioned his spasticity, he referred it to as "Brownian motion."[8]

While the operation was risky, Eigner reassured Corman that it was "less risky thn flying, and may be like having a tooth pulled-sort of." As a dark joke, he added, "come to think of it, i still have all my teeth (some of em patched up to be sure), while i lost some brains in '41," a reference to the operation he'd had in middle school.[9]

Luckily, his family brought his typewriter to the hospital, so he was able to keep up with his correspondence and write poems. He was annoyed, however, that rehabilitation took time away from writing. He wrote to Corman that everything he could do before physically took great effort. He expected the numbness to last for as much as six months, and his left side felt like dead weight: "sitting on knees to dress, its very easy to keel over . . . I'm wobbly, and a fight to get shirt over shoulder."[10] He described to Donald Allen the many side effects: "right now my rash is real bad again on a couple of fingers, neck, face and arms." He found it more difficult than ever to concentrate and complained that, as usual, his "folks" were not eager to help him "process literary data."[11] It was a difficult time for the family overall. He mentioned that his father also had to be admitted to the hospital, due to complications with an earlier prostate operation.

Once home, he got a new typewriter. He had trouble adjusting to the new machine and wrote to Robert Creeley that it "proved . . . a lemon."[12] During the recovery, he'd "set a mag . . . up on the typewriter" and would stand with his hand "on a slightly opened drawer, and read, slowly."[13] But his difficulties were not solely because of the typewriter. He wrote to Denise Levertov, "I am still, in the 56th week or so, numb, and being watched, etc., doing the roadwork (or shd be). It seems abt what expected anyway, the left arm being quite good, though the left fingers more or less clenched, and heaviness and vibration in leg. I dont mind the clench, such as it is, because of the numbness—and that I dont feel my heartbeat even when it must be a pounding."[14]

With his left side paralyzed, his relationship with the typewriter changed. In order to return the typewriter carriage, he had to reach across the machine with his right hand, which he had extreme difficulty controlling. Consequently, his words would progress horizontally down the right side of the page as the poem progressed, avoiding the left margin even more than his previous work:

```
blackbirds and sparrows
         what a mess
     garbage from the apple tree
         the dog noses
       the birds swerve in the wind
          branches    flowers
             now sunlight impounds shadows
           there's my own chimney
                 which was about to smoke
       the birds come back      more crumbs
           have been tossed out for them
                 a dying leaf is a wing¹⁵
```

Still, he continued to be diligent about spacing. When working with editors, Eigner would insist on hundreds of corrections, and even after poems were published, he would go through with a pencil and correct all the spacing errors made in the printing.[16] This is a testament to how he used spaces equally to words and punctuation and interacted with the page as though writing a music score. While recovering in the hospital, he had time to go through his published copy of *On My Eyes* line by line. Despite the lengthy process of making the book, he found many errors in the published text. Making corrections to line breaks and other aspects of published materials was something he would do throughout his life. Further, he confessed to Allen that he was still ambivalent about the selection; he felt a few of the poems were "below par" and admitted to only including them for the "sake of sequence." He found "a few boners in the bk," the biggest one he claimed as his own fault: an entire line from the poem "Cat's Ears" was missing.[17]

On My Eyes did not receive many reviews, although poet Galway Kinnell reviewed it in the September 1962 issue of *Poetry* magazine. The review wasn't very positive, and Eigner found it to be condescending. It reminded him of the letter that William Carlos Williams had written to Creeley upon reading *From the Sustaining Air* (1953). He was concerned that Kinnell had judged the poems through the lens of his disability or "uniqueness." Eigner's feeling was most likely valid. Kinnell was a neighbor and close friend of Levertov's, and he wrote the review upon her recommendation. His aesthetic was similar to hers, and he seemed to agree with her assessment that Eigner's form was the outcome of his impairments. In the review, he wrote scathingly that "if it were possible" for Eigner "to write without the simulation and camouflage of poetic devices—and I admit that maybe it is not—he would then at least have to face the real shortcoming of his poems." He continued with the complaint that the poems seemed "curiously unrealized, curiously broken off, as if the poet had underestimated his content, or, alternately, simply picked an unsuitable form."[18]

Kinnell wasn't the only one critical of Eigner's poems. Corman wrote that the poet Clayton Eshleman "begged" Corman to explain the work to him, and Donald Hall, another academic poet, "didn't get it at all." Corman complained of getting "weary" of explaining the work and in his cranky manner wrote that "a lazier world" of readers was "hard to imagine." However, Corman reported that others enjoyed the poems: "Equally far to the right comes word from James Dickey that you interest him very much, and he'll note the fact in one of their house organs, like Sewanee. Don Allen delighted too. And Duncan. And James Broughton."[19]

Even though *On My Eyes* was disappointing to Eigner in some ways, and Kinnell's lukewarm review must have been difficult to take, he continued to write poems even while in recovery. Although he generally avoided disability as a topic, his stay in the hospital led him to write some poems that approached the subject. The poems, which he referred to as the "hospital poems," would become a central part of his next major work, *Another Time in Fragments* (1967). He wrote a few poems about the doctors, the patients, and his time in the hospital bordering the line of confessional poetry that he so disliked. He wrote:

```
the Dr. saying
   I'll see you again

       what

          necessity
           is the mother
           of this time
```
[20]

In many ways, his situation at the hospital was barely manageable. He wrote to Corman that it felt like an "enormous labyrinth," with corridors as long as streets that reminded him of Grand Central Station. He felt that he didn't "know what to try and take in . . . everything gets scarey," and his memories of surgery were "a little too much now."[21] In the hospital, he fell victim to the surroundings, which he felt were chaotic and terrifying:

```
Screaming woman
 o god god please god
         beyond wall     angles
```
[22]

And, yet, always, he took his situation with a sense of humor. The operation took him many years to recover from, but he joked to Creeley that after healing, he was likely to "end up as an athlete . . . mostly, poised . . . on the verge of walking free and clear."[23] Ultimately, the surgery did help. With his left side in a state of partial paralysis, he could better control what he referred to as his "Brownian motion" and focus on the poems.

17

Another Time in Fragments

while hours may tick by
you remember from childhood
a bird
depending on the weather
—"the bird / of wire like a nest..." (*CP*, 2:370)

Throughout the early 1960s, Larry Eigner published a constant flow of chapbooks and broadsides. Despite his difficulties in finding a publisher for a full-length collection, Eigner continued to be popular in the little magazine world, with editors as diverse as Gerard Malanga (of Andy Warhol's Factory), Paul Auster, and Margaret Randall asking him for poems. His work appeared in numerous magazines and was translated into several languages. International journals such as *El corno emplumado* (the *Plumed Horn*) in Mexico published his poems. While he was happy about getting poems into small magazines and international journals, he was disheartened by the rejections his full-length manuscripts received. He wanted to publish with larger poetry presses, such as New Directions on the East Coast or City Lights on the West Coast.

Cid Corman, who was living in Europe and not publishing outside of his own magazine, *Origin*, assured him that the rejections had nothing to do with the poems' merits. He urged Eigner to stay focused on writing and to not get too caught up in finding places to publish. He also reminded Eigner to keep in mind that he had the support and respect of his peers: "I'm not sure how much of your gift you are aware of, nor do I feel sure it is necessary that you do know... I don't know, but as far as I can judge, you're having more 'success' getting printed than anyone else of the ORIGIN group these days, with the possible exception of [Irving] Layton . . . [John] Wieners (the youngster in Boston) writes me enthusiastically of your poems; he takes to them more than to Bob [Creeley] or Dennie [Levertov], so you come to have your devotees."[1]

A drawback of Eigner's submissions was the *way* he submitted work and subsequently interacted with editors. From the beginning, he didn't organize his own manuscripts. Rather, he would send a copious assortment of poems, sometimes in random order with handwritten corrections scribbled in the margins, such as those he had sent to Robert Creeley and Charles Olson when he began writing. Whoever agreed to publish the manuscript would also inherit the responsibility of editing the poems, deciding their order, and often retyping copies. The process was made more complex by the fact that Eigner rarely titled poems—except by date— and kept track of them with a complex, quirky numbering system. By the 1960s, Eigner had written hundreds of poems. He had great difficulty keeping track of them and devised a system in which poems were numbered, accompanied by letters. When he first began, the system was basic and orderly, but as time went on, it became something that only he could decipher.

Small press editors in his circle were understanding, as it wasn't completely unusual for poets and editors to help each other with the editorial process. Robert Duncan, for example, who would type and arrange Eigner's *Another Time in Fragments* (1967), had worked as a secretary, and had stellar typing skills. Other poets, such as Jack Spicer, could not type at all and still managed to put together magazines and publish collections with help from others.[2] However, many small press editors simply didn't have the time or patience required to bring an Eigner book to life. They were poets, like Corman, who were simultaneously trying to write and publish their own work.

Eigner wanted to pursue the larger presses, of course, in the hopes of getting recognition outside his immediate circle. When he approached New Directions with a manuscript, its editor, James Laughlin, responded, "I think there is a very fine quality, something almost Japanese, though very much your own, about these poems, and I have enjoyed them greatly. . . . They are uneven, as I'm sure you know, but some of the best are very good indeed."[3] Laughlin rejected the manuscript. New Directions would publish Creeley, William Carlos Williams, Duncan, and Denise Levertov, but it would never pick up Eigner as an author.

In 1965, Corman suggested that Doubleday, an even larger, more mainstream press, might "be seduced, though best not to bank on it."[4]

Eigner wrote to the press anyway and also sent work to Scribner's. He was rejected by both. In the 1960s, one of Doubleday's primary poets was Theodore Roethke, a more traditional poet. Eigner probably believed he had more of a chance with Scribner's because it published Creeley. He again began to worry about the quality of his work. He told Richard Morris, who published him in the small journal *Camels Coming*, that it was the second time an editor's letter had confirmed his worries about a manuscript's weakness.[5] Another issue that worked against him was that he was attempting to publish when the popularity of narrative and confessional poets was in full swing, and it was difficult to get attention for work outside these parameters.[6]

Despite these difficulties, Eigner's next major book, *Another Time in Fragments*, would be published in 1967. *Another Time in Fragments* was even more important than *On My Eyes* (1960) as it solidified his relationship with Duncan and brought his work to an international audience. While he was struggling to work with Jonathan Williams on getting *On My Eyes* into print, he was also corresponding with Stuart Montgomery, editor of Fulcrum Press in England. Montgomery was a medical student from Rhodesia who was interested in poetry. Fulcrum was founded in 1965, and Basil Bunting was the press's first author. It is unclear how Eigner first got in touch with Montgomery, but the connection most likely came through Duncan, who was also courting the press. Fulcrum would publish an edition of Duncan's selected poems, *Derivations*, the year after *Another Time in Fragments* came out. At the time, Duncan and Eigner were corresponding regularly. It was Duncan who helped make the book possible. Eigner wrote, "so out of the blue then in '61 and maybe '62, in two installments or else one, comes back the batch of what I'd mailed to him in 29 numbered pages of his own typing, for some reason (over a dozen years later, it probably was, I learned he was a typist, earned part of his living that way).... Two or three errata there—nearly perfect, perfectly congruent copying. All but 6 or 7 of these I put in my '67 book from Fulcrum Press in London, *Another Time in Fragments*."[7]

This collaboration was as beneficial for Duncan as it was for Eigner. When typing the poems, he came to internalize Eigner's use of space and the typewriter as a poetic device. Eigner later wrote of Duncan, "He took to my plainness or simplicity or whatever, in contrast to, I think he said 'relief from,' his own ornateness and complexity."[8] Notably, when Duncan published *Ground Work: Before the War* in 1984, he was insistent that the book be printed in the same font as his typewriter to maintain spacing.

The publication of *Another Time in Fragments* helped Eigner reach new readers in Europe. The French poet Claude Royet-Journoud, for example, first came to Eigner's work after discovering *Another Time in Fragments* on a visit to London. In Royet-Journoud's opinion, what made Eigner's work "so singular" was his "transparency of thought, something muscular & concrete on the page."[9] After returning to Paris, Royet-Journoud lent the collection to his friend Joseph Guglielmi, who also took an immediate interest in Eigner's work. Guglielmi's translations would become the first of many of Eigner's appearances in the French journal *Action poétique*.[10] The poet Jacques Roubaud would later republish the poems in the anthology *Vingt poètes américains* (1980).[11] Eigner kept up a lively correspondence with Guglielmi and Royet-Journoud, and eventually their letters were later collected in one of Eigner's many chapbooks.[12] One of the French poets showed Eigner's work to French schoolchildren, and he received a number of letters and drawings from the young students.[13] Although Eigner's work remained somewhat obscure in the United States, in a quirky way, the interest of French children showed how his work was beginning to reach a global audience. Later in his life, and posthumously, his work would be translated into many languages.

Meanwhile, Eigner continued to look for someone to act as a permanent publisher in the United States, and in 1966, he found someone who agreed to commit to publishing numerous books: John Martin of Black Sparrow Press. Having founded the press to promote the work of one author, Charles Bukowski, Martin hoped his press to be the eventual successor of New Directions. Although their work was extremely different, Bukowski championed Eigner's writing and at one point referred to him as one of the greatest living poets.[14]

Martin, who was used to working with difficult authors, found the process of editing an Eigner book exciting. After receiving the poems for the initial manuscript, he wrote to his new author, "I've been reading and re-reading your poems for several days now and they have begun to fall into a sequence for me. These are the first manuscript poems I've ever worked with where *space on the page* is so meaningful and where the *physical shape* of the poem is integral with meaning."[15]

He assured the poet that he could "count on at least three books next year, which is fine . . . the demand is certainly there."[16] Black Sparrow Books was based out of Los Angeles. *The- / Towards Autumn*, Eigner's first book with Black Sparrow, was edited by Martin himself and published in 1967, shortly after the release of *Another Time in Fragments*.[17] Martin went on to publish two Eigner pamphlets in 1968: *Air the Trees*, with drawings by Bobbie Creeley (Robert's wife), and *The Breath of Once*

Live Things in the Field with Poe. He published two more books with the press in the 1970s, and the poet Robert Grenier would edit two of Eigner's Black Sparrow books in subsequent decades: *Waters/Places/A Time* in 1983 and *Windows/Walls/Yard/Ways* in 1993. Although Eigner would publish many broadsides and chapbooks over the next many years, Black Sparrow would remain his primary publisher.

18

Denmark's a Prison

you don't realize
how mature you get
at 21
but you look back
whenever a summer
continue 70 seasons
—"LETTER FOR DUNCAN" (*CP*, 2:327)

As he entered his fortieth year, Larry Eigner became more and more frustrated by his parents' restrictions and the little control he had over his daily life. His home life was both "problematic and useful."[1] While Eigner felt that his life was too dictated by his parents, his circumstance also provided him with what could be considered luxuries for a poet: he never had to have a job or support a family. He had the freedom to focus his time and energy on reading and writing. Also, due to the sheltered environment, he was protected from the prejudice people with cerebral palsy often experience when they attempt to be part of mainstream culture. Something as simple as going out to dinner can be met with prejudice, particularly in the time in which Eigner lived and especially for those with any kind of speech impediment. The fact that he spent much time at home and could not move throughout the town freely protected him from being taunted. He wasn't completely immune, however, from the limited perceptions other poets had about his situation. He was quite affected by William Carlos Williams's letter of "celebration," which he read to be a commentary on his disability. But mostly, the poets kept their thoughts about his disability from him.[2]

Although this was the case, the circumstance was hard to view as a privilege. The poets in his circle were traveling and leading seemingly exciting lives. Cid Corman left Boston to spent time in Europe before settling down in Japan. Charles Olson moved away from the area to serve as distinguished professor at the State University of New York at Buffalo. Robert Creeley was in Mallorca in the 1950s, then the San Francisco Bay Area, and finally New Mexico, where he moved to teach at the University of New Mexico.

Eigner was frustrated at hearing all his friends' stories, and he often wrote in his letters "Denmark's a prison" as a way of describing his situation at home.[3] Corman, who understood the situation the best, wrote to him, "whatever freedom—release—you arrive at, you're going to have to struggle for, just like the rest of us—though, Lord knows, you have special restraints."[4]

The primary sticking point in the family continued to be summer vacation. Bessie wanted her son to attend summer camp when she traveled to Saint Louis to visit Joseph and Janet. Eigner viewed his mother's insistence that he go to summer camp as "all sorts of things stuffed down my throat, ever so subtly," or more like having a "kettle thrown at your at head—with which I've actually bn threatened in my time)." He told Corman that his mother had read about a new camp on Martha's Vineyard, Camp Jabberwocky, run by the South Shore Cerebral Palsy Society.[5] She was planning on sending him there.

This particular summer, 1965, Eigner wrote to Corman that the decision about going to camp—or not—felt like a matter of making the best out of socializing with disabled people or "playing dead" at home in Swampscott. He confessed to Corman that he was going to "sneak" a letter to the camp out of the house with the housekeeper.[6] He wanted to tell the directors to inform his mother that there were no vacancies left, so that he wouldn't have to go. He noted that it would not be the first time he went behind his mother's back, perhaps a reference to when he wrote letters in French to Jonathan Williams in the process of getting *On My Eyes* (1960) published so that his mother would not be able to read them. He must have been successful because he did not attend.

While he was arguing with Bessie about their summer plans, the poets he corresponded with were convening for the Berkeley Poetry Conference.[7] Organized by Robert Duncan and Thomas Parkinson, the conference was intended to be an extension of Donald Allen's *The New American Poetry* (1960). As a contributor, Eigner had good reason to want to be there. In retrospect, it would come to be regarded as one of the most important poetry conferences in the twentieth century. It was the first and only time most of the poets published in the anthology would come together in person. Eigner received word of the event from an advertisement in the journal *Wild Dog* (to which he was a contributor). Olson, Duncan, and Creeley were attending, along with Allen Ginsberg, LeRoi Jones (Amiri Baraka), John Wieners, and Jack Spicer. With Eigner's brother Richard living in San Francisco, there was a possibility that Eigner would have been able to attend the conference with his help. He wrote to Corman that it felt important to "chip in 2¢ wrth otherwise than by mail."[8] He wanted to interact with the poets he was publishing with in person.

In the end, he wasn't able to attend, but a few years later, he met some of the poets who participated. At the annual Jack Kerouac festival in Lowell, Massachusetts, he heard the Beat poets Allen Ginsberg and Gregory Corso read. After the event, Corso, Ginsberg, and Ginsberg's partner, Peter Orlovsky, visited 23 Bates Road. Eigner's brother Richard later said that the "entourage" was "quite a bit for my mother to take, her having grown up in Salem, Mass, influenced by Longfellow."[9] Bessie was apprehensive about meeting Ginsberg because she had never interacted with any openly gay men, and for once, she was at a loss for words. Ginsberg had recently slipped on the ice and broken his leg, and was on crutches. In his usual eccentric fashion, he "sat down on the floor to play his portable organ."[10] He chanted and sang "an Australian children's song."[11]

Although Eigner had poets visit him periodically, giving him much needed time to discuss poetry, he remained frustrated about living with his parents. He wrote to Corman that he was seriously thinking of relocating to San Francisco to live with Richard. Corman warned him not to be too hasty and advised that he "stay in Swampscott unless lots of <u>friends</u> are in sf. Too much life had gone into where you are. . . . And sf. is a costly move—a visit will do."[12]

In 1964, Eigner did set off on a visit to see his siblings, beginning by taking his first airline trip by himself to visit his younger brother Joseph (Joe) and his sister-in-law Janet in Saint Louis, Missouri.[13] Eigner had become close to his youngest brother and sister-in-law. He kept a lively correspondence with them. Joe was a scientist and provided his brother with a steady stream of reading material. Janet was interested in poetry and, in fact, wrote a paper at one point on her brother-in-law's work. This trip was followed by a visit to see Richard in the Bay Area. While Eigner was visiting Richard, who then lived in an apartment building in San Francisco's Japantown, he met Robert Duncan for the first time. Duncan came see him at his brother's apartment with Donald Allen.

Initially, Duncan told Denise Levertov that he was hesitant to spend time with Eigner in person.[14] He also told Eigner's bibliographer, Andrea Wyatt, that he found Eigner's home life "depressing," and that she should avoid going to Swampscott if she could.[15] Duncan made this judgment, however, without ever going to Swampscott. His opinion may have been based on Levertov's frustrations over driving Eigner to Maine in the summer, as well as her unsightly descriptions of him. Much of this was not unusual. Duncan, of course, lived on the West Coast and very rarely went all the way east. Correspondence was the primary way poets connected at the time. However, his hesitations also speak to the bigger issue of poets creating a disconnect between Eigner's disability and the desire to promote his poetry. The situation with Duncan was even more interesting as Duncan was close to other Eigner family members, and he visited Eigner's cousin Edwin numerous times.[16]

A few years later, when Eigner made a second trip to the Bay Area, he spent more time with Duncan. With Richard, they attended the Gathering of the Tribes / Human Be-In (1967) in Golden Gate Park. The poet had a number of new experiences on this trip. He rode a cable car with his sister-in-law Beverly and visited Muir Woods.[17] He met numerous poets in person, some for the first time. He wrote to David Gitin, another Bay Area poet with whom he had been corresponding, "Coming to your city. I expect in June, maybe next week!! . . . Don't know how much if at all I might be around, but I'm easy to spot, am in a whlchr as you know . . . life nowadays is full of blind dates."[18] He attended a reading organized by David Meltzer with Gitin, Kenneth Rexroth, and John Wieners. Of the reading, he hilariously wrote to Corman, "I can't say I got a lot out of the readings. Most of the poets mumbled or read long wearying accounts of something that had happened to them that afternoon."[19] Despite this, his desire to attend readings in person remained.

Back in Swampscott, he longed to continue the social life and independence he had experienced on the Bay Area trip. In letters, he reported the smallest victories in gaining independence. He relayed to his sister-in-law Janet that upon visiting the dentist he was able to sit in the chair "almost like anyone else." He learned to "go to bathroom without risk, myself (getting off seat was touch and go)." He had reached a point in his life where he wanted to be able to care for himself, "not to mention living all alone."[20] After quite a bit of coaxing, Bessie finally agreed to travel to Saint Louis without him. She was still reluctant to leave him alone with his father and asked a neighbor to look in on them daily.

In the 1970s, Eigner started to have a more regular social life when he met Sam Borash, who was his first close friend in Swampscott. Borash was a house painter, and the two began talking one day when Bessie was having work done on the house. Although Borash wasn't a writer, he was interested in poetry. Eigner invited him over later to hear him read from his favorite book, Olson's *The Maximus Poems* (1953). It could be argued that this friendship was as important to Eigner's life and poetry as was his receipt of the typewriter at his bar mitzvah. Of course, even before meeting Borash, he was able to go places with his family. But, with Borash to drive, help him navigate his wheelchair, and, most importantly, keep him company, Eigner could engage in the local poetry scene.

The ability to socialize regularly outside of the household changed him. It deepened his life, of course, but also brought new audiences to his work. With Borash, he attended readings on a regular basis and eventually started to give readings himself. According to the chronology in Eigner's *Collected Poems* (2010), the poet gave his first public reading in March 1973, at the Cambridge Artists' Cooperative.[21] However, his letters attest that he read publicly as early as 1971. At one of Vincent Ferrini's readings, a student read some of Eigner's work, the first time his poems were read aloud in public.[22] Eigner also gave informal readings at Borash's house and read at the Lynn, Massachusetts, YMCA as part of the National Poetry Day celebration.[23] With Borash, he attended a meeting of the New Hampshire Poetry Society in Concord. Eigner described this to the poet Robert Grenier: "Just today he took me to 3rd affair since I wrote last."[24] He also attended events at a bookstore in Marblehead, Massachusetts, and when the bookstore began hosting a writing workshop sponsored by the Water Field Free School, Eigner and Borash participated.[25]

Eigner was also close to Borash's wife, and he stayed with them for the three days when his parents attended his father's fifty-fifth-year class reunion.[26] It was a considerable change for Bessie to trust her son with them. In the past, she resisted leaving him alone with his father for even one day. At one point there was talk that the Borashes might move into the upstairs apartment to help with Eigner's caregiving.

Although the early 1970s were a fruitful time for Eigner, he suffered a profound loss. On January 10, 1970, Charles Olson died.[27] In the mid-1960s, Olson had left Gloucester for the State University of New York at Buffalo. He abandoned Gloucester due to his heartbreak over both gentrification and the budding tourism industry in the area. The latter was causing the demise of the fishing industry, which had been central to Gloucester for centuries. Olson had fought the changes to his city throughout the sixties; he wrote nearly daily "screams to the editor" published in the local newspaper. According to George F. Butterick, Olson's primary archivist and scholar, Olson rejected what he had once called "roots city." In the documentary *Polis Is This* (2007), Butterick recalled, "There was this sense that it hadn't come out right. It hadn't really worked in the way that he'd imagined in 1950 and in the intervening twenty years. Things just got worse as he lived on, and he wasn't really forging a republic on Watch House Point after all."[28]

Olson held the position at the State University of New York at Buffalo for two years.[29] While he was there, his second wife, Betty Kaiser, was killed in a car accident. The couple had a child, Charlie, that his father sent back to Gloucester to live with relatives. Eigner, and many others, worried that Olson never recovered from his wife's death. Eigner heard about Olson's depression and subsequent inattention to his health. For many years, Olson had been a heavy drinker and smoker, issues that became more prominent after Betty's death. Shortly before his death, he moved to Storrs, where he taught at the University of Connecticut for one year. There, he spent time with Butterick, who was building an archive of Olson's work at the Thomas J. Dodd Research Center on campus. Olson went to New York, where he was supposed to have surgery for liver cancer, but he died before the procedure.

When Eigner spoke about the death of people close to him in letters, as he would later when his parents passed away, he did so with distance and without emotion. With the exception of his mother's death, Olson's passing was probably the most profound Eigner would experience. Ways of applying Olson was something Eigner would think about for the rest of his life. With the amount of scholarship around Olson, there would be no lack of reading material. In the 1970s, Eigner studied *Maps* 4 (1971), John Taggert's magazine issue on Olson; *Olson's Push* (1978) by Sherman Paul; and scholarship by Ralph Maud. He also had a brief correspondence with Butterick as the scholar continued to build Olson's archive at the University of Connecticut. Butterick reached out to Eigner to obtain the letters Olson had written to him and, at one point, visited Bates Road. Eventually, Eigner would have his own small archive of materials alongside those of the poet who meant so much to him.[30]

19

A Temporary Language

a temporary language
as temporary things
and poetry the
math.. of
everyday
life
—"a temporary language . . ." (*CP*, 3:970)

The 1970s continued to be a time of change. Another major change occurred when Larry Eigner received a letter from the poet Robert Grenier, asking to come visit Bates Road.[1] This connection would begin an intense relationship that would last over twenty years. Grenier would become one of Eigner's closest friends, a supporter of his work, and eventually his caregiver and editor.

Raised in Minneapolis, Minnesota, Grenier attended Harvard as an undergraduate. After developing an interest in poetry, he moved to Iowa City to study with Robert Lowell at the Iowa Writers' Workshop. Although he was one of Lowell's best students, he rejected confessional poetry and turned to the work of Eigner's mentors, Charles Olson and Robert Creeley. After graduate school, Grenier moved back to the Boston area to teach at Tufts University. He came across Eigner's book *Another Time in Fragments* (1967) in the Grolier Poetry Book Shop in Cambridge.[2] He connected with the work immediately, finding echoes of Olson's work and what he was attempting to do with his own poetry. Soon after, he wrote to Eigner and asked whether he could visit. He hoped to solicit work for a magazine he was starting. He later described himself as a "a creepy little magazine editor trying to crawl in there and get a poem (for nothing!) for my (unpublished) 'periodical' *this*." Grenier noted that he asked Eigner to read his poems out loud so that he could "get used to" the poet's speech.³

After this initial visit in January 1971, Grenier returned to Swampscott regularly. He strongly believed in the strength of Eigner's work and wanted to do everything he could to help bring it into the world. He assisted with arranging papers, typing, and sending out work. Not one to throw things away, Eigner was in constant battle with his mother about how to organize his copious papers. Even though he kept them in his office, Bessie often intruded in his space. She was constantly worried about dust, and to be fair, her son was a pack rat. It is possible that she ended up throwing away some letters and even some poems. Eigner wrote to the editor James (Jim) Weil, "Monday night mother saw red at lots of dirt according to her announcement next morning . . . she was out to chuck any loose papers she came to in shelves. . . . Bugs she found again on Tuesday." A solution was proposed by Eigner's cousin Edwin, who was teaching at the University of Kansas. A librarian at the university offered to start an archive for the poet. Bessie was getting impatient with the situation and pressed him to get papers off to the archive. Eigner wrote to Weil, "So she was demanding I select stuff to pack. . . . Stuff now in a paper bag unhurriedly awaiting pickup by English teacher (met at UMass Salem). . . . Eyesore no more, ok). Her bite way smaller than her bark but the latter, wow!!!"⁴

The archive at Kansas would be the first of many Eigner archives; he later had archives at Stanford University, the Thomas J. Dodd Research Center at the University of Connecticut, and the New York Public Library. The Kansas archive was particularly important, and not just because it made his mother happy. The librarians catalogued his materials and assisted him with record keeping and sending out work for publication. Most crucially, in exchange for the original copies of poems he sent to the library, he received photocopies that he could use for submissions. Paper handling was always an issue: typing was laborious, he could not easily manage carbon copies, and he did not have access to a photocopier in Swampscott. He had enough trouble getting mail to the post office. However, Eigner would often edit the poems on the photocopies before sending them to publishers, which would later complicate the work for scholars.

In addition to helping get the poet organized, Grenier arranged speaking engagements for the poet. When they first met, Grenier was teaching at Tufts University, but soon after he moved on to Franconia College in New Hampshire. In spring 1972, he arranged for Eigner to give a reading and talk to his class. Sam Borash drove Eigner there and back. Eigner described the reading in a letter to his brother Joe and sister-in-law Janet. He was thrilled with the event and wrote that he couldn't "imagine any better circumstances" for getting people to pay attention to his work.[5] It was new territory for Eigner to speak in front of a class of young writers. Over the next few years, he visited Franconia a couple more times, and Grenier asked him to be a reader for a student's thesis.[6] When Eigner had a reading at the Cambridge Artists' Cooperative in March 1973, he read with Grenier, a few students from Franconia, and a local actor named Bob Teague, who read some of Eigner's poems.[7] Eigner's poems were also projected from slides at this reading.

After the visits to Franconia, Grenier encouraged Eigner to give more readings and try to get wider recognition. He also encouraged him to consider applying for teaching jobs. The idea wasn't completely unrealistic. Before moving to the East Coast, Grenier had been hired by Josephine Miles to teach at the University of California, Berkeley.[8] Miles, who also had a significant disability, was the first woman tenured in the English Department at Berkeley. The poet could not walk, refused to use a wheelchair, and, instead, enlisted students to help her around campus. But cerebral palsy, particularly as pronounced as Eigner's, with his significant speech impediment, created an extra level of complexity. If Eigner had lived after the Americans with Disabilities Act (1990), the prospect of finding a teaching job might have been feasible, although extremely difficult. He did, however, have another opportunity to speak to students. He gave a reading to his brother's class at Washington University in Saint Louis when he visited in fall 1972.[9]

As his social life expanded, he also found new publishing opportunities. During these years, he published two more books with John Martin at Black Sparrow Press, *Things Stirring Together or Far Away* in 1974 and *The World and Its Streets, Places* in 1977. Martin also published most of the poets in Eigner's circle, including Robert Creeley, Charles Olson, and Cid Corman, as well as the composer and novelist Paul Bowles, D. H. Lawrence, and other poets who would be influenced by Eigner later in life, including Michael McClure and Robert Kelly.

Despite his Black Sparrow Press publications, Eigner still had hundreds of unpublished pages of poetry and fiction. An opportunity presented itself when the poet and music critic Sam Charters reached out to him. Upon finding the poet's work, Charters immediately felt an affinity. After their first meeting, he wrote to Eigner that he felt he was a kindred spirit and that Eigner was the "First person I've met who is as involved with poetry . . . other poets are involved too [but] the involvement seems to center around themselves in a way that is different from your complete response to the poem itself [rather] I just like poetry, as you do."[10]

Charters had a chapbook series, Portents, and asked to publish two of Eigner's short stories—what would become *Farther North* (1969). He also began working with Charters on a collection of selected poems for Oyez, a Berkeley press that had published Olson. Eigner proposed writing an autobiography to be included with the poems. Corman planted the idea in his mind: "every poet should try one—even if he just decides to burn it along with the bad poems when it comes time to go through things. There is the notion that everything should be in the poems, but it isn't really true."[11] This was especially the case in Eigner's situation as the poems contained little, if any, biographical information. Ironically, the "autobiography" did not clear up many details about Eigner's life.[12] True to his resistance to confessional poetry or poetry that made the "I" central in poems, it was written in the third person and only gave a subtle feeling of his childhood, not many personal, concrete details. He saved personal details for letters not meant for public view.

Given this, it makes sense how resistant he was when a filmmaker named Leonard Henny approached the Eigner family about making a documentary about their son. Henny worked for a program called Films for Social Change at Washington University in Saint Louis, where Joseph was teaching microbiology, and Eigner's brother thought the documentary would be a good idea.[13] Eigner was against the film from the beginning. In his opinion, the project threatened to have an aura of *The Miracle Worker* (1962) about it. Worried about being reduced to a stereotype and used to inspire able-bodied people, he tried to talk Henny out of it. However, his brother Joe insisted.

The end product, *Getting It Together* (1973), was deeply frustrating to Eigner, who found it to be inaccurate and condescending.[14] The narrator described the poet as "almost completely paralyzed" and attributed the form of the poems to "one finger typing, which unfortunately, cannot keep pace with the speed of his thinking or poetic invention." Allen Ginsberg spoke about Eigner's work and used the same language Denise Levertov had: "Obviously, the form of the verse is dictated by his physical condition." Eigner was furious. Adding insult to injury, the narrator asserted that the poet's mother and brother Richard were the only people who could understand him. Additionally, Henny was concerned that Eigner's speech was not clear enough for viewers to understand, and he asked Ginsberg to read the poems rather than Eigner.[15] His speech was vastly different from Eigner's, and it would have been impossible for Ginsberg to read them accurately. Considering that Eigner's poems were based on Olson's "Projective Verse," the poet's individual voice and breath deeply mattered. The fragmentariness in Eigner's voice clearly reflected the spacing and punctuation in his poetry. In contrast, Ginsberg's long lines and passionate exclamations reflected his own breath. Therefore, Ginsberg was an odd choice, but Henny also probably chose Ginsberg to bring attention to the film as he was at the height of his popularity.

Upon receiving the final cut of the film, Eigner was very unhappy. He complained about the bad sound quality, which was very distorted and made the film nearly impossible to understand. The images that accompanied his poems, such as dolls, didn't make much sense, and he was unhappy with Ginsberg's introduction. The film had a few good qualities. It created footage of Eigner and his parents that would not otherwise exist. Some of the film was shot in the Marblehead bookstore where Eigner took his writing workshops. An audience gave him the opportunity to discuss his ideas about the environment. It is the only document existing on film of Eigner as a younger man. He was rarely recorded on film. The poet Bob Holman would film him many years later for a documentary for public television, *The United States of Poetry* (1996).

As Eigner was finding new outlets for his work, his home life was also changing. In 1978, his father, Israel, had a heart attack. Even with the help of a housekeeper, Bessie was unable to continue to care for both of them; Eigner wrote to Jim Weil that his father had become impossible for his mother to manage. Israel had been ill for quite some time. In a rare moment when his father was vocal, Eigner wrote to Paul Auster about Israel being scandalized by the mail: "(Paul) Buck still has at least 4 or5 things in hand. His porno '..... Not Fit For the Queen' came Saturday. Mother proposed I ask my friends to send no more of that kind of thing – a passing remark – she didn't see it, (zz) Dad just reported it to her in his vague fashion (all during life, not just his stroke at 77 1/2 18 months back) characterizing it as 'crazy stuff.'"[16]

Israel was moved to Salem Hospital from his home, and his son predicted that he would move to a nursing home so he could have around-the-clock aid. He wrote, "Heart still good (!) but poor circulation and of course wandering disoriented mind. Enough ups and downs, eg, wow!" Israel did move to a nursing home, but he passed away six weeks later. Eigner did not express much sorrow for the loss of his father in his letters. He found the outpouring of attention at his father's Shiva "a little striking, oddly so," as his father was "never the life of the party."[17] While this sentiment is harsh, it is clear that he was emotionally distant from his father. Although Israel advocated for the publication of *On My Eyes* (1960), he was never fully able to understand his son's dedication to poetry. Corman and Olson sufficed as more plausible father figures.

It is possible that at the back of his mind, Eigner viewed his father's death as an opportunity to move out of his parents' home as Bessie was aging and her health was getting fragile. Eigner wrote to Jonathan Williams that it had been four years since his mother had been diagnosed with angina.[18] As a consequence, his brothers began seriously looking at new places for him to live. They were exploring the possibility of having Eigner and Bessie move in with a nephew or niece in the area. Another relative suggested that Eigner stay in Swampscott and move into a local group home. There was still a debate as to whether Eigner should move to the West Coast to live near Richard, something Richard and Eigner had long been pushing for. By then, Eigner and Grenier were also close friends and Grenier had relocated to the Bay Area as well, so there was the possibility of being able to participate in more poetry circles. There was also discussion as to whether Bessie would move with him. In the end, all agreed that he would move to Berkeley, and Bessie would remain in Swampscott. In August 1978, at age fifty-one, he ventured into a life without his parents.

20

The Cornerstone House

there are so many memories
maybe numberless as the stars
—"our barren loves . . ." (*CP*, 1:142)

Once Larry Eigner left his parents' home to move to Berkeley, California, the groundwork for a different life was set. His brother Richard and sister-in-law Beverly became his legal guardians, and they set out to enable him to be as independent as possible. Richard had heard about the independent living movement in the area, and he had settled in the Bay Area with the thought that his brother might come to live with him someday.[1]

The independent living movement began in 1962, when the activist Edward Roberts applied to the University of California, Berkeley. The university dean told him, "We have tried cripples before and it didn't work."[2] In addition to inaccessible classrooms and libraries, a major roadblock for Roberts was the school's lack of a dormitory that could support the iron lung he slept in as treatment for polio. With Roberts's persistence, however, the school was forced to provide a residence for him on the third floor of Cowell Hospital, and he enlisted peers to help him navigate campus.[3] He joined with others to form the activist group the Rolling Quads. When the Quads faced eviction from Cowell, they organized a revolt that led to the creation of curb cuts and other accessibility improvements—both on and off campus.

Out of this struggle came the first center for independent living. The goal of the independent living movement was to enable people with disabilities to be in control of where they lived, a decision that had previously been made for them. The idea behind the movement wasn't so much that people with severe disabilities were expected to live alone, but that they would have a say in where they lived and whom they hired as caregivers. While Eigner wasn't a disability activist himself, the move was another opportunity for him to experience progressive spaces for people with disabilities as he had when he spent time at Camp Jened.

Eigner's move was a big change for both mother and son, and it must have involved letting go on Bessie's part. She was resistant throughout her son's life for anyone else helping with his caregiving, and the move was made out of necessity. When Eigner came to the Bay Area, his brother and sister-in-law tried to get the poet involved with the local center for independent living and United Cerebral Palsy (UCP), an organization that helped people with cerebral palsy find housing and other resources. However, neither proved to be a good match. Part of the issue was Eigner's poor conversation skills. His sister-in-law Beverly noted, "We found that he needed [to learn] some social interaction outside of us because we would cater to his needs and not everyone would. So that was a problem, socially."[4] Not surprisingly, his speech reflected the kind of monologue used in letter writing, the way he had communicated for so many years. When Beverly took him to a social group at the center for independent living, the other participants found him to be "spoiled" and difficult to get along with. When she took him to UCP to find out what services it had, Eigner told the staff that he didn't need (or want) any help.[5]

His reaction was to be expected, given how his mother had impressed on him never to receive help outside the family, and his negative reaction to UCP was most likely derived from growing up in the era of the first telethons. Starting in 1950, the UCP Telethon, the first of its kind, relied heavily on pity to get donations; children would be brought onstage using crutches or wheelchairs to sing the theme song:

> Look at us, we're walking!
> Look at us, we're talking!
> We who've never walked or talked before.
> Look at us, we're laughing.
> We're happy and we're laughing.
> Thank you from our hearts, forever more.
> But the fight has just begun.
> Your dollars make dreams come true.

Until the time Eigner moved to Berkeley, his family resisted taking any sort of help, financial or otherwise, from any such organization, harking back to Bessie's steadfast belief that her family was her responsibility.[6] For his part, Eigner continued to resist being associated with other disabled people. Despite his misgivings with these organizations, in September 1978 he moved into a group home on La Loma Avenue in Berkeley. He nicknamed it the Cornerstone House. The house was owned and run by a "palsied woman," Anna Johnson, who provided room and board for people with disabilities (as well as several able-bodied students from the nearby campus).[7]

While the house was billed as independent living, the residents there required and received twenty-four-hour care. Eigner, for example, was still not able to dress himself or eat by himself. He was not able to shop or cook and could not be left alone at night in case he fell or needed help with the bathroom. Although his brother and sister-in-law's intentions were good, the living situation turned out to be a disaster. In letters, Eigner constantly complained about his housemates and the attendants as well his frustrations with the "commune" environment. The house functioned as a democracy, with its fourteen residents voting on policies concerning "neatness, routine, and privacy," but these rules were constantly broken.[8] He described the house as an environment of endless drama with a loud, partylike atmosphere and continuously rotating residents and attendants. His living situation was also complicated by the fact that it was difficult to maintain good caregivers, who were often underpaid workers or untrained students working in exchange for housing. People in the house were "living it up, leaving unused tv, radio, lights on, smoking pot and 'hash,' doing jigs, going around . . . everyone on the town, wow! Quite a few ppl in and out."[9]

Growing up in the quiet, sheltered environment of his parents' house, Eigner couldn't stand the noise. He had particular difficulty with the fact that people left the television on, something that annoyed him the most about his parents' home. Eigner never had to deal with or tolerate other people's habits. After being cared for all his life, and bound by his mother's restrictions, he didn't have the skills needed to relate to living with strangers. He didn't get along with many of the other residents, and relationships were often strained. He complained about a "new roomer" who lashed "out with tongue if any of us in whchrs says a word to him or otherwise inadvertently bother him."[10]

Eigner described to Corman feeling constantly pressured by attendants to participate in house activities when he just wanted to write: "I just got lectured for not getting girl next door a birthday present o card- 26-yr-old attendant . . . saying its a disgrace and he's ashamed of me."[11] Although he was clearly experiencing pressure, he was mostly upset by being asked to leave the typewriter. He wrote poems about the situation, and his longing for quiet:

```
    silence

       however brief

          gap    lightening¹²
```

He described to a most likely confused and worried Bessie that there was "disco again this morning"[13] and said that an attendant "on the town, goes in for loud disco and gospel shouting."[14] Poet Ron Silliman recalled, "They were not tending to his needs was the way he expressed it to me, because they were actively having sex in the hallways. I think the partying side of it (or the cruising side) was more a problem for Larry than any question of orientation. It was very much a poppers and cocaine type of scene, at least that's how the one person who worked there whom I knew (through his lover, a poet in my writer's workshop in SF) described it to me."[15]

The residents suffered constant neglect. Eigner wrote to his mother, "the phone's been disconnected again, 2nd time this year," and one attendant charged a housemate to have him read to her.[16] It was rare that Eigner reported a day that was "normal, peaceful," and sometimes, it was "rather amazing to see how things straighten out and meals get taken care of." Often, he did not have access to a regular shower or meals. He told his mother, "At the end of the first yr" it was "tolerable," but "all the same wild enough," and the attendants were "unpredictable . . . cranky and rather domineering."[17] The noisy environment made it into his poems:

```
    D   i   s   c   o

       like new yr's eve

          all year through

                there's a typewriter    sound

       what of the day¹⁸
```

Eigner complained to his mother that Anna Johnson, the "palsied proprietress" who lived with them and managed the household, had her lover move into the house after she met someone in a lonely hearts advertisement in the local paper. She wanted to retire from running the household and "get a man to lean on," as Eigner described it to Corman. She hired a twenty-six-year-old able-bodied man to replace her. Eigner found the new manager to be abusive, "a minute or two later I back into the hallway, headed for living room to make a phone call and see him right there say, surprised, 'Boy! I didn't see you here.' He said, 'Larry, get out of there. I don't want to hear a word from you! I've got my own problems.' 3rd such incident. Well, last Sat. night I heard I'm not the only one after all."[19] His mother distanced herself from the difficult situation, writing, "Sorry to hear about your problems, but I'm sure Rich and Beverly are working on a solution which I hope will be satisfactory all around."[20]

Despite the problems Eigner experienced, he made friends with other disabled people and learned about the prejudices they suffered. He joined a disability "rap session," which was kind of like a support group.[21] He wrote to his mother that he learned how difficult it was for someone with cerebral palsy to find their own apartment, even in the relatively disability-friendly Bay Area. A friend of his was "having a hard engh time hunting apts via phone partly bcz some ppl hang up thinking she's a kid."[22]

He was forced into learning how to navigate new social situations and make new friends. He formed a bond with his housemate Adele, and related to his mother that he was "regaling Adele, talking, reciting, and reading to her."[23] From his letters, it seems like he might have had a romantic interest in her, but he did not mention those feelings directly. Although the people around him, able-bodied and disabled, were having romantic relationships, sexuality and dating remained a complete mystery to him. He wrote to his mother that when a woman complained in the rap group that the nursing home where she resided wouldn't let her young son live with her, he was convinced the woman "cd be fantasizing or fabricating." He couldn't believe that someone with such pronounced impairments could have a relationship, let alone a child. He sent along a copy of the *National Enquirer* that Robert Grenier gave him for laughs; it had a story about a disabled couple having a child.[24]

The poet Robert Grenier, Eigner's good friend, moved to the Bay Area around the same time Eigner did. He lived above the Berkeley Zen Center, run by the poet Norman Fischer, with his partner, Kathleen Frumkin. Frumkin was also a poet, and Grenier and Frumkin were centered socially in the Berkeley poetry scene. Through them, Eigner started to meet many new poets, who came to visit him at the Cornerstone House: "Ron Silliman here Sunday invited me to read at the end of Oct. . . . Grenier was here with Lyn [Hejinian] and Kit Robinson." He told his mother, "I've been asked to read together with a guy [Norman Fischer] now dwelling above Grenier, Aug 29 . . . 364 days after I came here. Another anniversary, wow!"[25]

While Eigner was living at the Cornerstone House, Richard bought him an electric typewriter, an IBM Selectric, but the typewriter keys were too difficult to use with his spasticity, and he switched back to his Royal manual typewriter.[26] He had a similar situation with his new electric wheelchair, which Richard had given him to increase his independence. Working the chair wasn't an easy adjustment. Before learning how to use it effectively, he took off one day to visit Grenier and Frumkin at the Berkeley Zen Center. The trip was downhill, and Frumkin received a call from a stranger who rescued the poet from a crash on the street.[27] Eigner later complained to Bessie about the uselessness of the chair, as it would not "fold and the batteries, a big job to move, make it too heavy to lift. We agreed, too, it's not so good for around the house. For instance, I can push backward with my feet, but not forward, it's soo hvy, and my hand is kept rather busy driving."[28] Although the wheelchair was difficult to use at first, he felt like it gave him some freedom.[29] He wrote to his mother about his deepening relationship with Grenier and Frumkin. He told her, "Past few month I've had more or less of a secretary desultory engh in this freelance miscellaneous willy-nilly life what we do we figure as we go along, mostly we gab, a few hours a wk." He described Frumkin as a "friend of Bob Grenier's, lively. She came along with us here 2-3 wks ago to Angel Island one day, she and her 7-year-old son. I drove around pretty well on the ferryboat, sf wharf, and on the isle, road in a couple of stretches two ways."[30]

Although Eigner described their relationship as primarily social, with Frumkin he had the assistance he needed to work. She helped him organize his work space, even though he was writing less since the house's pervasive chaos and noise impeded his concentration. He described Frumkin as "a bright fun-filled woman . . . has bn helping with papers the past couple of weeks . . . 15$ a week she's getting, it sounds quite a sum to me, but evidently it's a going rate and her and Bob need it."[31] Frumkin's father was in the shoe business, and she used discarded shoe boxes to organize Eigner's massive collection of paper. With the help of the shoeboxes, they created a method in which the poet could easily access his books and papers while continuing to write new poems.

In 1978, Eigner had the opportunity to spend time with Cid Corman in person when he traveled to the Bay Area. He relayed to Bessie, "Lyn Hejinian took me to see Cid (for the first time in over 20 yrs) at Tom Mandel's, director of SF Poetry Center." There he also met poets George and Mary Oppen as well as Corman's wife, Shizumi, whom he told his mother, "Hardly knows English after all, she isn't conversant in the language anyway, and seem an unassuming or quiet person."[32]

As Eigner spent more time with Grenier and in poetry circles, it became clear that the living situation at the group home was not working well. Grenier attested that the last straw came when Eigner got into a fistfight with another resident over the volume of a television set.[33] Grenier still felt passionately about the poet's work and wanted to help create a situation where he could write. As Grenier and Frumkin also had two children, Amy and Ezra, they wanted to live in a regular house and move from living on a busy street. Frumkin agreed that they would all move into a house with Eigner and take over his care.[34]

21

McGee Avenue

the man comes up
and straightens him out

it's quite the ball..
—"THE ST. BERNARD LOOKING AT THE TOY" (*CP*, 1:227)

Once Robert Grenier and Kathleen Frumkin decided that they were going to live with Larry Eigner, they went about the task of setting up house. Richard Eigner bought his brother a large house on McGee Avenue in Berkeley near the campus in 1980. In exchange for caregiving, Grenier and Frumkin (and their respective children, Amy and Ezra) lived rent free and received a small stipend from social security. Grenier noted that the house "was uniquely structured because there were two kitchens back-to-back. Separate bathrooms. . . . It had doors that you could open or shut so that you could eat together in one kitchen."[1] There was a large yard with a live-in cottage occupied by a philosophy student, Jay Ryneck, and his partner, Diane, both of whom also helped out.[2] Also living at the house on McGee was Grenier's dog, Boom, whom Eigner described:

```
the dog

   comes

out of the door

   of course

   lifts his

         back leg
```

```
doesn't like
          wet

   some days³
```

The house on McGee had two floors so that the family had their own private space upstairs. Downstairs, Eigner had his own bedroom and study; there was a communal living room and kitchen. Grenier worked nights as a proofreader in San Francisco, and Frumkin worked in the university library at Berkeley, where she also attended school. The couple arranged their schedules so that someone would always be home as Eigner couldn't be alone in case he fell or had an emergency. Despite their complicated schedule, everyone shared at least one meal a day, usually breakfast. Grenier felt that Eigner needed to brush up on his conversation skills. As Grenier described it, the poet eventually got used to being able to "give and take among the discussion . . . without trying to dominate the conversation."[4] Eigner's lack of social skills wasn't a product of his disability but a consequence of his having grown up with his parents. He often complained about not having enough interaction with other people, and as much as his parents supported him, they certainly had no interest in talking about poetry. Although his life changed significantly when he became friends with Sam Borash, his way of relating to others was already settled into his personality. He was so thrilled to discuss poetry when people visited it was difficult not to launch into a monologue, a habit that he had throughout his life. Grenier and Frumkin both wanted to help him change this habit and get used to being in conversation with others.

With their help, Eigner's physical skills also improved. He wrote to his mother, "I've put my stockings on evry morning lately and this wk have tightened and tied myself gunboat shoes (loop at the back does seem essential for putting on, though . . . so good news! And, as you figured, something here really learned." Among his other accomplishments was learning to get in and out of his bed and manual wheelchair. He could get on and off the toilet, which he described to his mother as "quite an achievement."[5] He learned to dress and undress himself and to use a fork and spoon. Grenier related that Eigner "traversed in his electric wheelchair down the ramp (around corners) & around & about in much of Berkeley."[6] Most importantly, he could make his own schedule. He had always been a night owl, and now he could go to bed and get up when he wanted. Grenier recalled, "He could stay up as late as he was wanted which was something he was never able to do at his parents' house . . . he was free in a way that he hadn't been. I envied his freedom when I went to work. I had this mind-numbing proofreading job."[7] In poet Ron Silliman's opinion, these developments made Eigner a "more authoritative (or, alternately, demanding) presence."[8] For the first time, he was experiencing a level of control, independence, and privacy.

One thing that frustrated Eigner was Richard and Beverly's insistence that he continue physical therapy.[9] In Berkeley, it wasn't quite as brutal as what he had experienced as a child. He went to speech therapy and swimming classes. He participated in the "Wilderness Project," an organization that helped people with disabilities get out into nature.[10] He took two trips with the organization, to Yosemite National Park and to Calistoga, California, where he went on a twenty-minute ride on a glider. He wrote to his brother Joe and sister-in-law Janet about a camping trip with Grenier and Frumkin, "Just got back from Kings Canyon last night, where we pitched 3 tents 11 pm or so Tuesday night, I guess we were all asleep by the smallest hour wdnsday. I had a whopping time as usual, of crs, there are always all kinds of differences and similarities. I never got into a sleeping bag before, for one thing, and hadnt got to ask how far dow[n] it opened up – all the way, ah, so a cinch to lie in, and Bob has it was pretty easy to haul me into and out tent."[11]

Eigner was happy with his new life. The best part was that Grenier and Frumkin had a constant stream of poets and students visiting, and Eigner was able to immerse himself in discussions about poetry. Grenier found students to help with the secretarial work that he and Frumkin no longer had time to do. Robert Kocik was one student who came to the house to help Eigner. Kocik assisted with writing and mailing letters, including cover letters to publishers. He retyped poems and followed up with submissions. Kocik was careful to "never be the scribe for his poems or letters 'firsthand'" as he knew typing was integral to Eigner's process. He remembered:

> One of the most important roles I had was to mediate, de-isolate and circulate. I.e. it was social. I took Larry to readings, out for lunch, visits. Also, to "interpret" when someone wanted to visit Larry, as many people feared their inability to understand what Larry was saying (and I never or rarely had a problem with this, as I already had a background in disability and caregiving and the like). So, to take some of the load off of Bob. Secretarial. And then, after a short while, it was just friendship and being a bit of the household. I don't recall when the work-study officially ended, but I just kept doing what I was doing, as what I wanted to do, introduced many people to Larry, got his work around, etc.[12]

With so many people around to assist him, and given the accessible landscape of Berkeley, Eigner was able to attend events regularly. In the years he lived with Grenier and Frumkin, the poetry he was exposed to expanded greatly. He attended readings by Alice Notley, Joanne Kyger, Michael Palmer, Tom Raworth, Ronald Johnson, and Philip Whalen. He attended the Modern Language Association (MLA) Annual Convention, where he heard Robert Creeley and Warren Tallman read.[13] Eigner also heard Gary Snyder read with Robert Bly. Periodically, poets came to stay at the house on McGee. Robert and Penelope Creeley spent a week with the family, as did Anselm Hollo.[14] Eigner also started to give more readings. Soon after he moved in with Frumkin and Grenier, he was invited by Norman Fischer to read at the Tassajara Zen Mountain Center.[15] In 1983, he traveled with Grenier to New York City. There, they gave a reading and taught a workshop at St. Mark's Poetry Project in the East Village.[16] It was on this trip that he met Charles Bernstein, and they visited the American Museum of Natural History.[17]

In the mid-1980s, Eigner began spending a lot of time with the poet Jack Foley, who would become his closest friend in his later years.[18] Foley ran a reading series at the blues club Larry Blake's on Telegraph Avenue in Berkeley. Eigner attended the reading series weekly and read there periodically himself. According to Foley's description, when Eigner would attend the reading, he would move directly to the front, just inches away from the reader.[19] He had difficulty hearing, something he linked to the palsy. Doctors diagnosed that he could "hear lower pitches easier than high – a condition I was told has been to bn rather common among CPs." But the trouble was "too slight to warrant a hearing aid."[20] However, Foley attested that Eigner would promptly fall asleep at the readings and sometimes begin to snore loudly. Eigner wrote about these events:

```
fight the background
   chatter as
     the people
   eat more

     and there's the music
        across the street
           or listen in

             why not
```
[21]

While Eigner was busy socializing with the poets in the Bay Area, the quantity of his correspondence waned. Now that he was able to attend readings and have people over nearly daily, he didn't have to live in letters. He did, however, keep in touch with Cid Corman through writing. Corman was permanently settled in Japan. He had long since suspended publishing *Origin*, mostly out of financial difficulties. In the early years of their relationship, Corman served as a mentor, but later in life their relationship shifted significantly. Throughout Corman's life, he had significant money problems, and he attempted to get the Eigners wrapped up in his financial troubles. In a letter wishing her son a "happy fifty-fifth birthday," Bessie wrote, "I'm also sorry that I cannot take on Cid Corman's finances. As I remember it is a bottomless hole, and I don't have Daddy around to sustain me." At the bottom of the letter, Eigner wrote in both script and type, "Please shred (dispose of) after a bit."[22]

Now that he no longer had full days at the typewriter, Eigner was also writing less poetry. Being away from the house made it impossible for him to "type things right off" as soon as they came into his head, and he probably wished again for the "pocket size" typewriter he once mentioned to Creeley.[23] He wrote to Joe and Janet, "too bad you cant do everything – as, now I go out quite a lot, I dont type things right off, but scribble in a notebk, still as it turns out illegibly engh, and in general, too, the more I see the less I remember and write down. Ok though. Like to see how sizeably you can manage."[24] He wrote about the difference between Swampscott and Berkeley, saying, "A few years back I could feel in things a lot more than I've been able to since I moved to Berkeley . . . it seems, I felt the world a neighborhood, or two dozen square miles."[25]

Something that did not change was Eigner's habitual reading. He always had a book in his hand, or he would carry books around in his wheelchair next to his thigh. At this point, his vision had begun to fade from age, and he used a magnifying glass to read, showing his passion and dedication. Books were not only something to be read, but something to be carried and lived with, objects to be kept close at all times. Consequently, his books were full of crumpled pages, scrawled notes, and broken spines. The constant stream of books arriving by mail included, as always, new poetry collections, magazines, and chapbooks. In addition, his brother and sister-in-law picked up books covering a wide variety of subject matter at yard sales or in used bookstores: mathematics, science, and history. He described his reading habits as "wolfing down" information; his curiosity was such that he found himself hardly able "even yet to skip a word" of what was in front of him. In just one letter to Corman he mentioned reading Will Durant's *The Renaissance* (1953) and *The Age of Louis XIV* (1963), a handful of books from the Mechanics' Institute Library, and copies of *Scientific American*. He asked his brother to get a copy of Richard Morris's *Light* (1979).[26] He also remained dedicated to studying Charles Olson's work.

One significant absence from the social scene at the McGee house was Robert Duncan. Frumkin remembered that despite his early championing of Eigner's work and the close association Eigner felt to him, Duncan never came to visit.[27] He certainly had the opportunity, as they shared many friends, and Duncan and the artist Jess lived just on the other side of the bay. It may have Duncan's discomfort with Eigner's disability. Another possible contributing factor was the generational, aesthetic split in that happened in American poetics in the 1980s. Duncan landed on one side, with Grenier on the other. The scholar George Hart notes, "Olson's death in 1970 might be considered the turning point between these generations—he was the 'strong' precursor figure to be both embraced and contested. His 'Projective Verse' manifesto is the dominant statement for open-form poetics after *The New American Poetry*, and the next generation defined itself by both accepting and rejecting aspects of Olson's projective verse."[28]

Poets of this new generation came to be referred to as the Language poets, and they considered Grenier to be a predecessor; many people cited Grenier's essay "On Speech" (1971) as the beginning of the new poetics. In it, he wrote, "why imitate 'speech'? Various vehicle that American speech is in the different mouths of any of us, possessed of particular powers of colloquial usage, rhythmic pressure, etc., it is only such. To me, all speeches say the same thing or: why not exaggerate, as Williams did, for our time proclaim an abhorrence of 'speech' designed as was his castigation of 'the sonnet' to rid us, as creators of the world, from reiteration of the past dragged on in formal habit. I HATE SPEECH. . . . I want writing what is thought/where feeling is/words are born."[29]

Although the so-called Language poets were creating something vastly different from Duncan's generation, Grenier considered Creeley and Olson to be mentors. It's clear that Grenier was influenced by Olson's "Projective Verse" and, subsequently, Eigner's work. Grenier reminds the reader that "speech is in the different mouths of any of us," a thought directly derived from Olson's insistence that the poem should come from the poet's individual breath and leanings.[30]

In a history of Language poetry, Lee Bartlett wrote, "Probably the first use of the term 'Language Poetry' . . . appeared in [Ron] Silliman's selection of poems by nine poets (including Bruce Andrews, Robert Grenier, Clark Coolidge, and Silliman himself) in *Alcheringa* in 1975."[31] The goal of language-based poetics, if any at all, was to "privilege critical intelligence" over what had become the popular, "orphic, bardic impulse in American poetry."[32]

While descendants of Ezra Pound resisted poetry written in traditional forms, poets such as Denise Levertov and Olson did rely on romanticism and narrative to a certain degree. Eigner's work leaned more toward Grenier's desire for "writing what is thought/where feeling is/words are born." Silliman thought Eigner to be "the first man to isolate words/phrases/perceptions in such a way as to force the attention onto them, not to the context."[33] In addition, there is also Eigner's nontypical speech to consider. His speech patterns and the labor of reading aloud are reflected in his "isolation" of individual words, his fragmentary syntax, and the wandering nature of the poems, all of which are also evident in his letters. Again, this can be read not as a reflection of his disability, but as a reflection of his individual voice and breath.

In the late 1970s, when Bruce Andrews and Charles Bernstein were compiling the magazine $L=A=N=G=U=A=G=E$, they looked toward Eigner as an influence and opened the first issue with his essay "Approaching Things / Some Calculus / How figure it / Of Everyday Life Experience" (1978).[34] The journal was devoted to "poetics—whether essays, notes, or reviews—and the 'house style' was, to say the least, usually as elliptic as Eigner's."[35] Bernstein later explained that they had hoped to emphasize, "a spectrum of writing that places its attention primarily on language and ways of making meaning, that takes for granted neither vocabulary, grammar, process, shape, syntax, program, or subject matter."[36] This, of course, could be an accurate description of Eigner's work as well as his belief that "immediacy and force" had to take precedence.[37]

Language poetry rejected the self as the center of the poem. As Bernstein wrote, "It's a mistake, I think, to posit the self as the primary organizing feature of writing. As many others have pointed out, a poem exists in a matrix of social and historical relations that are more significant to the formation of an individual text than any personal qualities of the life or voice of an author."[38] As Bartlett noted, from the beginning, the Language poets' goal was to resist "a Wordsworthian sense of the poem's task—[which was] to recall through a fixed and definable identity" or "a poem [that] exists, that is, primarily to convey from writer to reader an experience."[39]

What is interesting about Eigner is that he created a bridge across these two poetic landscapes. Despite the poets' dislike of each other [and the other's work] they all took Eigner's poetry seriously. Even after Grenier and Eigner parted ways, those associated with Language poetry worked hard to have Eigner's work published and remain in print. Throughout the 1980s and 1990s Eigner had books or chapbooks published by James

Sherry's Roof Books, Lyn Hejinian's Tuumba Press, and Doug Messerli's Green Integer.[40] When Silliman edited *In the American Tree* (1986), an anthology of Language poets, he dedicated it to Eigner, whom he directly referred to as a predecessor.[41] In the long run, Grenier accomplished what he set out to do. He built a solid circle of people who would support Eigner and his work.

22

Later Life

you'll always go to sleep
more times than you'll wake
—"LETTER FOR DUNCAN" (*CP*, 2:327)

After Larry Eigner had spent nearly a decade with Robert Grenier and Kathleen Frumkin, his living situation began to unravel. Remembering that time, Frumkin noted, "We were also ten years older, and our children were older. And I started commuting to UC Davis."[1] In the late 1980s, both children had left the household to attend college. The stress of years of running a household and facing financial problems had taken its toll on the relationship between Grenier and Frumkin. Grenier spent many years looking for a full-time teaching job with no success. Frumkin was studying at the University of California, Davis, and had a long commute. Their relationship with each other, and their role as Eigner's caregiver, became too complicated. In 1989, Frumkin moved out. Later that fall, Grenier moved to Bolinas, California. It is unclear whether Frumkin or Grenier spent time with Eigner after they moved out, but it is unlikely as Eigner does not mention them visiting in his letters. Although they parted ways, Grenier remained dedicated to publishing Eigner's work for many years.

As the family owned the house, Eigner remained living there, but it was a difficult transition. In some respects, his living situation reverted to a chaotic state, one similar to when he lived in the group home upon first moving to Berkeley. Richard and Beverly had a difficult time finding someone to live with him as a full-time caregiver.[2] They relied on an agency to send caregivers to the house on a day-by-day basis. It was difficult for Eigner to make clear the urgency of the situation since whenever his brother or anyone else came to visit there was "no brickbats or hot water or anything like that to be seen." He wrote in letters that the situation was creating a lot of stress between Richard and Beverly; his brother accused him of exaggerating the situation or lying and blamed him for not being able to get along with people. Still, he preferred complexity over loneliness: "I have thought in recent weeks quite a few times that a battleground is better than a vacuum, for me anyway."[3]

The fact that Eigner had a different person taking care for him every day made stability difficult. He wrote to his mother that he was only able to have occasional quiet when "rollcoaster isnt here (brought once or twice a day by characters living with me." He developed a sort of Buddhist resolve to his living situation, and he often mentioned in his letters feeling entertained by the constant changes. He wrote, "If life, things, weren't so interesting, it, they would kill me." The chaos, however, made it difficult for him to write, and it felt "less and less likely things will settle down enough here for me to feel like looking out a window and reaching for a poem."[4] Throughout these years, he wrote considerably fewer and shorter poems.

Eigner's ability to use the typewriter was declining, which he described as "a little problematic," adding that he "really mistype[d] a lot of words as well as faintly, nowadays." While cerebral palsy is not degenerative, the stress on Eigner's muscles from a lifetime of spasticity made aging a difficult process. On the other hand, he wrote that he was "still in good health at 68." The primary problem was the divergence and distraction caused by a living situation that made it difficult to concentrate. Eigner described the situation as "both good and not so good -- i.e. a rough tumble harem scarem life I's subjected to." He reported constantly getting "into hot water with my 4 of 5 helpers."[5]

During the last few years of his life, Eigner did have a few caregivers whom he liked. For a short period, Eigner bonded with a woman named Monica Nowak, whom he referred to as "Saint Monica." His only complaint about her was that when she typed letters for him to his mother, she resisted sharing anything other than good news. After Monica, he lived with a Polish filmmaker, Marek, whom he liked almost as well. There were not as many poets coming by to visit in these years. Ben Friedlander had worked extensively with Eigner editing a book of his essays, *Areas Lights Heights* (1989), throughout the 1980s.[6] Despite coming to the McGee house daily when Eigner lived with Grenier, he now felt uncomfortable visiting.

Although Eigner wasn't getting help from the community with his caregiving as he had in the past, he still had many poet friends who continued to support his work. Eigner continued to spend a lot of time with Jack Foley and his partner, Adelle. Foley interviewed the poet on his radio program on KPFA. Eigner spoke about his writing process, reiterating the importance of what he called "immediacy and force" in his poems. Foley respectfully repeated the poet's comments. The recording was testament to Eigner's stream of consciousness in his speaking and writing.

For Eigner's sixtieth birthday, the community set up a huge celebration at the University Art Museum and the Pacific Film Archive, located at the University of California, Berkeley, with the poem "Again Dawn" projected on the wall outside the museum. The projection was part of an art exhibit titled *Matrix 159*. In a pamphlet, the curators explained how the poem was ideal for this kind of display as they found it to be "spatially open and variable as well as concise."[7] They put the poem in the context of the work of artists Jenny Holzer and Barbara Kruger. This was one of the first readings of an Eigner poem as an art object.

On January 23, 1993, Eigner's mother, Bessie, died at the age of ninety-two. By then, Eigner was in his sixties, dealing with the situation of not having stable caregiving and facing his own health issues. Eigner had Jack Foley transcribe a letter to Cid Corman: "Sad enough news, I guess, and still kind of too bad I couldn't cheer her up, whenever I tried to, she took it I was downplaying all she did for me."[8] In his letters, he showed the same kind of emotional distance he had when his father died. Clearly, he loved his mother and must have recognized how she made it possible for him to be a serious poet. He also felt stifled by her, as any man would living under the circumstances of a child. He felt that being a poet, particularly an experimental poet, was a kind of rebellion. If he had gone the path, say, of Robert Lowell, he may have been able to fulfill their idea of "writ[ing] greeting cards," something that paid.

Given his association with the Language poets and their claim of Gertrude Stein as a predecessor, it is fitting that Eigner's last public appearance was at a marathon reading of Gertrude Stein's *Three Lives* (1909).[9] The event, arranged by Lyn Hejinian, took place at the New College of California on November 17, 1995. Jack Foley, who spent the last few weeks of Eigner's life with him, told Hejinian that Eigner genuinely did not want to do it. He went and read a passage with his magnifying glass. Foley held open the book. In a later interview, Foley spoke about the last time he saw the poet whom he considered to be one of his best friends.

Eigner died on February 3, 1996, at Alta Bates Hospital in Berkeley, due to complications from pneumonia. He was sixty-eight years old. His traditional Jewish funeral and burial was attended by his family, including his brother Richard and sister-in-law Beverly, who had worked so hard to take care of him and make his life comfortable. At the ceremony Richard spoke about how his parents, the children of immigrants from the Jewish

Pale of eastern Europe to New England, became invested in New England culture—Bessie in literature and art, Israel in baseball and television—which translated into their son's poetry. Richard described his brother as strong willed, with "a determination to be a giving as well as receiving person but on his own terms." He spoke about the poet's "insight, coupled with a healthy irreverence, which enabled him to perceive the ironies of life, an ear for hearing, and an eye and mind for seeing the sounds, sights, and patterns of his world."[10]

On Eigner's grave, lines from two of his poems are inscribed: "from the sustaining air" and "there is the clarity of a shore," from the poem he worked so hard on with Robert Creeley, and "o i walk, i walk," from the poem "Open," which includes the lines "But I flower myself. / or can't change" and "the flowers seem to nod." And for Larry Eigner, the flowers do indeed "nod."

Abbreviations

Berg	Henry W. and Albert A. Berg Collection of English and American Literature, Special Collections, New York Public Library.
Brown	John Hay Library, Brown University, Providence, Rhode Island.
CP	Larry Eigner, *The Collected Poems of Larry Eigner*, edited by Curtis Faville and Robert Grenier, 4 vols. (Stanford, CA: Stanford University Press, 2010).
Dodd	Archives and Special Collections, Thomas J. Dodd Research Center, University of Connecticut, Storrs.
HRC	Harry Ransom Center, University of Texas at Austin.
KU	Department of Special Collections, Kenneth Spencer Research Library, University of Kansas, Lawrence.
NYU	Fales Library and Special Collections, New York University.
Stanford	Department of Special Collections, Stanford University Libraries, Stanford, California.
UB	Poetry Collection of the University Libraries, University at Buffalo, State University of New York.
UCSD	Special Collections and Archives, University of California, San Diego.

Notes

Larry Eigner's Calendar
   1. References for events prior to 1953 from Curtis Faville and Robert Grenier, "Larry Eigner Chronology," in *The Collected Poems of Larry Eigner* (*CP*), ed. Curtis Faville and Robert Grenier (Stanford, CA: Stanford University Press, 2010), 1:xxi–xxii.
   2. Larry Eigner to Cid Corman, May 9, 1953, Cid Corman collection, HRC (see list of abbreviations and bibliography for archival sources). Also see Larry Eigner to Alexandra Mason, August 1979, Larry Eigner poems and papers, KU: "x2 I must've done right after Spring '53 drive to NYC down through Connecticut and back home where we found ORIGIN #8, Olson's In Cold Hell, . . . in the mailbox."
   3. Larry Eigner to Cid Corman, June 26, 1953, Cid Corman collection, HRC.
   4. Larry Eigner to Paul Blackburn, May 6, 1954, in *Momentous Inconclusions: The Life and Work of Larry Eigner*, ed. Jennifer Bartlett and George Hart (Albuquerque: University of New Mexico Press, 2020), 224–26.
   5. Larry Eigner, "The dinosaur connected to the . . ." (Larry Eigner to George Butterick, February 22, 1970), in *Areas Lights Heights: Writings, 1954–1989*, by Larry Eigner, ed. Benjamin Friedlander (New York: Roof Books, 1989), 108. Also see Larry Eigner to Cid Corman, June 1, 1954, Cid Corman collection, HRC.
   6. "Larry Eigner had been alerted to Olson's coming and his father duly delivered him." Cid Corman, introduction to *The Gist of Origin, 1951–1971: An Anthology*, ed. Cid Corman (New York: Grossman, 1975), xxviii–xxix.
   7. Larry Eigner to Vincent Ferrini, October 9, 1955, Vincent Ferrini papers, Dodd.
   8. Larry Eigner to Judson Crews, July 10, 1957, Judson Crews papers, HRC; Larry Eigner to Jonathan Williams, July 19, 1957, letter 22, in *Letters to Jargon: The Correspondence between Larry Eigner and Jonathan Williams*, ed. Andrew Rippeon (Tuscaloosa: University of Alabama Press, 2019), 44.
   9. Larry Eigner to Jonathan Williams, May 31, 1958, letter 34, in Eigner and Williams, *Letters to Jargon*, 56.
   10. Larry Eigner to Don Allen, September 17, 1958, Donald Allen collection, UCSD; Larry Eigner to Jonathan Williams, September 9, [1958], letter 35, in Eigner and Williams, *Letters to Jargon*, 56.
   11. Regarding the poem "F o l d s o f t h e d e s e r t" (*CP*, 2:292–93), Eigner wrote,

"when I came home from being up in Olson's Fort Sq. Gloucester flat." Larry Eigner to Alexandra Mason, August 1979, Larry Eigner, poems and papers, KU. Also see Faville and Grenier, "Larry Eigner Chronology," *CP*, 1:xxiii.

12. Regarding the poem "There is no tomorrow, her . . ." (*CP*, 2:29), Eigner wrote, "I got during ride home from our visit to MacFarland and M and D Levertov in Friendship, Maine." Larry Eigner to Alexandra Mason, August 1979, Larry Eigner poems and papers, KU. Also see Larry Eigner to Jonathan Williams, [August] 26, [1959], letter 42, in Eigner and Williams, *Letters to Jargon*, 64.

13. The date of the visit could also be 1958. "I guess it's entirely possible Olson sent you the ms copy he borrowed when he and Wms were down here." Larry Eigner to Don Allen, October 3, 1958, Donald Allen collection, UCSD.

14. Larry Eigner to Cid Corman, May 25, 1960, in "Larry Eigner: Six Letters," by Larry Eigner, ed. Jennifer Bartlett and George Hart, *Poetry*, December 2014; Larry Eigner to Jonathan Williams, April 16, 1960, letter 53, in Eigner and Williams, *Letters to Jargon*, 79.

15. Larry Eigner to Cid Corman, November 4, 1960, Cid Corman collection, HRC; Larry Eigner to Jonathan Williams, October 31, 1960, letter 63, in Eigner and Williams, *Letters to Jargon*, 90.

16. Larry Eigner to Jonathan Williams, February 21, 1961, letter 70, in Eigner and Williams, *Letters to Jargon*, 100.

17. Larry Eigner to Denise Levertov, December 1, 1961, Denise Levertov papers, Stanford.

18. Larry Eigner to Cid Corman, aerogram dictated to Bessie Eigner, October 4, 1962, Cid Corman collection, HRC.

19. Larry Eigner to unknown recipient, August 28–29, 1963, Louis Zukofsky collection, HRC. The letter, which discusses contents of the summer 1963 issue of *Kulchur*, is held in Zukofsky's papers but not apparently addressed to him.

20. Larry Eigner to Jonathan Williams, December 20, 1964, letter 81, in Eigner and Williams, *Letters to Jargon*, 130.

21. Larry Eigner to Terrence Williams, August 25, 1966, Larry Eigner poems and papers, KU. Also mentioned in Larry Eigner to Margaret and Sergio Mondragon, April 24, 1966, *El corno emplumado* (*Plumed Horn*) records, HRC: "Brother flying here to escort me, there and back. Airlines wont take me alone."

22. Faville and Grenier, "Larry Eigner Chronology," *CP*, 1:xxiii.

23. Larry Eigner to Denise Levertov, September 1, 1968, Denise Levertov papers, Stanford.

24. Larry Eigner to Denise Levertov, April 10, 1972, Denise Levertov papers, Stanford.

25. Larry Eigner to Robert Wilson, January 5, 1977, uncatalogued manuscripts, Berg; Larry Eigner to Vincent Ferrini, October 27, 1970, Vincent Ferrini papers, Dodd; Larry Eigner, "'Responsibility is to keep / the ability to respond,'" in Eigner, *Areas Lights Heights*, 114.

26. Larry Eigner to George Butterick, June 4, 1974, George Butterick collection, UB.

27. Larry Eigner to Vincent Ferrini, October 27, 1970, Vincent Ferrini papers, Dodd. Apparently Eigner participated in the readings; see Larry Eigner to Jonathan Williams, February 18, 1971, letter 92, in Eigner and Williams, *Letters to Jargon*, 151.

28. Larry Eigner to Vincent Ferrini, October 27, 1970, Vincent Ferrini papers, Dodd.

29. Larry Eigner to Paul Auster, July 15, 1975, Paul Auster papers, Berg; Larry Eigner, "an original eye . . . ," *CP*, 3:1021.

30. Larry Eigner to Cid Corman, July 29, 1971, Cid Corman papers, Berg; Larry Eigner, "A i r," *CP*, 3:1025.

31. Larry Eigner to Alexandra Mason, August 15, 1971, Larry Eigner poems and papers, KU. Also mentioned in Larry Eigner to Cid Corman, [c. September 1971], Cid Corman papers, Berg.

32. Larry Eigner to Robert Grenier, October 8, 1971, Larry Eigner poems and papers, KU.

33. "A notice in the paper tonight says the theme of the celebration will be ecology!" Larry Eigner to Robert Grenier, October 8–15, 1971, Larry Eigner poems and papers, KU. In the same letter, Eigner later reports: "Theme of ecology a farce, considering – yet a few things were very pointed and incisive as to that!"

34. Eigner wrote: "just today he took me to 3rd affair since I wrote last." Larry Eigner to Robert Grenier, March 26, 1972, Larry Eigner poems and papers, KU.

35. Larry Eigner to Ron Silliman, October 21, 1972, in Bartlett and Hart, *Momentous Inconclusions*, 254–56. Also described in detail in Larry Eigner to [Eigner family], May 15, 1972, Larry Eigner poems and papers, KU. Eigner dates the reading as May 6, 1972, in Larry Eigner to Jerome Rothenberg, April 21, 1974, Jerome Rothenberg papers, UCSD.

36. Larry Eigner to Robert Grenier, May 14, 1972, Larry Eigner poems and papers, KU.

37. Larry Eigner to Robert Grenier, September 23, 1972, Larry Eigner poems and papers, KU. This letter also mentions Eigner's parents' homophobia.

38. Larry Eigner to Robert Grenier, November 30, 1972, Larry Eigner poems and papers, KU. About the October 11 visit, Eigner wrote: "I had readings there, too, unexpectedly." Larry Eigner to Ron Silliman, October 21, 1972, Ron Silliman papers, UCSD. Also mentioned in Larry Eigner to Robert Grenier, November 30, 1972, Larry Eigner poems and papers, KU.

39. Larry Eigner to Robert Grenier, November 30, 1972, Larry Eigner poems and papers, KU. Eigner dates the event as November 16 in Larry Eigner to Jim Weil, March 26, 1973, Fales manuscript collection, NYU.

40. This event was identified as Eigner's "first public reading" in Faville and Grenier, "Larry Eigner Chronology," *CP*, 1:xxiv; Larry Eigner to Jim Weil, March 26, 1973, Fales manuscript collection, NYU. Also see Faville and Grenier, "Larry Eigner Chronology," *CP*, 1:xxiv.

41. Larry Eigner to Alexandra Mason, April 19, 1973, Larry Eigner poems and papers, KU. Eigner writes that Ginsberg and Orlovsky visited on April 5 in Larry Eigner to Jackson Mac Low, May 1, 1973, Jackson Mac Low papers, UCSD.

42. Larry Eigner to Ron Silliman, August 28, 1973, Ron Silliman papers, UCSD.

43. Eigner to Silliman, August 28, 1973.

44. Eigner wrote: "since Dec 14, when on returning here from 33 days at my brother's in St. Louis, where I got to see Diane Wakoski read and talk with her and others of the audience at The Mary Institute, this girls' school." Larry Eigner to George Butterick, June 4, 1974, in Bartlett and Hart, *Momentous Inconclusions*, 257. Exact dates mentioned in Larry Eigner to Jonathan Williams, April 3, 1974, letter 95, in Eigner and Williams, *Letters to Jargon*, 160.

45. Larry Eigner to George Butterick, November 6, 1974, George Butterick collection, UB.

46. Larry Eigner to Robert Grenier, October 6, 1974, Larry Eigner poems and papers, KU.

47. Larry Eigner to Alexandra Mason, September 23, 1974, Larry Eigner poems and papers, KU.

48. Larry Eigner to Robert Grenier, October 6, 1974, Larry Eigner poems and papers, KU.

49. "Bob Grenier some weeks ago wrote asking me up to Franconia College again, and now a student ('Examiner' of whose Thesis of poems and photo..s I've agreed to be, also) is to drive down here to pick me up Dec 5 and bring me back the 7th." Larry Eigner to George Butterick, November 6, 1974, George Butterick collection, UB.

50. Larry Eigner to Joseph Eigner, January 29, 1975, Larry Eigner papers, Stanford.

51. Larry Eigner to Ron Silliman, postcard, November 9, 1975, Ron Silliman papers, UCSD. Trip briefly described by Barrett Watten in Rae Armantrout et al., *The Grand Piano: An Experiment in Collective Autobiography; San Francisco, 1975–1980*, part 10 (Detroit: Mode A, 2010), 201.

52. Larry Eigner to Jonathan Williams, July 20, 1978, letter 97, in Eigner and Williams, *Letters to Jargon*, 163.

53. Eigner to Williams, July 20, 1978, 164.

54. Lisa Jarnot, *Robert Duncan: The Ambassador from Venus; A Biography* (Berkeley: University of California Press, 2012), 362.

55. Larry Eigner to Cid Corman, July 30, 1979, Cid Corman papers, Berg.

56. Larry Eigner to Cid Corman, November 30, 1979, Cid Corman papers, Berg.

57. Faville and Grenier, "Larry Eigner Chronology," *CP*, 1:xxv.

58. Larry Eigner to Arthur McFarland, January 7, 1980, in Bartlett and Hart, *Momentous Inconclusions*, 268–70.

59. Larry Eigner to Cid Corman, April 10, 1980, Cid Corman papers, Berg.

60. Eigner wrote: "(at a sr cit.. place whr still i can maybe move ǂthe possibility came to light during my mother's 17-day visit in feb..ǂ I'd have 1/3 the space I have here)." Larry Eigner to Cid Corman, November 20, 1980, Cid Corman papers, Berg.

61. Larry Eigner to Cid Corman, April 10, 1980, Cid Corman papers, Berg. Eigner mentioned hearing about the Citizens Party in Larry Eigner to Cid Corman, October 24, 1979, Cid Corman papers, Berg.

62. Larry Eigner to Joe and Janet Eigner ("dear folks"), June 10, 1980, Larry Eigner papers, Stanford.

63. Larry Eigner to Cid Corman, November 11, 1980, Cid Corman papers, Berg.

64. Eigner to Corman, November 11, 1980.

65. Eigner to Corman, November 11, 1980. Also see Jarnot, *Robert Duncan*, 391: "In the second week of November, Duncan gave an extracurricular talk at [New College] titled 'Shakespeare: Lear and Prospero.'"

66. Larry Eigner to Cid Corman, December 28, 1981, Cid Corman papers, Berg.

67. Eigner to Corman, December 28, 1981.

68. Larry Eigner to Clayton Eshleman, May 21, 1982, in Bartlett and Hart, *Momentous Inconclusions*, 271–73; Larry Eigner, #1324, *CP*, 4:1456. Also mentioned in Larry Eigner to Cid Corman, June 2, 19[8]2, Cid Corman papers, Berg.

69. Larry Eigner to Clayton Eshleman, May 21, 1982, in Bartlett and Hart, *Momentous Inconclusions*, 271–73.

70. Larry Eigner to Ruth Polansky Bloom, August 3, 1992, in Bartlett and Hart, 276.

71. Larry Eigner, "Some Priorities   Ah, Hierarchy," in Eigner, *Areas Lights Heights*, 39. Previously published as Larry Eigner to Tony Green and Judi Stout, April 26, 1985, in *Jimmy & Lucy's House of "K,"* no. 4 (June 1985).

72. Larry Eigner to Clayton Eshleman, March 29, 1985, Clayton Eshleman papers, UCSD.

73. Larry Eigner to Ron Silliman, January 24, 1986, Ron Silliman papers, UCSD.

74. Larry Eigner to Jim Weil, October 28, 1988, contemporary manuscripts collection, UB.

75. Larry Eigner to Charles Bernstein, September 15, 1989, Charles Bernstein papers, UCSD. Also see Larry Eigner, #1667, *CP*, 4:1623.

76. Larry Eigner, #1687b, *CP*, 4:1632.

77. "Working in collaboration with the museum Designer, Nina Zurier, Eigner designed the layout of his text on the museum facade." *Larry Eigner: MATRIX/BERKELEY 159*, exhibition brochure, University of California, Berkeley Art Museum and Pacific Film Archive, June 15–October 15, 1993.

78. Jack Foley to Lyn Hejinian, handwritten letter, October 11, 1995, Lyn Hejinian papers, UCSD.

79. Larry Eigner to Lyn Hejinian, handwritten letter, dictated to Jack Foley, November 4, 1995, Lyn Hejinian papers, UCSD.

Chapter 1

1. "Polis" is from Olson's poem "Maximus to Gloucester, Letter 27 [withheld]," in *The Maximus Poems*, by Charles Olson, ed. George F. Butterick (Berkeley: University of California Press, 1983), 184–85.

2. "NWS Boston—The Great New England Hurricane of 1938," National Weather Service, Boston/Norton, MA, office (website), accessed August 10, 2016.

3. Larry Eigner, "This," in *The Collected Poems of Larry Eigner* (*CP*), ed. Curtis Faville and Robert Grenier (Stanford, CA: Stanford University Press, 2010), 1:57. Eigner's poems are cited by title, number, or first line as indicated in the index of *CP*.

4. Larry Eigner, "Rambling (in) Life," in *Areas Lights Heights: Writings, 1954–1989*, by Larry Eigner, ed. Benjamin Friedlander (New York: Roof Books, 1989), 131.

5. "History of Swampscott," Town of Swampscott, MA (website), accessed June 6, 2015.

6. Stephen G. Mostov, *Immigrant Entrepreneurs: Jews in the Shoe Trades in Lynn, 1885–1945* ([Marblehead, MA]: Jewish Historical Society of the North Shore, 1982), chap. 2.

7. Unless otherwise indicated, information about Eigner's early life in this chapter is from Richard Eigner, interview by the author, July 2011, Berkeley, CA. See also Richard Eigner, "An Origin and a Setting," *CP*, 4:xxxv–xxxvii.

8. Larry Eigner, "'Keep at it,' they say when they see L . . . ," *CP*, 1:49. For typescript, see *CP*, 4:1696.

9. Larry Eigner, "europe a map," in Eigner, *Areas Lights Heights*, 24.

10. Larry Eigner to [Joseph Guglielmi], date unknown, in *Larry Eigner Letters (to Joseph Guglielmi and Claude Royet-Journoud)*, ed. Robert Kocik and Joseph Simas (Paris: Moving Letters Press, 1987), n.p.

11. Larry Eigner, "Life/puzzles," in Eigner, *Areas Lights Heights*, 133.

12. Eigner, "Rambling (in) Life," 127.

13. Larry Eigner, "Has Enough Seemed Nobody with a Pretty Strange Language or Just Accent Can Think Much at All," in Eigner, *Areas Lights Heights*, 14; Benjamin Friedlander, "Larry Eigner (6 August 1926–3 February 1996)," in *American Poets since World War II*, 6th ser., ed. Joseph Mark Conte, vol. 193 of *Dictionary of Literary Biography* (Detroit: Gale Research, 1998), Electronic Poetry Center, University of Pennsylvania.

14. R. Eigner, "An Origin and a Setting," *CP*, 4:xxxv.

15. Larry Eigner, "b l a n k - b l," *CP*, 1:77.

Chapter 2

1. Larry Eigner, "Rambling (in) Life," in *Areas Lights Heights: Writings, 1954–1989*, ed. Benjamin Friedlander (New York: Roof Books, 1989), 129.
2. "Cerebral Palsy: What to Look for If You Think Your Child Has Cerebral Palsy," CP Family Network (website), accessed August 15, 2022.
3. Eigner wrote: "and at Boston's Children's Hospital where I was found to have a high IQ or somewhere else it was said I had a 'photographic memory.'" Eigner, "Rambling (in) Life," 129.
4. Baby's Year Book, Larry Eigner papers, Dodd (see list of abbreviations and bibliography for archival sources). Unless otherwise noted, Bessie's observations on Eigner's childhood in this chapter are from this source.
5. Eigner stated: "My left side was wild; arms and legs, until a few weeks after my 35th birthday in '62. I had cryosurgery that tamed and numbed it." Larry Eigner, "Larry Eigner," interview by Marian Kindel, *Kaleidoscope*, no. 5 (Spring 1982): 11.
6. Richard Eigner, "An Origin and a Setting," in *The Collected Poems of Larry Eigner* (*CP*), ed. Curtis Faville and Robert Grenier (Stanford, CA: Stanford University Press, 2010), 4:xxxvi.
7. Richard Eigner, interview by the author, July 2011, Berkeley, CA.
8. Eigner, "Rambling (in) Life," 131–32.
9. Richard Eigner in Larry Eigner et al., "Virtually Enough: Videoconference [. . .] December 29, 1995," in "Larry Eigner," ed. Shelly Andrews, in *Contemporary Authors Autobiography Series*, ed. Joyce Nakamura, vol. 23 (Detroit: Gale Research, 1996), 50.
10. Larry Eigner, "Omnipresent to Some Extent: Jack Foley's Radio Interview with Larry Eigner, Recorded for KPFA-FM's Poetry Program, March 9, 1994," in Eigner, "Larry Eigner," ed. Andrews, 32.
11. Eigner, "Rambling (in) Life," 133.

Chapter 3

1. Andrea DenHoed, "The Forgotten Lessons of the Eugenics Movement," *New Yorker*, April 27, 2016.
2. Buck v. Bell, 274 U.S. 200 (1926).
3. Adam Cohen, *Imbeciles: The Supreme Court, American Eugenics, and the Sterilization of Carrie Buck* (New York: Penguin Books, 2017).
4. David Goode et al., *A History and Sociology of the Willowbrook State School* (Washington, DC: American Association on Intellectual and Developmental Disabilities, 2013), 201.
5. Paul A. Offit, *Vaccinated: One Man's Quest to Defeat the World's Deadliest Diseases* (Washington, DC: Smithsonian Books, 2008), 27.
6. "Child Neurology Residency Training Program: History," Boston Children's Hospital (website), accessed August 10, 2022.
7. Elizabeth Evans Lord, *Children Handicapped by Cerebral Palsy: Psychological Factors in Management*, with medical explanation by Bronson Crothers (New York: Commonwealth Fund, 1937).
8. Larry Eigner, "Rambling (in) Life," in *Areas Lights Heights: Writings, 1954–1989*, by Larry Eigner, ed. Benjamin Friedlander (New York: Roof Books, 1989), 130.
9. Larry Eigner, "L e n g t h," in *The Collected Poems of Larry Eigner* (*CP*), ed. Curtis Faville and Robert Grenier (Stanford, CA: Stanford University Press, 2010), 1:72.
10. Eigner, "Rambling (in) Life," 129.
11. Larry Eigner, "Larry Eigner," interview by Marian Kindel, *Kaleidoscope*, no. 5 (Spring 1982): 11.

12. Larry Eigner, "What a Time Distance: The Autobiography," in *Larry Eigner: Selected Poems*, ed. Samuel Charters and Andrea Wyatt (Berkeley, CA: Oyez Press, 1972), 123.

13. Gladys Gage Rogers and Leah C. Thomas, *New Pathways for Children with Cerebral Palsy* (New York: Macmillan, 1935), 3.

14. Larry Eigner, "the proper arm's-length . . . ," *CP*, 3:1070.

15. Rogers and Thomas, *New Pathways for Children with Cerebral Palsy*, 37.

16. Rogers and Thomas, 37.

Chapter 4

1. Larry Eigner, "Qs & As (?) Large and Small / Parts of a Collaborate," in *Areas Lights Heights: Writings, 1954–1989*, by Larry Eigner, ed. Benjamin Friedlander (New York: Roof Books, 1989), 162.

2. Larry Eigner, "not / forever / serious," in Eigner, *Areas Lights Heights*, 26 (original emphasis).

3. Larry Eigner, "O n e o f a S e r i e s," in *The Collected Poems of Larry Eigner* (*CP*), ed. Curtis Faville and Robert Grenier (Stanford, CA: Stanford University Press, 2010), 1:54.

4. Eigner, "Qs & As (?) Large and Small / Parts of a Collaborate," 162.

5. Richard Eigner, in Larry Eigner et al., "Virtually Enough: Videoconference [. . .] December 29, 1995," in "Larry Eigner," ed. Shelly Andrews, in *Contemporary Authors Autobiography Series*, ed. Joyce Nakamura, vol. 23 (Detroit: Gale Research, 1996), 50.

6. Larry Eigner, "Rambling (in) Life," in Eigner, *Areas Lights Heights*, 129.

7. Eigner, 127.

8. Larry Eigner, "Larry Eigner," interview by Marian Kindel, *Kaleidoscope*, no. 5 (Spring 1982): 11.

9. Eigner, "Rambling (in) Life," 128.

10. Larry Eigner, "Mother's Day Present," *CP*, 1:36.

11. I reviewed issues of *Child Life* magazine at the New York Public Library. One issue of note was September 1937, featuring cover art by movie art director Robert B. Usher.

12. Larry Eigner, "When All Sleep," *CP*, 1:35; clipping of Larry Eigner, "When All Sleep," *Child Life* 16, no. 9 (September 1937): 436, box 23, folder 3, Larry Eigner papers, Stanford (see list of abbreviations and bibliography for archival sources).

13. Larry Eigner, "Good Citizenship on Halloween," *Child Life* 18, no. 10 (October 1939): 474, box 23, folder 3, Larry Eigner papers, Stanford.

Chapter 5

1. Curtis Faville and Robert Grenier, "Larry Eigner Chronology," in *The Collected Poems of Larry Eigner* (*CP*), ed. Curtis Faville and Robert Grenier (Stanford, CA: Stanford University Press, 2010), 1:xxii; Richard Eigner, "An Origin and a Setting," *CP*, 4:xxxvi.

2. "History," Pappas Rehabilitation Hospital for Children (formerly Massachusetts Hospital School) (website), accessed March 2, 2021.

3. Richard Eigner, in Larry Eigner et al., "Virtually Enough: Videoconference [. . .] December 29, 1995," in "Larry Eigner," ed. Shelly Andrews in *Contemporary Authors Autobiography Series*, ed. Joyce Nakamura, vol. 23 (Detroit: Gale Research, 1996), 56.

4. Larry Eigner, short story (for course taken by distance from the University of Chicago, instructor Frances S. Nipp), April 1946, box 27, folder 3, Larry Eigner papers, Stanford (see list of abbreviations and bibliography for archival sources).

5. Eigner, short story, April 1946.

6. Eigner et al., "Virtually Enough," 55.
7. Eigner, short story, April 1946, box 27, folder 3, Larry Eigner papers, Stanford.
8. Larry Eigner, "Rambling (in) Life," in *Areas Lights Heights: Writings, 1954–1989*, by Larry Eigner, ed. Benjamin Friedlander (New York: Roof Books, 1989), 131.
9. Larry Eigner, "ALTER yr . . . ," *CP*, 1:70.
10. Arnold Goldman, interview by the author, March 2013, Skype.
11. Eigner, "Rambling (in) Life," 130.
12. Eigner, 128.
13. *Poems by Laurence Joel Eigner* (Canton, MA: privately printed, 1941); for a facsimile of this chapbook, see *CP*, 1:3–32.
14. Larry Eigner, "Rain," *CP*, 1:13.
15. Faville and Grenier, "Larry Eigner Chronology," *CP*, 1:xxii.
16. Eigner, "Rambling (in) Life," 127.
17. Richard Eigner, "An Origin and a Setting," *CP*, 4:xxxvi; Faville and Grenier, "Larry Eigner Chronology," *CP*, 1:xxii.
18. Larry Eigner, rejected application for Guggenheim grant, 1972, box 15, folder 5, Larry Eigner papers, Stanford.
19. Larry Eigner, "I," *CP*, 1:47; for typescript, see *CP*, 4:1695.
20. Eigner, "Rambling (in) Life," 128.
21. Faville and Grenier, "Larry Eigner Chronology," *CP*, 1:xxii.
22. Walter Blair and W. K. Chandler, eds., *Approaches to Poetry* (New York: Appleton-Century-Crofts, 1935).
23. Larry Eigner, "Larry Eigner," interview by Marian Kindel, *Kaleidoscope*, no. 5 (Spring 1982): 12. Eigner also mentions this incident in "Rambling (in) Life," 133: "In the Versification course one time I asked the instructor what 'free verse' was, or what was there to it really if anything, something I was puzzled over for some years, and he called it meretricious, there was nothing to it."
24. Larry Eigner, correspondence classes taken at University of Chicago, 1945–46, box 27, folders 2 and 3, Larry Eigner papers, Stanford.
25. Eigner, correspondence classes taken at University of Chicago, 1945–46.

Chapter 6

1. Richard Eigner, "An Origin and a Setting," in *The Collected Poems of Larry Eigner* (*CP*), ed. Curtis Faville and Robert Grenier (Stanford, CA: Stanford University Press, 2010), 4:xxxvi.
2. Richard and Beverly Eigner, interview with author, June 23, 2012, Berkeley, CA.
3. Cid Corman, "Communication: Poetry for Radio," *Poetry* 81, no. 3 (1952): 212.
4. Kevin Bowen, "Reclaiming Corman: Cid Corman's Dorchester Past," in "Mass: Raw Poetry from the Commonwealth of Massachusetts," ed. Jim Dunn and Kevin Gallagher, special feature, *Jacket2*, December 24, 2012.
5. Quoted in Eigner's biographical note in Donald Allen, ed., *The New American Poetry* (Berkeley: University of California Press, 1999), 436.
6. Cid Corman to Charles Olson, January 19, 1952, in *Charles Olson & Cid Corman: Complete Correspondence, 1950–1964*, ed. George Evans (Orono, ME: National Poetry Foundation, 1987), 1:229.
7. Richard and Beverly Eigner, interview with author, June 23, 2012, Berkeley, CA.
8. Cid Corman to Larry Eigner, April 27, 1950, Larry Eigner papers, Dodd (see list of abbreviations and bibliography for archival sources).
9. Larry Eigner, "A Wintered Road," *CP*, 1:48.

10. Cid Corman to Larry Eigner, April 27, 1950, Larry Eigner papers, Dodd.
11. Cid Corman to Larry Eigner, June 9, 1950, Larry Eigner papers, Dodd.
12. Cid Corman to Larry Eigner, November 5, 1950, Larry Eigner papers, Dodd.
13. Richard Eigner, "An Origin and a Setting," *CP*, 4:xxxvi.
14. Lee Bartlett, interview by the author, May 15, 2015, Las Cruces, NM.
15. Cid Corman to Larry Eigner, December 5, 1951, Larry Eigner papers, Dodd.
16. Larry Eigner, "Be minimal then . . . ," in *Areas Lights Heights: Writings, 1954–1989*, by Larry Eigner, ed. Benjamin Friedlander (New York: Roof Books, 1989), 8.
17. Larry Eigner, "not / forever / serious," in Eigner, *Areas Lights Heights*, 25.
18. Larry Eigner, to Joseph Guglielmi, May 11, 1973, in *Larry Eigner Letters (to Joseph Guglielmi and Claude Royet-Journoud)*, ed. Robert Kocik and Joseph Simas (Paris: Moving Letters Press, 1987), 5.
19. Cid Corman to Larry Eigner, April 27, 1950, Larry Eigner papers, Dodd.
20. William Carlos Williams, introduction to *The Wedge* (1944), in *The Collected Poems of William Carlos Williams*, ed. Christopher MacGowan, vol. 2, *1939–1962* (New York: New Directions, 1991), 53.
21. "—Say it, no ideas but in things—": William Carlos Williams, *Paterson*, rev. ed., ed. Christopher MacGowan (New York: New Directions, 1995), 6; Cid Corman to Larry Eigner, November 5, 1950, Larry Eigner papers, Dodd.
22. Louis Zukofsky, "An Objective," in *Prepositions: The Collected Critical Essays of Louis Zukofsky*, exp. ed. (Berkeley: University of California Press, 1981), 12.
23. Richard Eigner, interview by the author, July 2011, Berkeley, CA.
24. Sherman Paul, *Olson's Push: Origin, Black Mountain, and Recent American Poetry* (Baton Rouge: Louisiana State University Press, 1978).
25. Larry Eigner, "Has Enough Seemed Nobody with a Pretty Strange Language or Just Accent Can Think Much at All," in Eigner, *Areas Lights Heights*, 15.
26. Eigner first saw Williams read in person in 1952: "1952—Goes to Brandeis University to hear William Carlos Williams read his poetry." Curtis Faville and Robert Grenier, "Larry Eigner Chronology," *CP*, 1:xxii.

Chapter 7

1. "When I read on Cid's program, my business in Boston was, simply, the Boston Poultry Show." Robert Creeley to Larry Eigner, [c. February 1950], in *The Selected Letters of Robert Creeley*, ed. Rod Smith, Peter Baker, and Kaplan Harris (Berkeley: University of California Press, 2014), 24.
2. Larry Eigner to Robert Creeley, [1950?], and Robert Creeley to Larry Eigner, [c. February 1950], in *The Selected Letters of Robert Creeley*, 24.
3. Robert Creeley to Larry Eigner, [c. February 1950], in *The Selected Letters of Robert Creeley*, 24.
4. Robert Creeley to Larry Eigner, [undated, 1951], in *The Selected Letters of Robert Creeley*, 86.
5. Larry Eigner to Robert Creeley, August 12, 1951, Larry Eigner papers, Dodd (see list of abbreviations and bibliography for archival sources).
6. Robert Creeley to Larry Eigner, [undated, 1951], in *The Selected Letters of Robert Creeley*, 86.
7. Robert Creeley to Larry Eigner, undated, 1950, Larry Eigner papers, Dodd.
8. Larry Eigner, "Method from Happenstance," in *Areas Lights Heights: Writings, 1954–1989*, by Larry Eigner, ed. Benjamin Friedlander (New York: Roof Books, 1989), 6.

9. Larry Eigner to Robert Creeley, July 21, 1951, in Robert Creeley and Larry Eigner, "Selected Correspondence, July–September 1951," *Chicago Review* 58, no. 2 (2014): 55.

Chapter 8

1. Tom Clark, *Charles Olson: The Allegory of a Poet's Life* (New York: W. W. Norton, 1991), 50–70.

2. Robert von Hallberg, *Charles Olson: The Scholar's Art* (Cambridge, MA: Harvard University Press, 1978), 5. See also Clark, *Charles Olson*, 72–89, 99–100.

3. Ann Charters, *Olson/Melville: A Study in Affinity* (Berkeley, CA: Oyez Press, 1968), 9, quoted in Von Hallberg, *Charles Olson*, 5.

4. George F. Butterick, *A Guide to the Maximus Poems of Charles Olson* (Berkeley: University of California Press, 1978), xxvi.

5. Charles Olson, "Projective Verse," in *Collected Prose: Charles Olson*, ed. Donald Allen and Benjamin Friedlander (Berkeley: University of California Press, 1997), 239, first published as "Projective Verse vs. the Non-Projective," *Poetry New York*, no. 3 (1950): 13–22.

6. Eleanor Berry and Alan Golding, "Projective Verse," in *The Princeton Encyclopedia of Poetry and Poetics*, 4th ed., ed. Roland Greene et al. (Princeton, NJ: Princeton University Press, 2012), 1109.

7. Robert Creeley to Larry Eigner, undated, 1951, Larry Eigner papers, Dodd (see list of abbreviations and bibliography for archival sources).

8. Berry and Golding, "Projective Verse," 1109.

9. Olson, "Projective Verse," 239, 242.

10. Larry Eigner to Ina Forster, February 11, 1987, in Larry Eigner, "Unpublished Letter to Ina Forster," February 11–20, 1987, ed. Benjamin Friedlander, in "Larry Eigner Issue," ed. Benjamin Friedlander and Christopher Funkhouser, special issue, *Passages: A Technopoetics Journal*, no. 5 (April 1998), Electronic Poetry Center, University of Pennsylvania.

11. Larry Eigner, "Method from Happenstance," in *Areas Lights Heights: Writings, 1954–1989*, Larry Eigner, ed. Benjamin Friedlander (New York: Roof Books, 1989), 6.

12. Larry Eigner, "Has Enough Seemed Nobody with a Pretty Strange Language or Just Accent Can Think Much at All," in Eigner, *Areas Lights Heights*, 15.

13. Cid Corman to Larry Eigner, November 15, 1950, Larry Eigner papers, Dodd.

14. Larry Eigner, "O p e n," *CP*, 1:113.

15. Cid Corman to Larry Eigner, April 27, 1957, Cid Corman collection, HRC.

Chapter 9

1. Larry Eigner to Cid Corman, May 25, 1965, Cid Corman collection, HRC (see list of abbreviations and bibliography for archival sources).

2. In an interview with the author, Robert Grenier recalled that Eigner did not want to associate with other disabled people. He saw himself as different from others because of his poetry. He preferred to be in the company of able-bodied poets. Other than during his time at Robin Hood's Barn and the Massachusetts Hospital School, he did not have many daily interactions with other disabled people, and the rare times he mentioned disability in his poetry, he used negative language. Interview, June 2016, Berkeley, CA.

3. Larry Eigner to Robert Creeley, June 1953, Larry Eigner papers, Stanford.

4. Larry Eigner to Cid Corman, August 26, 1953, Cid Corman collection, HRC.

5. A history of Camp Jened and its connection to the disability rights movement

is detailed in the film *Crip Camp: A Disability Revolution*, directed by Nicole Newnham and Jim LeBrecht (Higher Ground Productions, 2020, 108 min.). This documentary film centers on the 1960s, over a decade after Eigner attended the camp, and the film was released after I had been researching the camp for six years. In my early research, there was very limited information about the camp. The time in which Eigner attended, shortly after it opened, remains undocumented, but one can assume that the camp was liberal and oriented toward social justice from its inception.

6. Larry Eigner to Robert Creeley, August 29, 1953, Robert Creeley papers, Stanford.

7. Larry Allison, "Personal Background and the Camp Jened Years, 1965–1973," interview by Denise Sherer Jacobson, July 14, 2001, transcript, in *New York Activists and Leaders in the Disability Rights and Independent Living Movement*, vol. 1 (Berkeley: Regional Oral History Office, Bancroft Library, University of California, 2004), Online Archive of California.

8. Larry Eigner to Bessie and Israel Eigner, August 11, 1953, Larry Eigner papers, Stanford.

9. Allison, "Personal Background and the Camp Jened Years, 1965–1973."

10. Larry Eigner, *Through, Plain*, revised manuscript prepared by Hillary Gravendyk and Rebecca Gaynos. "To the Plain" (retitled "Through, Plain"), with revisions, [1953, 1974], box 13, folder 4, Larry Eigner papers, Stanford.

11. Larry Eigner to Bessie and Israel Eigner, August 11, 1953, Larry Eigner papers, Stanford.

12. Eigner, *Through, Plain*, 14, Larry Eigner papers, Stanford.

13. Larry Eigner to Bessie and Israel Eigner, August 11, 1953, Larry Eigner papers, Stanford.

14. Larry Eigner, "Now I put her away, combustible beauty . . . ," in *The Collected Poems of Larry Eigner (CP)*, ed. Curtis Faville and Robert Grenier (Stanford, CA: Stanford University Press, 2010), 1:60.

Chapter 10

1. For the history of the *Lititz Review*, I relied on Jacob Leed, ed., "Robert Creeley and 'The Lititz Review': A Recollection with Letters," *Journal of Modern Literature* 5, no. 2 (1976): 243–59.

2. Robert Creeley to Jacob Leed, February 1950, in Leed, 245. For solicitation of Marianne Moore's work, see Robert Creeley to Jacob Leed, [c. April 1950], in Leed, 252–53.

3. Robert Creeley to Jacob Leed, April 24, 1950, in Leed, 255–56.

4. Dorothy Pound to Robert Creeley, c. 1950, in Leed, 249.

5. Robert Creeley to Jacob Leed, [c. April 1950], in Leed, 252–53.

6. Leed, 250, 256.

7. Leed, 257.

8. Cid Corman to Larry Eigner, September 16, 1950, Larry Eigner papers, Dodd (see list of abbreviations and bibliography for archival sources).

9. Larry Eigner to Cid Corman, May 13, 1954, Cid Corman collection, HRC.

10. Charles Olson, *Letters for Origin, 1950–1956*, ed. Albert Glover (New York: Cape Goliard Press, 1970). See also Cid Corman, ed., *The Gist of Origin, 1951–1971: An Anthology* (New York: Grossman, 1975).

11. Charles Olson to Cid Corman, October 21, 1950, in Olson, *Letters for Origin*, 8.

12. Charles Olson to Cid Corman, December 8, 1950, in Olson, 21.

13. Charles Olson to Cid Corman, March 1, 1951, in Olson, 35.

14. Larry Eigner, "Act," *Origin* 1, no. 9 (1953): 24–31; Eigner, "Quiet," *Origin* 1, no. 10 (1953): 88–91. Details for Eigner periodical appearances are taken from Irving P. Leif, *Larry Eigner: A Bibliography of His Works* (Metuchen, NJ: Scarecrow Press, 1989). Scans of *Origin* are available through Independent Voices: An Open Access Collection of an Alternative Press.

15. Larry Eigner, "Around," *Origin* 1, no. 12 (1954): 235–51; Eigner, "The Eye Doctor," *Origin* 1, no. 19 (1956): 61–62; Eigner, "A Bus to Bermuda," *Origin* 1, no. 19 (1956): 62–63.

16. Larry Eigner, "in the blackout," *Goad* 1, no. 3 (1952): 11. See also Eigner, "in the blackout . . . ," in *The Collected Poems of Larry Eigner* (*CP*), ed. Curtis Faville and Robert Grenier (Stanford, CA: Stanford University Press, 2010), 1:58.

17. Ekbert Faas, *Robert Creeley: A Biography*, with Maria Trombacco (Hanover, NH: University Press of New England, 2001), 123–32.

18. Robert Creeley to Larry Eigner, November 20, 1952, Larry Eigner papers, Dodd.

19. Robert Creeley to Larry Eigner, January 31, 1953, Larry Eigner papers, Dodd.

20. Eigner never completely edited his manuscripts by himself. As noted, he would send a pile of poems to an editor who would compile a chapbook or book on his behalf. Often, he worked with other poets who would arrange books for him. He worked extensively with Robert Grenier, Ben Friedlander, and Robert Kocik on such projects.

21. Robert Creeley to Larry Eigner, January 31, 1953, Larry Eigner papers, Dodd.

22. Larry Eigner to Robert Creeley, date unknown, Larry Eigner papers, Dodd.

23. William Carlos Williams to Robert Creeley, December 4, 1953 (retyped by Eigner, sent to Jonathan Williams), box 574, folder 19, Jargon Society collection, UB. For provenance of the typescript, see *Letters to Jargon: The Correspondence between Larry Eigner and Jonathan Williams*, ed. Andrew Rippeon (Tuscaloosa: University of Alabama Press, 2019), 225, note for "My ma said . . ." The letter was used as promotional copy for Larry Eigner, *On My Eyes: Poems*, photo. Harry Callahan, intro. Denise Levertov (Highlands, NC: Jargon Press, 1960); and printed on the dust jacket of Larry Eigner, *Another Time in Fragments* (London: Fulcrum Press, 1967).

24. Larry Eigner to Cid Corman, January 18, 1954, Cid Corman collection, HRC.

25. Cid Corman to Larry Eigner, January 10, 1954, Larry Eigner papers, Dodd.

26. Larry Eigner to Cid Corman, January 7, 1953, Cid Corman collection, HRC.

27. Lee Bartlett, interview by the author, June 2015, Las Cruces, NM.

28. Larry Eigner to Robert Creeley, February 17, 1954, Larry Eigner papers, Stanford.

29. Larry Eigner, "THE CARICATURE," *CP*, 1:122.

30. Lee Bartlett, interview by the author, summer 2012, Las Cruces, NM.

31. "Interesting Adult Books for Young People, 1955," *Educational Horizons* 34, no. 4 (1956): 314.

32. Larry Eigner to Cid Corman, September 17, 1971, uncatalogued manuscripts, Berg.

Chapter 11

1. Larry Eigner to Cid Corman, September 22, 1953, Cid Corman collection, HRC (see list of abbreviations and bibliography for archival sources).

2. Larry Eigner, "M o r e," in *The Collected Poems of Larry Eigner* (*CP*), ed. Curtis Faville and Robert Grenier (Stanford, CA: Stanford University Press, 2010), 1:53.

3. Richard Eigner, "An Origin and a Setting," *CP*, 4:xxxvi.

4. Larry Eigner to Sam Charters, June 14, 1969, Larry Eigner papers, Dodd.

5. Larry Eigner to Paul Blackburn, May 6, 1954, in *Momentous Inconclusions: The Life and Work of Larry Eigner*, ed. Jennifer Bartlett and George Hart (Albuquerque: University of New Mexico Press, 2020), 224–26.

6. Robert Grenier, interview by the author, July 2011, Bolinas, CA.

7. Larry Eigner to Sam Charters, June 14, 1969, Larry Eigner papers, Dodd.

8. Larry Eigner, "Company," *CP*, 1:55.

9. Larry Eigner to Cid Corman, March 15, 1970, uncatalogued manuscripts, Berg.

10. Larry Eigner to Cid Corman, May 25, 1965, Cid Corman collection, HRC.

11. Larry Eigner to Sam Charters, June 14, 1969, Larry Eigner papers, Dodd.

12. Larry Eigner to Cid Corman, May 25, 1965, Cid Corman collection, HRC.

13. Larry Eigner to David Gitin, May 30, 1970, Larry Eigner papers, Dodd.

14. Larry Eigner, "O n t h e W i d e S h o r e," *CP*, 1:143.

15. Arthur Goldman, interview by the author, March 2013, Skype.

16. Larry Eigner to Charles Olson, September 1, 1954, Larry Eigner papers, Dodd.

17. Larry Eigner to Jonathan Williams, February 10, 1960, letter 49, in *Letters to Jargon: The Correspondence between Larry Eigner and Jonathan Williams*, ed. Andrew Rippeon (Tuscaloosa: University of Alabama Press, 2019), 75–76.

18. Larry Eigner, "A P r i m e," *CP*, 1:106.

19. Larry Eigner to Robert Creeley, June 9, 1953, Robert Creeley papers, Stanford.

Chapter 12

1. Tom Clark, *Charles Olson: The Allegory of a Poet's Life* (New York: W. W. Norton, 1991), 15–40.

2. Robert Creeley to Cid Corman, January 18, 1954, Cid Corman collection, HRC (see list of abbreviations and bibliography for archival sources).

3. The first volume of the first series of *Origin* was largely dedicated to Charles Olson's work. Olson had corresponded heavily with Corman as the magazine was coming to fruition. He was, in fact, heavy handed about his own publications. The first issue, published in spring 1951, featured excerpts from *The Maximus Poems*. The issue also included work by William Carlos Williams, William Bronk, and Vincent Ferrini, as well as an essay on Hart Crane by Robert Creeley.

4. Larry Eigner to Cid Corman, January 18, 1954, Cid Corman Collection, HRC.

5. Larry Eigner to Robert Creeley, August 12, 1951, Larry Eigner papers, Dodd.

6. Larry Eigner to Cid Corman, May 13, 1954, Cid Corman collection, HRC.

7. Larry Eigner to Charles Olson, October 20, 1956, Larry Eigner papers, Dodd.

8. Larry Eigner to Cid Corman, January 18, 1954, Cid Corman collection, HRC.

9. Larry Eigner, "Has Enough Seemed Nobody with a Pretty Strange Language or Just Accent Can Think Much at All," in *Areas Lights Heights: Writings, 1954–1989*, by Larry Eigner, ed. Benjamin Friedlander (New York: Roof Books, 1989), 15.

10. Larry Eigner to Cid Corman, January 18, 1954, Cid Corman collection, HRC.

11. Eigner to Corman, January 18, 1954.

12. Larry Eigner to Charles Olson, October 20, 1956, Charles Olson collection, Dodd.

13. Larry Eigner to Jonathan Williams, May 31, 1958, letter 34, in *Letters to Jargon: The Correspondence between Larry Eigner and Jonathan Williams*, ed. Andrew Rippeon (Tuscaloosa: University of Alabama Press, 2019), 56.

14. Robert Creeley to Larry Eigner, October 14, 1954, Larry Eigner papers, Dodd.

15. Larry Eigner to Charles Olson, June 7, 1956, Larry Eigner papers, Dodd.

16. Charles Olson to Larry Eigner, June 20, 1956, in *Selected Letters: Charles Olson*, ed. Ralph Maud (Berkeley: University of California Press, 2001), 236.

17. "The phrase first was used by Olson in a poem entitled 'For R.C.' which he sent Creeley on 16 January 1953 and rewrote the next day: 'the figure of outward . . . all things stand by him, and all the others / are the better known.' In his letter to Creeley containing the poem, Olson reports how 'the first senses of it got written in the dark on the white, and scratched-on, wall!'" George F. Butterick, *A Guide to the Maximus Poems of Charles Olson* (Berkeley: University of California Press, 1978), 3–4.

18. Larry Eigner to Charles Olson, February 17, 1957, Larry Eigner papers, Dodd.

19. Robert Creeley, quoted in Ann Charters, introduction to *The Special View of History*, by Charles Olson, ed. Ann Charters (Berkeley, CA: Oyez Press, 1970), 5–6.

20. The decision for Eigner to be part of the Black Mountain College group of poets was somewhat circumstantial. His correspondence with Corman led to correspondence with Creeley. His relationship with Olson developed in part through Corman and in part due to the fact that he lived and wrote in the same area, Boston's North Shore. Eigner also had a long-term correspondence with another Gloucester poet, Vincent Ferrini. The Black Mountain College circle was largely made up of white men, save for a few exceptions: Amiri Baraka was briefly part of the group, and Denise Levertov and a few other women were also involved.

Chapter 13

1. Dana Greene, *Denise Levertov: A Poet's Life* (Urbana: University of Illinois Press, 2012).

2. Robert Duncan to Denise Levertov, June 1953, letter 1, in *The Letters of Robert Duncan and Denise Levertov*, ed. Robert J. Bertholf and Albert Gelpi (Stanford, CA: Stanford University Press, 2004), 3–5.

3. Lisa Jarnot, *Robert Duncan: The Ambassador from Venus; A Biography* (Berkeley: University of California Press, 2012).

4. Robert Duncan to Denise Levertov, August 25, 1957, letter 50, in *The Letters of Robert Duncan and Denise Levertov*, 66.

5. Larry Eigner, "BRINK," in *The Collected Poems of Larry Eigner* (*CP*), ed. Curtis Faville and Robert Grenier (Stanford, CA: Stanford University Press, 2010), 1:212.

6. Robert Duncan, "Three Poems in *Measure* One: An Open Letter," [c. 1957], p. 3 of typescript, box 28, Robert Duncan collection, UB (see list of abbreviations and bibliography for archival sources). "*Measure* One" refers to the first issue of the magazine *Measure* (1957), where the three poems addressed in Duncan's essay appeared: "One" by Edward Marshall, "The Rick of Green Wood" by Edward Dorn, and "Brink" by Larry Eigner.

7. Duncan, 3.

8. Robert Duncan to Denise Levertov, August 25, 1957, letter 50, in *The Letters of Robert Duncan and Denise Levertov*, 66.

9. Robert Duncan to Denise Levertov, November 30, 1957, letter 59, in *The Letters of Robert Duncan and Denise Levertov*, 76.

10. "I had the double reminder always, the vertical and horizontal displacements in vision that later became separated, specialized into a near and a far sight. One image to the right and above the other. Reach out and touch. Point to the one that is really there." Robert Duncan, "A Sequence of Poems for H.D.'s Birthday," in *Roots and Branches*, by Robert Duncan (New York: Charles Scribner's Sons, 1964), 14. For further informa-

tion on Duncan's visual disability, see Lisa Jarnot, *Robert Duncan*, 438; Ekbert Faas, *Young Robert Duncan: Portrait of the Poet as Homosexual in Society* (Santa Barbara, CA: Black Sparrow Press, 1983), 18–20.

11. Denise Levertov to Robert Duncan, November 25, 1957, letter 57, in *The Letters of Robert Duncan and Denise Levertov*, 75.

12. Denise Levertov, "A Note on Larry Eigner's Poems," in *On My Eyes: Poems*, by Larry Eigner, photo. Harry Callahan (Highlands, NC: Jargon Press, 1960), n.p., previously published in *Migrant*, no. 3 (1959): 5–9.

13. Denise Levertov, interview by Sybil Estess, October 1977 and March 1978, in *Conversations with Denise Levertov*, ed. Jewel Spears Brooker (Jackson: University Press of Mississippi, 1998), 93.

14. Denise Levertov to Robert Duncan, November 25, 1957, letter 57, in *The Letters of Robert Duncan and Denise Levertov*, 75.

15. Robert Duncan to Denise Levertov, August 25, 1957, letter 50, in *The Letters of Robert Duncan and Denise Levertov*, 66–67.

16. Denise Levertov to Robert Duncan, July 13/14, 1959, letter 129, in *The Letters of Robert Duncan and Denise Levertov*, 184; Denise Levertov to Robert Duncan, August 4, 1958, letter 92, in *The Letters of Robert Duncan and Denise Levertov*, 127.

17. Denise Levertov to Robert Duncan, August 4, 1958, letter 92, in *The Letters of Robert Duncan and Denise Levertov*, 127 (original emphasis).

18. Arthur McFarland to Larry Eigner, date unknown, Larry Eigner papers, Stanford.

19. Denise Levertov to Robert Duncan, July 13/14, 1959, letter 129, in *The Letters of Robert Duncan and Denise Levertov*, 184.

20. Larry Eigner to Cid Corman, November 3, 1961, Cid Corman collection, HRC.

21. Cid Corman to Larry Eigner, May 5, 1960, uncatalogued manuscripts, Berg.

22. Robert Duncan to Larry Eigner, July 22, 1959, Robert Duncan collection, UB.

23. Larry Eigner to Robert Duncan, August 31, 1959, Robert Duncan collection, UB.

24. Robert Duncan to Denise Levertov, August 25, 1957, letter 50, in *The Letters of Robert Duncan and Denise Levertov*, 66.

25. Larry Eigner to Donald Allen, August 26, 1958, Donald Allen collection, UCSD.

26. Donald Allen to Larry Eigner, December 18, 1957, Donald Allen collection, UCSD.

27. Robert Duncan, "Ideas of the Meaning of Form," in *Robert Duncan: Collected Essays and Other Prose*, ed. James Maynard (Berkeley: University of California Press, 2019), 82.

Chapter 14

1. Larry Eigner to Robert Creeley, April 1, 1954, Robert Creeley papers, Stanford (see list of abbreviations and bibliography for archival sources).

2. Larry Eigner, "the music, the rooms . . . ," in *The Collected Poems of Larry Eigner* (*CP*), ed. Curtis Faville and Robert Grenier (Stanford, CA: Stanford University Press, 2010), 2:634.

3. Larry Eigner, "Rambling (in) Life," in *Areas Lights Heights: Writings, 1954–1989*, by Larry Eigner, ed. Benjamin Friedlander (New York: Roof Books, 1989), 128.

4. Larry Eigner to Robert Creeley, April 1, 1954, Robert Creeley papers, Stanford.

5. Lee Bartlett, interview by the author, April 7, 2012, Las Cruces, NM.

6. Larry Eigner, "D e   L i m i t s," *CP*, 1:75.

7. Alison Kafer, *Feminist, Queer, Crip* (Bloomington: Indiana University Press, 2013).

8. Eigner, "Rambling (in) Life," 128.

9. Larry Eigner, "Again Dawn," *CP*, 2:357. For typescript, see *CP*, 4:1700.
10. George Hart, *Finding the Weight of Things: Larry Eigner's Ecrippoetics* (Tuscaloosa: University of Alabama Press, 2022).
11. Larry Eigner, "Arrowhead of Meaning," in Eigner, *Areas Lights Heights*, 48.
12. Larry Eigner, "Statement on Words," in Eigner, 3.
13. Eigner, "Be minimal then . . . ," in Eigner, 8.
14. Larry Eigner to Jack Lorts, November 1, 1961, private collection.
15. Eigner, "Poet & Critic," in Eigner, *Areas Lights Heights*, 16.
16. Robert Grenier, interview by the author, July 2011, Bolinas, CA.
17. Hart, *Finding the Weight of Things*, 60.
18. Wikipedia, s.v. "Leonard Bernstein," last modified April 7, 2021.
19. Leonard Bernstein, "Forever Beethoven," *Young People's Concerts*, season 11, episode 2, prod. and dir. Roger Englander, aired January 28, 1968, on CBS.
20. J. W. N. Sullivan, *Beethoven: His Spiritual Development* (New York: Alfred A. Knopf, 1936), 258.
21. Larry Eigner, *CP*, 2:361.
22. Larry Eigner, "A l o n g   L i n e s   O f," *CP*, 1:127.
23. Larry Eigner to Cid Corman, April 19, 1965, Cid Corman collection, HRC.
24. Eigner to Corman, April 19, 1965 (original emphasis).
25. Hart, *Finding the Weight of Things*, 95.
26. Paul R. Ehrlich, *The Population Bomb*, rev. ed. (New York: Ballantine Books, 1971), 130–31.
27. Larry Eigner, letter to the editor (unpublished), *Saturday Evening Post*, April 25–May 2, 1963, in "Letters to the Editor, 1963–69," by Larry Eigner, ed. George Hart, *PMLA* 131, no. 3 (2016): 778–79.
28. Between 1962 and his death in 1970, Charles Olson wrote seventeen letters to the editor of the *Gloucester Daily Times*, primarily focused on his fight against the gentrification of Gloucester. The letters are collected in *Maximus to Gloucester: Letters and Poems of Charles Olson to the Editor of the Gloucester Daily Times, 1962–1969*, ed. Peter Anastas (Gloucester: Ten Pound Island Books, 1992).

Chapter 15

1. Larry Eigner to Jonathan Williams, March 19, [1956?], letter 9, in *Letters to Jargon: The Correspondence between Larry Eigner and Jonathan Williams*, ed. Andrew Rippeon (Tuscaloosa: University of Alabama Press, 2019), 25.
2. Larry Eigner to Robert Duncan, March 29, 1957, Robert Duncan collection, UB (see list of abbreviations and bibliography for archival sources). Eigner writes about Williams and Olson's visit in this letter: "Olson and Williams here last Friday." He also mentions Richard's visit to San Francisco: "My brother heading for S F next week, and wd like to look you up . . . he wants to settle if he can in Cal."
3. Larry Eigner to Jonathan Williams, July 20, 1956, letter 12, in Eigner and Williams, *Letters to Jargon*, 29.
4. Larry Eigner to Charles Olson, September 1, 1959, Charles Olson research collection, Dodd.
5. Larry Eigner to Jonathan Williams, July 20, 1956, letter 12, in Eigner and Williams, *Letters to Jargon*, 29.
6. Eigner to Olson, September 1, 1959.
7. Larry Eigner to Jonathan Williams, August 10, 1956, letter 13, in Eigner and Williams, *Letters to Jargon*, 30.

8. Cid Corman to Larry Eigner, March 18, 1960, Cid Corman collection, HRC.
9. Corman to Eigner, March 18, 1960.
10. Denise Levertov to Jonathan Williams, May 23, 1958, Jargon Society collection, UB.
11. Larry Eigner to Jonathan Williams, February 7, 1957, letter 17, in Eigner and Williams, *Letters to Jargon*, 37.
12. Jonathan Williams to Charles Olson, August 15, 1957, Charles Olson research collection, Dodd.
13. Larry Eigner to Jonathan Williams, November 19, 1957, letter 25, in Eigner and Williams, *Letters to Jargon*, 46.
14. Denise Levertov to Jonathan Williams, May 23, 1958, Jargon Society collection, UB.
15. Larry Eigner to Jonathan Williams, [December 6, 1957], letter 27, in Eigner and Williams, *Letters to Jargon*, 48.
16. Larry Eigner to Jonathan Williams, November 19, 1957, letter 25, in Eigner and Williams, 47.
17. Larry Eigner to Jonathan Williams, March 19, [1956?], letter 9, in Eigner and Williams, 25.
18. Larry Eigner to Robert Duncan, July 15, 1959, Robert Duncan collection, UB.
19. Larry Eigner to Jonathan Williams, March 25, 1959, letter 38, in Eigner and Williams, *Letters to Jargon*, 59.
20. Eigner and Williams, 241, note for "and since you . . ."
21. Larry Eigner to Jonathan Williams, February 10, 1960, letter 49, in Eigner and Williams, 76.
22. "Eigner also began occasionally to write potentially sensitive content in French. And, on at least one occasion, Eigner enlisted the help of the Eigners' cleaning woman to smuggle letters out of the home without the knowledge of his parents (see card dated January 29, 1960)." Eigner and Williams, 7.
23. Denise Levertov to Larry Eigner, March 21, 1960, Larry Eigner papers, Stanford.
24. Denise Levertov, "A Note on Larry Eigner's Poems," in *On My Eyes: Poems*, by Larry Eigner (Highlands, NC: Jargon Press, 1960), n.p., previously published in *Migrant*, no. 3 (1959): 5–9.
25. Denise Levertov to Robert Duncan, July 13/14, 1959, letter 129, in *The Letters of Robert Duncan and Denise Levertov*, ed. Robert J. Bertholf and Albert Gelpi (Stanford, CA: Stanford University Press, 2004), 184 (original emphasis).
26. See Irving P. Leif, *Larry Eigner: A Bibliography of His Works* (Metuchen, NJ: Scarecrow Press, 1989), 5–6. A copy of *Look at the Park* (Swampscott, MA: privately printed, 1958) is available in the Berg Collection at the New York Public Library.
27. Cid Corman to Larry Eigner, March 10, 1957, uncatalogued manuscripts, Berg.
28. Larry Eigner to Cid Corman, May 25, 1960, Cid Corman collection, HRC.
29. Eigner to Corman, May 25, 1960.
30. Larry Eigner to Cid Corman, September 6, 1960, Cid Corman collection, HRC.

Chapter 16

1. Larry Eigner to Cid Corman, May 25, 1960, Cid Corman collection, HRC (see list of abbreviations and bibliography for archival sources).
2. See Larry Eigner's calendar at the front of this volume: entries for September 20, 1960; January 23, 1961; and September 21, 1962.
3. "And, my left arm and leg pretty wild till I had cryosurgery about 6 weeks into

my 36th year, I had to keep my attention away from myself to sit still, yet not too far away either." Larry Eigner, "Rambling (in) Life," in *Areas Lights Heights: Writings, 1954–1989*, by Larry Eigner, ed. Benjamin Friedlander (New York: Roof Books, 1989), 128.

4. Larry Eigner to Cid Corman, June 26, 1963, Cid Corman collection, HRC.

5. Cid Corman to Larry Eigner, late 1960, Larry Eigner papers, Dodd.

6. Larry Eigner to Jonathan Williams, January 29, 1962, letter 73, in *Letters to Jargon: The Correspondence between Larry Eigner and Jonathan Williams*, ed. Andrew Rippeon (Tuscaloosa: University of Alabama Press, 2019), 107.

7. Jack Foley, in Larry Eigner et al., "Virtually Enough: Videoconference [. . .] December 29, 1995," in "Larry Eigner," ed. Shelly Andrews, in *Contemporary Authors Autobiography Series*, ed. Joyce Nakamura, vol. 23 (Detroit: Gale Research, 1996), 54.

8. *Larry Eigner Letters (to Joseph Guglielmi and Claude Royet-Journoud)*, ed. Robert Kocik and Joseph Simas (Paris: Moving Letters Press, 1987), n.p.

9. Larry Eigner to Cid Corman, September 14, 1962, Cid Corman collection, HRC.

10. Larry Eigner to Cid Corman, October 19, 1962, Cid Corman collection, HRC.

11. Larry Eigner to Donald Allen, October 1961, Donald Allen papers, UCSD.

12. Larry Eigner to Robert Creeley, July 30, 1965, Robert Creeley papers, Stanford. This letter was addressed to Creeley at the Berkeley Poetry Conference.

13. Larry Eigner to Robert Creeley, February 17, 1964, Robert Creeley papers, Stanford.

14. Larry Eigner to Denise Levertov, October 15–18, 1963, Denise Levertov papers, Stanford.

15. Larry Eigner, "blackbirds and sparrows," in *The Collected Poems of Larry Eigner* (*CP*), ed. Curtis Faville and Robert Grenier (Stanford, CA: Stanford University Press, 2010), 2:672.

16. Eigner's diligence in notating changes in every book and magazine that published his work attests to the fact that his spacing was calculated, not, as Levertov noted, merely a typo or product of his inability to use the typewriter in a typical way.

17. Larry Eigner to Donald Allen, January 27, 1962, Donald Allen papers, UCSD.

18. Galway Kinnell, "Seeing and Being," rev. of *On My Eyes*, by Larry Eigner, *Poetry* 100, no. 6 (September 1962): 402.

19. Cid Corman to Larry Eigner, December 13, 1960, uncatalogued manuscripts, Berg.

20. Larry Eigner, "the Dr. saying," *CP*, 2:439.

21. Larry Eigner to Cid Corman, October 4, 1962, Cid Corman collection, HRC.

22. Larry Eigner, "Screaming woman," *CP*, 2:432.

23. Larry Eigner to Robert Creeley, February 17, 1964, Larry Eigner papers, Dodd.

Chapter 17

1. Cid Corman to Larry Eigner, October 7, 1956, uncatalogued manuscripts, Berg (see list of abbreviations and bibliography for archival sources).

2. Kevin Killian, email message to author, April 9, 2018. Spicer edited a magazine called *J*. It was his intention to only publish Bay Area poets, yet he felt so strongly about Eigner's work and that of a few other poets not on the West Coast that he solicited them for poems. *J* ran for eight issues. The first five were edited by Spicer, the next two by George Stanley, and the last by Harold Dull. Spicer published Eigner in the fifth issue, which was released in 1959.

3. James Laughlin to Larry Eigner, February 6, 1963, Larry Eigner papers, Dodd.

4. Cid Corman to Larry Eigner, September 11, 1965, Larry Eigner papers, Dodd.

5. Larry Eigner to Richard Morris, date unknown, Fales manuscript collection, NYU.

6. While it remains difficult for any poet who writes experimental work to gain mainstream attention in the United States, it is particularly difficult for poets with disabilities. The publishing world tends toward writers who write about their disability as a tragedy, something that Eigner always resisted.

7. Larry Eigner, "Letter for Duncan," in *Areas Lights Heights: Writings, 1954–1989*, by Larry Eigner, ed. Benjamin Friedlander (New York: Roof Books, 1989), 117.

8. Eigner, 118.

9. Claude Royet-Journoud, email message to author, March 6, 2014.

10. Eigner's first appearance in a French publication was in *Action poétique*, no. 56 (December 1973): 86–93.

11. Jacques Roubaud and Michel Deguy, eds., *Vingt poètes américains* ([Paris]: Gallimard, 1980).

12. *Larry Eigner Letters (to Joseph Guglielmi and Claude Royet-Journoud)*, ed. Robert Kocik and Joseph Simas (Paris: Moving Letters Press, 1987).

13. Cards and correspondence to Larry Eigner from French schoolchildren who read his poems in class, [undated], box 23, folder 4, Larry Eigner papers, Stanford.

14. Charles Bukowski, "Charles Bukowski Speaks Out," interview by Arnold L. Kaye, *Chicago Literary Times* 2, no. 4 (March 1963), Bukowski.net.

15. John Martin to Larry Eigner, December 7, 1967, box 1, folder 38, Larry Eigner papers, Brown (original emphasis).

16. Martin to Eigner, December 7, 1967.

17. Larry Eigner, *The- / Towards Autumn* (Los Angeles: Black Sparrow Press, 1967).

Chapter 18

1. Robert Grenier, interview by the author, July 2011, Bolinas, CA.

2. In Denise Levertov's and Robert Duncan's letters about Larry Eigner, they often spoke about his disability in ways that could be considered disrespectful or prejudiced. They certainly did not have an idea of disability justice or the mundane way in which Eigner felt about his own disability. Of the poets he corresponded with, Cid Corman understood Eigner's situation the best as they were close and Corman had a lot of insight into Eigner's relationship with his parents.

3. Larry Eigner to Cid Corman, May 25, 1965, Cid Corman collection, HRC (see list of abbreviations and bibliography for archival sources).

4. Cid Corman to Larry Eigner, September 11, 1965, uncatalogued manuscripts, Berg.

5. Larry Eigner to Cid Corman, May 25, 1965, Cid Corman collection, HRC.

6. Eigner to Corman, May 25, 1965.

7. For more on the Berkeley Poetry Conference, see Libbie Rifkin, "Making It / New: Institutionalizing Postwar Avant-Gardes," *Poetics Today* 21, no. 1 (2000): 129–50.

8. Larry Eigner to Cid Corman, May 25, 1965, Cid Corman collection, HRC.

9. Richard Eigner, in Larry Eigner et al., "Virtually Enough: Videoconference [. . .] December 29, 1995," in "Larry Eigner," ed. Shelly Andrews, in *Contemporary Authors Autobiography Series*, ed. Joyce Nakamura, vol. 23 (Detroit: Gale Research, 1996), 53.

10. L. Eigner et al., 53. Andrews notes that part of this quote is sourced from a letter from Larry Eigner, dated January 3, 1996.

11. Larry Eigner, "Qs & As (?) Large and Small Parts of a Collaborate," in *Areas Lights Heights: Writings, 1954–1989*, ed. Benjamin Friedlander (New York: Roof Books, 1989), 154.

12. Cid Corman to Larry Eigner, September 11, 1965 (original emphasis), uncatalogued manuscripts, Berg.

13. Larry Eigner to Jonathan Williams, December 20, 1964, letter 81, in *Letters to Jargon: The Correspondence between Larry Eigner and Jonathan Williams*, ed. Andrew Rippeon (Tuscaloosa: University of Alabama Press, 2019), 130.

14. Robert Duncan to Denise Levertov, August 25, 1957, letter 50, in *The Letters of Robert Duncan and Denise Levertov*, ed. Robert J. Bertholf and Albert Gelpi (Stanford, CA: Stanford University Press, 2004), 67–68.

15. Andrea Wyatt, email message to author, August 3, 2015.

16. Duncan makes at least two visits to the University of Kansas in Lawrence, where he spent time with Edwin Eigner (May 1965 and April 1967). See Lisa Jarnot, *Robert Duncan: The Ambassador from Venus; A Biography* (Berkeley: University of California Press, 2012), 241–42, 266–67.

17. See Larry Eigner's calendar at the front of this volume: entry for June 26–August 22, 1966.

18. Larry Eigner to David Gitin, May 30, 1970, Larry Eigner papers, Dodd.

19. Larry Eigner to Cid Corman, June 23, 1968, uncatalogued manuscripts, Berg.

20. Larry Eigner to Janet Eigner, December 16, 1962, Larry Eigner papers, Stanford.

21. "March 25, 1973 - First public reading, at Artists' Cooperative in Cambridge, MA, organized by George Groesbeck who taught at the University of Massachusetts, Salem." Curtis Faville and Robert Grenier, "Larry Eigner Chronology," in *The Collected Poems of Larry Eigner* (*CP*), ed. Curtis Faville and Robert Grenier (Stanford, CA: Stanford University Press, 2010), 1:xxiv.

22. Larry Eigner to Denise Levertov, April 10, 1972, Denise Levertov papers, Stanford; and see Larry Eigner's calendar at the front of this volume: entry for June 6, 1970.

23. Larry Eigner to Robert Grenier, October 8, 1971, Larry Eigner papers, KU; and see Larry Eigner's calendar at the front of this volume: entries for September 12, 1971; and October 17, 1971.

24. Larry Eigner to Robert Grenier, March 26, 1972, Larry Eigner papers, KU.

25. Larry Eigner to Vincent Ferrini, October 27, 1970, Larry Eigner papers, Dodd.

26. Larry Eigner to Cid Corman, July 29, 1971, uncatalogued manuscripts, Berg.

27. Henry Ferrini, dir., *Polis Is This: Charles Olson and the Persistence of Place*, written by Ken Riaf (Gloucester, MA: Ferrini Productions, 2007), 56 min.; Tom Clark, *Charles Olson: The Allegory of a Poet's Life* (New York: W. W. Norton, 1991).

28. Ferrini, *Polis Is This*.

29. Ferrini.

30. Eigner's work is primarily collected in archives at the University of Kansas and Stanford University. In the 1960s, through his cousin Edwin, he arranged to have the archive at the University of Kansas. This collection primarily houses typescripts of poems. After his death, Robert Grenier arranged to have Eigner's papers taken by Stanford. In my studies, I found that Eigner had smaller archives at the University of Connecticut Dodd J. Research Center and in the Berg Collection at the New York Public Library. It is my assumption that the Berg Collection came to be because Cid Corman was selling his letters to dealers in New York. After these letters stopped being profitable, they were donated to the library. I have no information as to how Eigner's papers came to the Dodd J. Research Center, whose collection includes early letters from Corman and Robert Creeley. I was given the last of Eigner's possessions from his family, which included many photographs, Eigner's Social Security card, and a few letters. These have all been donated to the Dodd J. Research Center.

Chapter 19

1. Robert Grenier, interview by the author, July 2013, Bolinas, CA.
2. Grenier, interview.
3. Robert Grenier, introduction to *The Collected Poems of Larry Eigner* (*CP*), ed. Curtis Faville and Robert Grenier (Stanford, CA: Stanford University Press, 2010), 1:vii. Grenier coedited *this* with Barrett Watten. Although neither of them remember the derivation of the magazine's title, both Charles Olson and Larry Eigner have poems by the same name.
4. Larry Eigner to Jim Weil, May 28, 1977, box 1, folder 36, Larry Eigner papers, Brown (see list of abbreviations and bibliography for archival sources).
5. Larry Eigner to Joe and Janet Eigner, May 15, 1972, Larry Eigner papers, KU.
6. See Larry Eigner's calendar at the front of this volume: entries for October 6, 1974; and December 5–7, 1974.
7. See Larry Eigner's calendar at the front of this volume: entry for March 25, 1973.
8. Robert Grenier, interview by the author, July 2013, Bolinas, CA.
9. See Larry Eigner's calendar at the front of this volume: entry for October 4–18, 1972.
10. Sam Charters to Larry Eigner, April 22, 1968, Larry Eigner papers, Dodd.
11. Cid Corman to Larry Eigner, date unknown, Cid Corman collection, HRC.
12. See Larry Eigner, "What a Time Distance: The Autobiography," in *Larry Eigner: Selected Poems*, ed. Samuel Charters and Andrew Wyatt (Berkeley, CA: Oyez Press, 1972), 111–25.
13. Richard Eigner, interview by the author, July 2015, Berkeley, CA.
14. Leonard M. Henny and Jan Boon, dirs., *Getting It Together: A Film on Larry Eigner, Poet*, text by Michael F. Podulke (Saint Louis, MO: Films for Social Change, 1973), 16 mm, 18 min.; Jack Foley, ed., "Transcript of *Getting It Together: A Film of Larry Eigner, Poet* (1973) with Commentary by Larry Eigner (1989)," in "Larry Eigner," ed. Shelly Andrews, in *Contemporary Authors Autobiography Series*, ed. Joyce Nakamura, vol. 23 (Detroit: Gale Research, 1996), 40–47. Quotations from the film come from this published transcript.
15. For archival records and correspondence related to *Getting It Together*, see the archival collection (film, transcripts, and letters) relating to *Getting It Together: A Film on Larry Eigner, Poet*, KU.
16. Larry Eigner to Paul Auster, February 11, 1974, Paul Auster papers, Berg.
17. Larry Eigner to Jim Weil, date unknown, 1978, box 1, folder 37, Larry Eigner papers, Brown.
18. Larry Eigner to Jonathan Williams, July 20, 1978, letter 97, in *Letters to Jargon: The Correspondence between Larry Eigner and Jonathan Williams*, ed. Andrew Rippeon (Tuscaloosa: University of Alabama Press, 2019), 164.

Chapter 20

1. Beverly Eigner and Richard Eigner, interview by the author, July 2015, Berkeley, CA.
2. Jon Oda (Edward Roberts's attendant for three years), "Highlights from Speeches by Ed Roberts" (unpublished manuscript), April 1995, quoted in Doris Zames Fleischer and Frieda Zames, *The Disability Rights Movement: From Charity to Confrontation*, updated ed. (Philadelphia: Temple University Press, 2011), 38.
3. Fleischer and Zames, 37–40.
4. Beverly Eigner and Richard Eigner, interview by the author, July 2015, Berkeley, CA.
5. B. Eigner and R. Eigner, interview.

6. The Eigner family graciously allowed me access to Eigner's copy of *The Maximus Poems* published by Jargon. The book is very worn, which attests to the lengthy time that Eigner spent with it. He also made numerous notes in the margins.

7. Larry Eigner to Cid Corman, July 30, 1979, uncatalogued manuscripts, Berg (see list of abbreviations and bibliography for archival sources).

8. Larry Eigner to Cid Corman, September 12, 1978, uncatalogued manuscripts, Berg. Although Beverly and Richard Eigner had the best of intentions in suggesting independent living arrangements to Eigner, after growing up in the constant care of his mother he did not have the skills to care for himself independently. From his letters, it is apparent that the people who worked for the residents at this group home could be negligent, so much so that Eigner complained at times of not getting enough to eat or having to go a number of days without a shower.

9. Larry Eigner to Cid Corman, September 12, 1978, uncatalogued manuscripts, Berg.

10. Larry Eigner to Cid Corman, July 30, 1979, uncatalogued manuscripts, Berg.

11. Eigner to Corman, July 30, 1979.

12. Larry Eigner, "clouds moving together . . . ," in *The Collected Poems of Larry Eigner* (*CP*), ed. Curtis Faville and Robert Grenier (Stanford, CA: Stanford University Press, 2010), 4:1361.

13. Larry Eigner to Bessie Eigner, date unknown, Larry Eigner papers, Stanford.

14. Larry Eigner to Cid Corman, July 30, 1979, uncatalogued manuscripts, Berg.

15. Ron Silliman, email message to author, April 20, 2015.

16. Larry Eigner to Bessie Eigner, September 6, 1978, Larry Eigner papers, Stanford.

17. Larry Eigner to Bessie Eigner, September 22, 1978, Larry Eigner papers, Stanford.

18. Larry Eigner, "D i s c o," *CP*, 4:1362.

19. Larry Eigner to Cid Corman, July 30, 1979, uncatalogued manuscripts, Berg.

20. Bessie Eigner to Larry Eigner, September 17, 1979, Larry Eigner papers, Stanford.

21. Larry Eigner to Bob Wilson, January 4, 1979, uncatalogued manuscripts, Berg.

22. Larry Eigner to Bessie Eigner, September 6, 1978, Larry Eigner papers, Stanford.

23. L. Eigner to B. Eigner, September 6, 1978.

24. Larry Eigner to Bessie Eigner, June 15, 1981, Larry Eigner papers, Stanford.

25. Larry Eigner to Bessie Eigner, September 6, 1978, Larry Eigner papers, Stanford.

26. Beverly Eigner and Richard Eigner, interview by the author, July 2015, Berkeley, CA.

27. For Eigner's description of this accident, see Larry Eigner, "Course Matter," in *Areas Lights Heights: Writings, 1954–1989*, Larry Eigner, ed. Benjamin Friedlander (New York: Roof Books, 1989), 141.

28. Larry Eigner to Bessie Eigner, January 6, 1978, Larry Eigner papers, Stanford.

29. Eigner did eventually learn to use the electric wheelchair, and many people recall seeing him move around town.

30. Larry Eigner to Bessie Eigner, January 6, 1978, Larry Eigner papers, Stanford.

31. Larry Eigner to Cid Corman, December 28, 1981, uncatalogued manuscripts, Berg.

32. Larry Eigner to Bessie Eigner, date unknown, Larry Eigner papers, Stanford.

33. "LE said he got into his only real / 'physical' *fight* with another guy in a wheelchair there, who wouldn't turn down volume on his t.v." Robert Grenier, preface to "Berkeley (1978–1995)," *CP*, 4:1350 (original emphasis).

34. Robert Grenier, interview by the author, July 2013, Bolinas, CA.

Chapter 21

1. Robert Grenier, interview by the author, July 2013, Bolinas, CA.
2. Larry Eigner to Bessie Eigner, July 25, 1981, Larry Eigner papers, Stanford (see list of abbreviations and bibliography for archival sources).
3. Larry Eigner, "the dog / comes . . . ," in *The Collected Poems of Larry Eigner* (*CP*), ed. Curtis Faville and Robert Grenier (Stanford, CA: Stanford University Press, 2010), 3:1201.
4. Robert Grenier, interview by the author, July 2013, Bolinas, CA.
5. Larry Eigner to Bessie Eigner, date unknown, Larry Eigner papers, Stanford.
6. Robert Grenier, "So Quick Bright Things Come to Confusion," in "Larry Eigner Issue," ed. Benjamin Friedlander and Christopher Funkhouser, special issue, *Passages: A Technopoetics Journal*, no. 5 (April 1998), Electronic Poetry Center, University of Pennsylvania.
7. Robert Grenier, interview by the author, July 2013, Bolinas, CA.
8. Ron Silliman, email message to author, January 24, 2012.
9. Larry Eigner, "Course Matter," in *Areas Lights Heights: Writings, 1954–1989*, ed. Benjamin Friedlander (New York: Roof Books, 1989), 141; Robert Grenier, interview by the author, July 2013, Bolinas, CA.
10. Larry Eigner to Clayton Eshelman, May 21, 1982, in *Momentous Inconclusions: The Life and Work of Larry Eigner*, ed. Jennifer Bartlett and George Hart (Albuquerque: University of New Mexico Press, 2020), 271.
11. Larry Eigner to Joe and Janet Eigner, August 23, 1980, Larry Eigner papers, Stanford.
12. Robert Kocik, email message to author, January 28, 2014.
13. See Larry Eigner's calendar at the front of this volume: entries for April 1980; and December 27–30, 1979.
14. See Larry Eigner's calendar at the front of this volume: entries for December 27–30, 1980; and August 1980.
15. See Larry Eigner's calendar at the front of this volume: entry for May 12, 1980.
16. See Larry Eigner's calendar at the front of this volume: entry for March 1983.
17. Charles Bernstein, "Again Eigner and 'The Only World We've Got,'" in Friedlander and Funkhouser, "Larry Eigner Issue."
18. Jack Foley, interview by the author, June 2014, Berkeley, CA.
19. Jack Foley, "A Tribute to Larry Eigner," based on a version read by Jack and Adelle Foley, November 19, 2010, *Poetry Flash*, n.d.
20. Larry Eigner to Bessie Eigner, date unknown, Larry Eigner papers, Stanford.
21. Larry Eigner, "fight the background . . . ," *CP*, 4:1609.
22. Bessie Eigner to Larry Eigner, August 7, 1983, uncatalogued manuscripts, Berg.
23. Larry Eigner to Robert Creeley, July 21, 1951, in Robert Creeley and Larry Eigner, "Selected Correspondence, July–September 1951." *Chicago Review* 58, no. 2 (2014): 54.
24. Larry Eigner to Joe and Janet Eigner, August 23, 1980, Larry Eigner papers, Stanford.
25. Larry Eigner, "not / forever / serious," in Eigner, *Areas Lights Heights*, 25–26.
26. Larry Eigner to Cid Corman, date unknown, uncatalogued manuscripts, Berg.
27. Kathleen Frumkin, interview by the author, summer 2014, Berkeley, CA.
28. George Hart, *Finding the Weight of Things: Larry Eigner's Ecrippoetics* (Tuscaloosa: University of Alabama Press, 2022), 161.
29. Robert Grenier, "On Speech," in *In the American Tree*, ed. Ron Silliman (Orno, ME: National Poetry Foundation, 1986), 496, previously published in *This*, no. 1 (1971): n.p.

30. Grenier, 496.
31. Lee Bartlett, "What Is 'Language Poetry'?," *Critical Inquiry* 12, no. 4 (1986): 742.
32. Stephen Freedman, quoted in Bartlett, 742.
33. Ron Silliman to Bruce Andrews, date unknown, in *The Language Letters: Selected 1970s Correspondences of Bruce Andrews, Charles Bernstein, and Ron Silliman*, ed. Matthew Hofer and Michael Golston (Albuquerque: University of New Mexico Press, 2019), 26.
34. Larry Eigner, "Approaching Things / Some Calculus / How figure it / Of Everyday Life Experience," *L=A=N=G=U=A=G=E*, no. 1 (February 1978): n.p., Eclipse Archive.
35. Bartlett, "What Is 'Language Poetry'?," 743.
36. Charles Bernstein and Bruce Andrews, "Repossessing the Word," in *The L=A=N=G=U=A=G=E Book*, ed. Bruce Andrews and Charles Bernstein (Carbondale: Southern Illinois University Press, 1987), ix.
37. Larry Eigner, "Qs & As (?) Large and Small Parts of a Collaborate," in Eigner, *Areas Lights Heights*, 135.
38. Charles Bernstein, interview by Tom Beckett, *Difficulties* 2, no. 1 (1982): 41, Eclipse Archive.
39. Bartlett, "What Is 'Language Poetry'?," 744–45.
40. Irving P. Leif, *Larry Eigner: A Bibliography of His Works* (Metuchen, NJ: Scarecrow Press, 1989).
41. Silliman, *In the American Tree*, dedication page.

Chapter 22

1. Kathleen Frumkin and Robert Grenier, interview by the author, summer 2014, Berkeley, CA.
2. Beverly Eigner and Richard Eigner, interview by the author, July 2015, Berkeley, CA.
3. Larry Eigner to Bessie Eigner, date unknown, Larry Eigner papers, Stanford (see list of abbreviations and bibliography for archival sources).
4. L. Eigner to B. Eigner, date unknown.
5. L. Eigner to B. Eigner, date unknown.
6. Ben Friedlander, interview by the author, June 12, 2015, Orono, ME.
7. *Larry Eigner: MATRIX/BERKELEY 159* (exhibition brochure), University of California, Berkeley Art Museum and Pacific Film Archive, June 15–October 15, 1993.
8. Larry Eigner to Cid Corman, date unknown, uncatalogued manuscripts, Berg.
9. A recording of this reading is available online; see Larry Eigner, "Last Public Reading, November 17, 1995," film clip, 11:39, at *Larry Eigner: Sacred Materials* (web page), PennSound: Center for Programs in Contemporary Writing, University of Pennsylvania, accessed August 14, 2022. This clip was filmed by Kush of Cloud House; Kush's reflection on Eigner's reading is linked from the same page.
10. See Larry Eigner, "Jewish Ground Ceremony, February 6, 1996," film clip, 66:32, at *Larry Eigner: Sacred Materials* (web page).

Bibliography

Archival Sources

Berg: Henry W. and Albert A. Berg Collection of English and American Literature, Special Collections, New York Public Library

Auster, Paul. Papers.
Uncatalogued manuscripts.
Corman, Cid. Papers.

Brown: John Hay Library, Brown University, Providence, Rhode Island

Eigner, Larry. Papers. MS 79.10.

Dodd: Archives and Special Collections, Thomas J. Dodd Research Center, University of Connecticut, Storrs

Eigner, Larry. Papers. MSS 1974-0001.
Ferrini, Vincent. Papers. MSS 1997-0107.
Olson, Charles. Research collection. MSS 1969-0001.

HRC: Harry Ransom Center, University of Texas at Austin

Corman, Cid. Collection. MS-00930.
Crews, Judson. Papers, 1935–81.
El corno emplumado (*Plumed Horn*). Records. MS-00933.
Zukofsky, Louis. Collection, 1910–85.

KU: Department of Special Collections, Kenneth Spencer Research Library, University of Kansas, Lawrence

Eigner, Larry. Poems and papers. MS 39.
Film, transcripts, and letters relating to *Getting It Together: A Film on Larry Eigner, Poet*. MS 122.

NYU: Fales Library and Special Collections, New York University

Fales manuscript collection. MSS 001.

Stanford: Department of Special Collections, Stanford University Libraries, Stanford, California

Creeley, Robert. Papers. M0662.
Eigner, Larry. Papers. M0902.
Levertov, Denise. Papers. M0601.

UB: Poetry Collection of the University Libraries, University at Buffalo, State University of New York

Butterick, George. Collection. In processing.
Contemporary manuscripts. Collection. PCMS-0001.
Duncan, Robert. Collection. PCMS-0110.
Jargon Society. Collection. PCMS-0019.

UCSD: Special Collections and Archives, University of California, San Diego

Allen, Donald. Collection. MSS 3.
Bernstein, Charles. Papers. MSS 0519.
Eshleman, Clayton. Papers. MSS 21.
Hejinian, Lyn. Papers. MSS 74.
Mac Low, Jackson. Papers. MSS 180.
Rothenberg, Jerome. Papers. MSS 10.
Silliman, Ron. Papers. MSS 75.

Published and Secondary Sources

Allen, Donald, ed. *The New American Poetry, 1945–1960.* Berkeley: University of California Press, 1999. First published 1960 by Grove Press.

Allison, Larry. "Personal Background and the Camp Jened Years, 1965–1973." Interview by Denise Sherer Jacobson, July 14, 2001. Transcript. In *New York Activists and Leaders in the Disability Rights and Independent Living Movement*, vol. 1. Berkeley: Regional Oral History Office, Bancroft Library, University of California, 2004. Online Archive of California.

Andrews, Bruce, Charles Bernstein, and Ron Silliman. *The Language Letters: Selected 1970s Correspondence of Bruce Andrews, Charles Bernstein, and Ron Silliman.* Edited by Matthew Hofer and Michael Golston. Albuquerque: University of New Mexico Press, 2019.

Armantrout, Rae, Steve Benson, Alan Bernheimer, Carla Harryman, Lyn Hejinian, Tom Mandel, Ted Pearson, Bob Perelman, Kit Robinson, Ron Silliman, and Barrett Watten. *The Grand Piano: An Experiment in Collective Autobiography; San Francisco, 1975–1980.* Part 10. Detroit: Mode A, 2010.

Bartlett, Jennifer, and George Hart, eds. *Momentous Inconclusions: The Life and Work of Larry Eigner.* Albuquerque: University of New Mexico Press, 2020.

Bartlett, Lee. "What Is 'Language Poetry'?" *Critical Inquiry* 12, no. 4 (1986): 741–52.

Bernstein, Charles. "Again Eigner and 'The Only World We've Got.'" In Friedlander and Funkhouser, "Larry Eigner Issue," n.p.

———. Interview by Tom Beckett. *Difficulties* 2, no. 1 (1982): 29–42. Eclipse Archive.

Bernstein, Charles, and Bruce Andrews. "Repossessing the Word." In *The L=A=N=G=U=A=G=E Book*, edited by Bruce Andrews and Charles Bernstein, ix–xi. Carbondale: Southern Illinois University Press, 1987.

Bernstein, Leonard. "Forever Beethoven." *Young People's Concerts*, season 11, episode 2. Produced and directed by Roger Englander. Aired January 28, 1968, on CBS.

Berry, Eleanor, and Alan Golding. "Projective Verse." In *The Princeton Encyclopedia of Poetry and Poetics*, 4th ed., edited by Roland Greene, Stephen Cushman, Clare Cavanagh, Jahan Ramazani, and Paul Rouzer, 1109–10. Princeton, NJ: Princeton University Press, 2012.

Blair, Walter, and W. K. Chandler, eds. *Approaches to Poetry*. New York: Appleton-Century-Crofts, 1935.

Bowen, Kevin. "Reclaiming Corman: Cid Corman's Dorchester Past." In "Mass: Raw Poetry from the Commonwealth of Massachusetts," edited by Jim Dunn and Kevin Gallagher, special feature, *Jacket2*, December 24, 2012.

Bukowski, Charles. "Charles Bukowski Speaks Out." Interview by Arnold L. Kaye. *Chicago Literary Times* 2, no. 4 (March 1963). Bukowski.net.

Butterick, George F. *A Guide to the Maximus Poems of Charles Olson*. Berkeley: University of California Press, 1978.

"Cerebral Palsy: What to Look for If You Think Your Child Has Cerebral Palsy." CP Family Network (website). Accessed August 15, 2022.

Charters, Ann. *Olson/Melville: A Study in Affinity*. Berkeley, CA: Oyez Press, 1968.

"Child Neurology Residency Training Program: History." Boston Children's Hospital (website). Accessed August 10, 2022.

Clark, Tom. *Charles Olson: The Allegory of a Poet's Life*. New York: W. W. Norton, 1991.

Cohen, Adam. *Imbeciles: The Supreme Court, American Eugenics, and the Sterilization of Carrie Buck*. New York: Penguin Books, 2017.

Corman, Cid. "Communication: Poetry for Radio." *Poetry* 81, no. 3 (1952): 212–15.

———, ed. *The Gist of Origin, 1951–1971: An Anthology*. New York: Grossman, 1975.

Creeley, Robert. *The Selected Letters of Robert Creeley*. Edited by Rod Smith, Peter Baker, and Kaplan Harris. Berkeley: University of California Press, 2014.

Creeley, Robert, and Larry Eigner. "Selected Correspondence, July–September 1951." *Chicago Review* 58, no. 2 (2014): 50–79.

DenHoed, Andrea. "The Forgotten Lessons of the Eugenics Movement." *New Yorker*, April 27, 2016.

Duncan, Robert. "Ideas of the Meaning of Form." In *Robert Duncan: Collected Essays and Other Prose*, edited by James Maynard, 68–83. Berkeley: University of California Press, 2019.

———. *Roots and Branches*. New York: Charles Scribner's Sons, 1964.

Duncan, Robert, and Denise Levertov. *The Letters of Robert Duncan and Denise Levertov*. Edited by Robert J. Bertholf and Albert Gelpi. Stanford, CA: Stanford University Press, 2004.

Ehrlich, Paul R. *The Population Bomb*. Rev. ed. New York: Ballantine Books, 1971.

Eigner, Larry. "Act." *Origin* 1, no. 9 (1953): 24–31.

———. *Another Time in Fragments*. London: Fulcrum Press, 1967.

———. "Approaching Things / Some Calculus / How figure it / Of Everyday Life Experience." *L=A=N=G=U=A=G=E*, no. 1 (February 1978): n.p. Eclipse Archive.

———. *Areas Lights Heights: Writings, 1954–1989*. Edited by Benjamin Friedlander. New York: Roof Books, 1989.

———. "Around." *Origin* 1, no. 12 (1954): 235–51.

———. "A Bus to Bermuda." *Origin* 1, no. 19 (1956): 62–63.

———. *The Collected Poems of Larry Eigner*. Edited by Curtis Faville and Robert Grenier. 4 vols. Stanford, CA: Stanford University Press, 2010.

———. "The Eye Doctor." *Origin* 1, no. 19 (1956): 61–62.

———. *Farther North*. N.p.: Samuel Charters, 1969.

———. *From the Sustaining Air*. Palma de Mallorca: Divers Press, 1953.

———. "in the blackout." *Goad* 1, no. 3 (1952): 11.

———. "Larry Eigner." Edited by Shelly Andrews. In *Contemporary Authors Autobiography Series*, edited by Joyce Nakamura, vol. 23, 19–62. Detroit: Gale Research, 1996.

———. "Larry Eigner." Interview by Marian Kindel. *Kaleidoscope*, no. 5 (Spring 1982): 10–14.

———. *Larry Eigner: Sacred Materials* (web page). PennSound: Center for Programs in Contemporary Writing, University of Pennsylvania. Accessed August 14, 2022.

———. *Larry Eigner: Selected Poems*. Edited by Samuel Charters and Andrea Wyatt. Berkeley, CA: Oyez Press, 1972.

———. "Letters to the Editor, 1963–69." Edited by George Hart. *PMLA* 131, no. 3 (2016): 774–86.

———. *Look at the Park*. Swampscott, MA: privately printed, 1958.

———. "Omnipresent to Some Extent: Jack Foley's Radio Interview with Larry Eigner, Recorded for KPFA-FM's Poetry Program, March 9, 1994." In L. Eigner, "Larry Eigner," ed. Andrews, 31–38.

———. *On My Eyes: Poems*. Photographs by Harry Callahan. Introduction by Denise Levertov. Highlands, NC: Jargon Press, 1960.

———. *Poems by Laurence Joel Eigner*. Canton, MA: privately printed, 1941.

———. "Quiet." *Origin* 1, no. 10 (1953): 88–91.
———. "Six Letters." Edited by Jennifer Bartlett and George Hart. *Poetry*, December 2014, 250–68.
———. *Things Stirring Together or Far Away*. Los Angeles: Black Sparrow Press, 1974.
———. *The- / Towards Autumn*. Los Angeles: Black Sparrow Press, 1967.
———. "Unpublished Letter to Ina Forster." February 11–20, 1987. Edited by Benjamin Friedlander. In Friedlander and Funkhouser, "Larry Eigner Issue," n.p.
———. "What a Time Distance: The Autobiography." In L. Eigner, *Larry Eigner: Selected Poems*, 111–25.
———. *The World and Its Streets, Places*. Santa Barbara, CA: Black Sparrow Press, 1977.
Eigner, Larry, Richard Eigner, Beverly Eigner, Jack Foley, and Shelly Andrews. "Virtually Enough: Videoconference [. . .] December 29, 1995." In L. Eigner, "Larry Eigner," ed. Andrews, 49–58.
Eigner, Larry, Joseph Guglielmi, and Claude Royet-Journoud. *Larry Eigner Letters (to Joseph Guglielmi and Claude Royet-Journoud)*. Edited by Robert Kocik and Joseph Simas. Paris: Moving Letters Press, 1987.
Eigner, Larry, and Jonathan Williams. *Letters to Jargon: The Correspondence between Larry Eigner and Jonathan Williams*. Edited by Andrew Rippeon. Tuscaloosa: University of Alabama Press, 2019.
Eigner, Richard. "An Origin and a Setting." In L. Eigner, *The Collected Poems of Larry Eigner*, vol. 4, xxxv–xxxvii.
Faas, Ekbert. *Robert Creeley: A Biography*. With Maria Trombacco. Hanover, NH: University Press of New England, 2001.
———. *Young Robert Duncan: Portrait of the Poet as Homosexual in Society*. Santa Barbara, CA: Black Sparrow Press, 1983.
Faville, Curtis, and Robert Grenier. "Larry Eigner Chronology." In L. Eigner, *The Collected Poems of Larry Eigner*, vol. 1, xxi–xxvi.
Ferrini, Henry, dir. *Polis Is This: Charles Olson and the Persistence of Place*. Written by Ken Riaf. Gloucester, MA: Ferrini Productions, 2007. 56 min.
Fleischer, Doris Zames, and Frieda Zames. *The Disability Rights Movement: From Charity to Confrontation*. Updated ed. Philadelphia: Temple University Press, 2011.
Foley, Jack, ed. "Transcript of *Getting It Together: A Film of Larry Eigner, Poet* (1973) with Commentary by Larry Eigner (1989)." In L. Eigner, "Larry Eigner," ed. Andrews, 40–47. Previously published in *Poetry USA*, no. 24 (1992): 2–5.
———. "A Tribute to Larry Eigner." Based on a version read by Jack and Adelle Foley, November 19, 2010. *Poetry Flash*, n.d.
Friedlander, Benjamin. "Larry Eigner (6 August 1926–3 February 1996)."

In *American Poets since World War II*, 6th ser., edited by Joseph Mark Conte, 114–26. Vol. 193 of *Dictionary of Literary Biography*. Detroit: Gale Research, 1998. Electronic Poetry Center, University of Pennsylvania.

Friedlander, Benjamin, and Christopher Funkhouser, eds. "Larry Eigner Issue." Special issue, *Passages: A Technopoetics Journal*, no. 5 (April 1998). Electronic Poetry Center, University of Pennsylvania.

Goode, David, Darryl Hill, Jean Reiss, and William Bronston. *A History and Sociology of the Willowbrook State School*. Washington, DC: American Association on Intellectual and Developmental Disabilities, 2013.

Greene, Dana. *Denise Levertov: A Poet's Life*. Urbana: University of Illinois Press, 2012.

Grenier, Robert. Introduction to L. Eigner, *The Collected Poems of Larry Eigner*, vol. 1, vii–xii.

———. "On Speech." In Silliman, *In the American Tree*, 496–97. Previously published in *This*, no. 1 (1971): n.p.

———. Preface to "Berkeley (1978–1995)." In L. Eigner, *The Collected Poems of Larry Eigner*, vol. 4, 1350.

———. "So Quick Bright Things Come to Confusion." In Friedlander and Funkhouser, "Larry Eigner Issue," n.p.

Hart, George. *Finding the Weight of Things: Larry Eigner's Ecrippoetics*. Tuscaloosa: University of Alabama Press, 2022.

Henny, Leonard M., and Jan Boon, dirs. *Getting It Together: A Film on Larry Eigner, Poet*. Text by Michael F. Podulke. Saint Louis, MO: Films for Social Change, 1973. 16 mm, 18 min.

"History." Pappas Rehabilitation Hospital for Children (formerly Massachusetts Hospital School) (website). Accessed March 2, 2021.

"History of Swampscott." Town of Swampscott, MA (website). Accessed June 6, 2015.

"Interesting Adult Books for Young People, 1955." *Educational Horizons* 34, no. 4 (1956): 314–15.

Jarnot, Lisa. *Robert Duncan: The Ambassador from Venus; A Biography*. Berkeley: University of California Press, 2012.

Kafer, Alison. *Feminist, Queer, Crip*. Bloomington: Indiana University Press, 2013.

Kinnell, Galway. "Seeing and Being." Review of *On My Eyes*, by Larry Eigner. *Poetry* 100, no. 6 (September 1962): 400–403.

Larry Eigner: MATRIX/BERKELEY 159. Exhibition brochure, University of California, Berkeley Art Museum and Pacific Film Archive, June 15–October 15, 1993.

Leed, Jacob, ed. "Robert Creeley and 'The Lititz Review': A Recollection with Letters." *Journal of Modern Literature* 5, no. 2 (1976): 243–59.

Leif, Irving P. *Larry Eigner: A Bibliography of His Works*. Metuchen, NJ: Scarecrow Press, 1989.

Levertov, Denise. Interview by Sybil Estess, October 1977 and March 1978.

In *Conversations with Denise Levertov*, edited by Jewel Spears Brooker, 87–100. Jackson: University Press of Mississippi, 1998.

———. "A Note on Larry Eigner's Poems." In L. Eigner, *On My Eyes: Poems*, n.p. Previously published in *Migrant*, no. 3 (1959): 5–9.

Lord, Elizabeth Evans. *Children Handicapped by Cerebral Palsy: Psychological Factors in Management*. With medical explanation by Bronson Crothers. New York: Commonwealth Fund, 1937.

Mostov, Stephen G. *Immigrant Entrepreneurs: Jews in the Shoe Trades in Lynn, 1885–1945*. [Marblehead, MA]: Jewish Historical Society of the North Shore, 1982.

Newnham, Nicole, and Jim LeBrecht, dirs. *Crip Camp: A Disability Revolution*. Higher Ground Productions, 2020. Film, 108 min.

"NWS Boston—The Great New England Hurricane of 1938." National Weather Service, Boston/Norton MA office (website). Accessed August 10, 2016.

Offit, Paul A. *Vaccinated: One Man's Quest to Defeat the World's Deadliest Diseases*. Washington, DC: Smithsonian Books, 2008.

Olson, Charles. *Letters for Origin, 1950–1956*. Edited by Albert Glover. New York: Cape Goliard Press, 1970.

———. *The Maximus Poems*. Edited by George F. Butterick. Berkeley: University of California Press, 1983.

———. *Maximus to Gloucester: Letters and Poems of Charles Olson to the Editor of the Gloucester Daily Times, 1962–1969*. Edited by Peter Anastas. Gloucester: Ten Pound Island Books, 1992.

———. "Projective Verse." In *Collected Prose: Charles Olson*, edited by Donald Allen and Benjamin Friedlander, 239–49. Berkeley: University of California Press, 1997. First published as "Projective Verse vs. the Non-Projective," *Poetry New York*, no. 3 (1950): 13–22.

———. *Selected Letters: Charles Olson*. Edited by Ralph Maud. Berkeley: University of California Press, 2001.

———. *The Special View of History*. Edited and introduced by Ann Charters. Berkeley, CA: Oyez Press, 1970.

Olson, Charles, and Cid Corman. *Charles Olson & Cid Corman: Complete Correspondence, 1950–1964*. Edited by George Evans. Vol. 1. Orono, ME: National Poetry Foundation, 1987.

Paul, Sherman. *Olson's Push: Origin, Black Mountain, and Recent American Poetry*. Baton Rouge: Louisiana State University Press, 1978.

Rifkin, Libbie. "Making It / New: Institutionalizing Postwar Avant-Gardes." *Poetics Today* 21, no. 1 (2000): 129–50.

Rogers, Gladys Gage, and Leah C. Thomas. *New Pathways for Children with Cerebral Palsy*. New York: Macmillan, 1935.

Roubaud, Jacques, and Michel Deguy, eds. *Vingt poètes américains*. [Paris]: Gallimard, 1980.

Silliman, Ron, ed. *In the American Tree*. Orno, ME: National Poetry Foundation, 1986.

Sullivan, J. W. N. *Beethoven: His Spiritual Development*. New York: Alfred A. Knopf, 1936.
Von Hallberg, Robert. *Charles Olson: The Scholar's Art*. Cambridge, MA: Harvard University Press, 1978.
Williams, William Carlos. Introduction to *The Wedge* (1944). In *The Collected Poems of William Carlos Williams*, edited by Christopher MacGowan, vol. 2, *1939–1962*, 53–55. New York: New Directions, 1991.
———. *Paterson*. Rev. ed. Edited by Christopher MacGowan. New York: New Directions, 1995.
Zukofsky, Louis. "An Objective." In *Prepositions: The Collected Critical Essays of Louis Zukofsky*, exp. ed., 12–18. Berkeley: University of California Press, 1981.

Index

Ableism, xi, 56
Action poetique, 104
Adele (Eigner's housemate, last name unknown), 122
Age of Louis XIV, The, 129
Air the Trees, 104
Albers, Anni, 63
Albers, Josef, 63
Alcheringa, 130
Allen, Donald, 40, 73, 97, 107, 108
Allison, Larry, 44
Alta Bates Hospital, 135
American Civil Liberties Union, 39
American Museum of Natural History, 128
Americans with Disabilities Act, 42
Amiri Baraka (LeRoi Jones), xiv, 44
Andrews, Bruce, 130
Angel Island, 123
Ann Arbor, Michigan, 42
Another Time in Fragments, 99–103
Areas Lights Heights, 134
ars poetica, 39
Artaud, Antonin, 85
Atlantic Ocean, 7–8
Atlantis, 69
Audubon, John James, 89
Auster, Paul, xv, 101, 116
Austro-Hungarian Empire, 8

Bakersfield, California, 69
bar mitzvah, x, 10, 21, 26, 110
Bartlett, Lee, xv, 130
Bates College, 10
Bay of Pigs, 90
Beethoven, Ludwig Van, 88
Bentley, Eric, 72
Berkeley Poetry Conference, 107
Berkeley University Art Museum, 135
Berkeley Zen Center, 122
Bern Porter Books, 91
Bernstein, Charles, xiii, 128, 131
Bernstein, Leonard, 87
Berryman, John, 49
Birds of America, 89
birth control, 72, 90
Bishop, Elizabeth, 54
Black Mountain College, 63, 66, 69, 91
Black Mountain Review, 92
Black Sparrow Press, ix, 104, 114
Blair, Walter, 27
blank verse, 30
Bly, Robert, 128
Bolinas, California, 133
Borash, Sam, 109–110, 113, 129
Boston Latin School, 29
Boston, Massachusetts, 8–9
Boston's North Shore, 7–8
Bowles, Paul, 114

Brandeis University, 29, 51
Breath of Once Live Things in the Field with Poe, The, 105
bris, 12
Broughton, James, 99
Brown, Christy, 54–55
Brownian Motion 97, 100
Buck, Carrie, 15
Buck, Paul, 116
Buck v. Bell, 16
Bukowski, Charles, 104
Bunting, Basil, 103
Butterick, George F., 110–111

Cage, John, 63
Calistoga, California, 127
Call Me Ishmael, 39
Cambridge Artists' Cooperative, 110, 114
Cambridge, Massachusetts, 72, 112
Camel Coming, 103
Camp Jabberwocky, 107
Camp Jened, 43, 57, 72, 119
Canada, 7
Candid Camera, 84
Canton, Massachusetts, 23
Cape Ann Trail, 65
Cape Verde Islands, 7
Carson, Rachel, 89
Catholicism, 90
Catskills, 43
Cerebral palsy, x, xv, 11–12, 16–18, 23–24
Chandler, W. K., 27
Charters, Sam, 58, 114
Child Life Magazine, 58
Children Handicapped by Cerebral Palsy, 16
Children's Hospital Boston, 16
Ciardi, John, 95
City Light's Press, 99, 101
Civil Rights, 43, 90
Clark University, 39
Cohen, Barney, 12

Cohen, Bee, 12
composition by field, 39
Concord, Massachusetts, 110
Confessional Poetry, x, 56, 99, 112, 115
Connelly, James B., 65
Contact Press, 92
Coolidge, Clark, 130
Corman, Cid, x, xi, xiv, xv, 29–36, 38, 40–43, 50–51, 53, 55, 57, 59–60, 62, 64, 68, 71–72, 85, 89–92, 93, 95–95
Corman, Shizumi, 123
Cornerstone House, 118, 120, 127
Corso, Gregory, 108
Cowell Hospital, 111
Creeley, Ann 52
Creeley, Bobbie, 104
Creeley, Penelope, 128
Creeley, Robert, x, ix, 29–30, 33–36, 38–39, 43, 47, 49, 50–54, 64–69, 71, 84, 97–98, 100–103, 107, 112, 114, 128–130
crip time, 86
Crothers, Bronson (doctor), 16
cryosurgery, 96
Cunningham, Merce, 63
Cummings, E. E., 32, 40

Dahlberg, Edward, 63
Dartmouth College, 29, 42
de Kooning, Elaine, 63
Dewey, John, 63
Dickey, James, 99
disability justice, xiv, 56
Divers Press, 52
Dorn, Edward, 64, 70
Doubleday Press, 102–103
Double Image, The, 68
Dublin, Ireland, 55
Duncan, Robert, 30, 64, 68–73, 91, 94, 99, 102–103, 106–109, 130, 133
Durant, Will, 129

East Village, 128
Ehrlich, Paul, 89

INDEX / 173

Eigner, Annie, 10
Eigner, Bessie, x, xv, 8, 10, 12–14, 16, 19, 21, 23, 26–27, 42–43, 47, 56, 58–61, 72, 94, 107, 109–110, 113, 116–117, 119, 121, 123, 129, 135–136
Eigner, Beverly, 109, 118–119, 122, 127, 134–135
Eigner, Celia, 9
Eigner, Edwin, 109, 113
Eigner, Israel, 9
Eigner, Janet, 42, 107–109, 114, 127, 129
Eigner, Joseph, xv, 11, 13, 43, 58, 107–108, 115
Eigner, Joseph, Sr., 8, 9
Eigner, Richard, xv, 9, 13–14, 20, 23, 29, 32, 42, 65, 92, 108, 115, 117, 118, 122–123, 125, 127, 134–135
El Corno Emplumado, 101
Eliot, T. S., 39, 68
Enslin, Theodore, 94
Eshlman, Clayton, 99
eugenics, 15
Europe, 9
Evergreen Review, 73
Everson, William, xiii

Farther North, 115
Ferlingetti, Lawrence, xiv, 92
Ferrini, Vincent, 49, 59, 61, 92, 110
"Figure of Outward," 67
Films for Social Change, 115
Fischer, Norman, 122–123
fishing industry, 7
Foley, Adelle, 134
Foley, Jack, 97, 128, 134–135
forced sterilization, 15, 89–90
Foreign Language Information Service, 39
France, 53
Franconia College in New Hampshire, 113–114
free verse, 27–28
French (language), 32, 94, 104, 107

French schoolchildren, 104
Friedlander, Ben, 134
Friendship, Maine, xiv, 71–71
From the Sustaining Air, 34, 52, 98, 136
Frost, Robert, x, 32–33
Frumkin, Ezra, 124–125
Frumkin, Kathleen, xi, 122, 125, 133
Fulbright, 53, 59
Fulcrum Press, 92, 103
Fuller, Buckminster, 63

Galway, Kinnell, 98
Gathering of the Tribes / Human Be-In (1967), 109
George Washington handpress, 49
Gerard Malanga, xiv, 101
Getting It Together, 115
Ginsberg, Allen, 104
Gitin, David, 109
Gloucester Chamber of Commerce, 65
Gloucester Daily Times, 90
Gloucester, Massachusetts, 7, 28, 49, 59, 61, 65, 67, 92, 110–111
Goad, 51
Golden Gate Park, 109
Goldman, Arnold, 24, 60
Gordon, Cairnie, 95
Grand Central Station, 99
Graves, Robert, 52
"Great Man," 64, 67
Great New England Hurricane, 7
Green Integer, 132
Grenier, Amy, 124–125
Grenier, Robert (Bob), ix, xiii, 59, 87, 105, 110, 112–114. 117, 122, 128, 130–134
Grolier Poetry Book Shop, 95, 112
Groundwork, 103
Grove Press, 73
Guggenheim grant, 26, 39
Guglielmi, Joseph, 104

Hall, Donald, 99
Halloween, 21, 95

174 / INDEX

Hentoff, Nat, 30
Harper's Bazaar, 39
Harrison, Lou, 63
Hart, George, vx, xvii, 87, 89, 130
Harvard University, ix, 39, 54, 95, 112
Harvard Yard, 95
Hawthorne, Nathaniel, 9
Heijinian, Lyn, 122
Henny, Leonard, 115–116
Hentoff, Nat, 30
Heumann, Judy, 43
His Spiritual Development, 88
Howdy Doody, 84
Hollo, Anselm, 128
Holman, Bob, 116
Holmes, Oliver Wendell, Jr., 15
Hopwood Award, 30
"hospital poems," 54, 99
House of the Seven Gables, The, 9

immediacy and force, 40, 90, 131, 135
independent living movement, 118
Inferno, 96
institutionalization, 15
In the American Tree, 132
Iowa City, Iowa, 112
Iowa Writers' Workshop, 112
Irving, Layton, 102

Jack Benny Program, The, 84
Jack Kerouac festival, 108
Jackson, Laura Riding, 52
Japan, 59, 92, 107, 129
Japantown, 108
Jargon Press Society, xi, 53, 64, 91–91, 94–95
Jewish Pale (settlement), 135–136
Johnson, Anna, 120–121
Johnson, Ronald, 128
Joyce, James, 29

Kaiser, Betty, 111
Kelly, Robert, 114
Kennedy, John F., 90

Kings Canyon, 127
Kinnell, Galway, 98
Kline, Franz, 63
Kocik, Robert, 127
Kooning, Willem de, 63
KPFA, 135
Kruger, Barbara, 135
Kyger, Joanne, 128

La Loma Avenue, 120
Language poets, ix, 130–132, 135
Larry Blake's, 128
Laughlin, James, 102
Lawrence, D. H., 114
Lawrence, Jacob, 63
Leed, Jacob, 49
left-hand margin, 35, 41
Levertoff, Paul, 68
Levertov, Denise, xi, xiv, 44, 64, 68–69, 91, 95, 97, 102, 108, 115, 131
Life Studies, 54
Light, 129
Lincoln Center, 87
Lithuania, 9
Lititz Review, 49–50
Littleton, New Hampshire, 34
London, England, 103–104
Longfellow, Robert Louis, 21, 25, 108
Look at the Park, 95
Lord, Elizabeth Evans, 16
Lord's Weary Castle, 54
Lorts, Jack, 87
Lowell, Massachusetts, 108
Lowell, Robert, 54, 56
Lynn Hospital, 11
Lynn, Massachusetts, 110, YMCA, 110

Malanga, Gerard, 101
Mallorca, Spain, 52
Mandel, Tom, 123
Maps 4, 111
Marblehead, Massachusetts, 110, 116
Marek (polish filmmaker, last name unknown), 134

Marshall, Edward, 70
Martha's Vineyard, 107
Martin, John, xiv, 104, 114
Massachusetts General Baker Memorial Hospital, 54, 96
Matrix 159, 135
Maud, Ralph, 111
Maximus of Tyre, 64
Maximus Poems, The, 38–39, 64–67, 110
Maya culture, 64
McClure, Michael, 114
McFarland, Arthur, xiv, 71–72
McGee Avenue, 125–126, 128, 130, 134
Meltzer, David, 109
Melville, Herman, 38–39
Messerli, Doug, 132
Metropolitan Museum, 85
Miles, Josephine, 114
Miller, Henry, 69
Miller, Vassar, 54
Minneapolis, Minnesota, 112
Miracle Worker, The, 115
Mitchell, Goodman, 68–69, 71–72
Moby Dick, 29
Modern Language Association Annual Convention, 128
Montgomery, Stuart, 103
Moore, Marianne, 32, 49
Morris, Richard (editor), 50
Morris, Richard (writer), 129
Muir Woods, 109
Murder Talk, 72
Mussolini, Benito, 64
My Left Foot, 55

National Book Award, 54
National Poetry Day, 110
New American Poetry, 43, 73, 91, 107, 130
New College of California, 135
New Deal, 39
New Directions, 63, 101–102, 104
New England, 8, 10
New Jersey, 65

New York Philharmonic, 88
New York Public Library, 113
New York City, 9
Newman, Dorothy, 64
Nin, Anaïs, 69
Norman, Dorothy, 64
North & South, 54
Not Fit for a Queen, 116
Notley, Alice, 128
Nowak, Monica, 134

Ocean House Hotel, 8
Olson, Charles, x–xi, xiii–xv, 7, 30, 33, 38–40, 49, 51, 56, 61, 63–67, 69, 71, 90–93, 95, 102, 107–108, 110, 111–112, 114–117, 129–131, 7
Olson, Charlie (Charles Olson's son), 111
Olson, Katherine (Katy), 39
Olson's Push, 111
On My Eyes, xi, 91, 95, 98–99, 103, 107, 116
On Speech, 130
Oppen, George, 123
Oppen, Mary, 123
Origin Magazine, 51–51, 93, 101–102, 129
Orlovsky, Peter, 108
Oyez (publisher), 115

Pacific Film Archive, 135
Palmer, Michael, 128
Parkinson, Thomas, 107
Paterson, 33, 64–65
Paterson, New Jersey, 64–65
Paterson Industrial Commission, 65
Paul, Sherman, 111
pidyon haben, 12
Pine Street, 13
Playwright as Thinker, The, 72
Poetry Center, San Francisco State University, 72, 123
Poetry (magazine), 98
Poetry New York, 39
Poets' Theatre, 72

176 / INDEX

Poland, 9
Polansky, Bessie, 9
Polansky, Tamara, 9
polis, 7
Polis is This, 110
Population Bomb, The, 89
Portents, 115
Port of Gloucester, The, 65
poultry, 34
Pound, Ezra, 30, 32, 39, 49–50, 64, 71, 131
Pound, Dorothy, 50
Projective Verse, 39–41, 56, 66, 71, 116, 130
Puerto Rico, 7
Pulitzer Prize, 54

Randall, Margaret, xiv, 101
Rauschenberg, Robert, 63
Raworth, Tom, 128
Red Sox, 85
Renaissance, The, 129
Revere Beach, 8
Rexroth, Kenneth, 109
Rhodesia, 103
Rice, John Andrew, 63
Rimbaud, Arthur, 32
Robert, Edward, 118
Robin Hood, 18
Robin Hood's Barn, 15, 18
Robinson, Kit, 122
Rock, John, 90
Rock Pool Farm, 34
Roethke, Theodore, 103
Rogers, Gladys Gage, 17
Rolling Quads, 118
Roof Books, 132
Roosevelt, Franklin Delano, 39
Roxbury, Massachusetts, 29
Royet-Journoud, Claude, 104
Ruscha, Jay, 125

St. Elizabeths Hospital, 64
St. Louis, Missouri, 42, 107–109, 114

Salem, Massachusetts, 9
Salem High School, 9
Salem Hospital, 116
San Francisco Bay Area, xi, 42
San Francisco Renaissance, 69
Sartre, John Paul, 73
Saturday Evening Post, 33, 90
Schribners, 103
Schwartz, Harvey, 51
Scientific American, 129
Seizen Press, 53
Seymour-Smith, Martin, 52
Sherry, James, 132
Silent Spring, 89
Silliman, Ron, 121–122, 127, 130–132
social Darwinism, 15
Sorbonne, 53
Souster, Raymond, 92
South Shore Cerebral Palsy, 107
"Special View of History, A," 67
Spenser, Edmund, 27
Spicer, Jack, xiv, 102, 108
Spooner-Jones, Beatrice, 69
State University New York, Buffalo, 107, 110–111
Stein, Gertrude, 32, 135
Steinbeck, John, 28
Stevens, Wallace, 49
Stevenson, Robert Louis, 19, 25
St. Mark's Poetry Project, 128
Sullivan, J.W.N., 88
Swampscott, Massachusetts, 7–9, 13, 24, 29–30, 44, 67, 72, 87, 92–93, 107–109, 113, 117, 129
Swampscott High School, 27
Swampscott Public Library, 87
Swampscotta, 27
Swanee Review, 99
Symmes, Edwin and Minnehaha, 69
Synder, Gary, 95, 128

Taggert, John, 111
Tallman, Warren, 128
Tassajara Zen Mountain Center, 128

Teague, Bob, 114
Temple Beth El, 10
Theatre of Cruelty, 85
Theosophists, 69
The- / Towards Autumn, 104
Things Stirring Together or Far Away, 114
This, 113
This Is Poetry (radio show), 71
Thomas, Dylan, 29
Thomas, Leah Coleman, 18
Thomas J. Dodd Research Center, 111, 113
Three Lives, 135
Through, Plain, 45
Totem Press, 92
Truman, Harry, 39
Tufts University, 112–113
Tuumba Press, 132
28 Fort Square, 66
23 Bates Road, 8–9, 13, 24, 26
Twombly, Cy, 63

UMass, Salem, 113
Under the Sea Wind, 89
United Cerebral Palsy, 119
United Cerebral Palsy Telethon, 119
United States of Poetry, The, 116
University of California, Berkeley, 69, 114, 118
University of California, Davis, 133
University of Chicago, 27, 30
University of Connecticut, 111
University of Kansas, 113
University of Michigan, 30
US Weather Bureau, 7

Vingt poetes americains, 104

Wake, 94
Washington, D.C., 39, 64
Washington University, Saint Louis, 42, 114–115
Watch House Point, 111
Water Field Free School, 110
Weil, Jim, xiv, 113, 116
Wesleyan University, 38
Whalen, Phillip, 95, 128
Wieners, John, 64, 67, 102, 108–109
Wilcock, Constance (Connie), 39
Wild Dog, 108
Wilderness Project, 127
Williams, Jonathan, 117
Williams, Richard (doctor), 11
Williams, William Carlos, 33, 39–40, 49–50, 53, 56, 64–65, 86, 90, 98, 102, 106
Willowbrook, 16
Windows/Walls/Yard/Ways, 105
WMEX, 29
Wordsworthian, 130
World and Its Streets, Places, The, 114
World War 1, 9
Wyatt, Andrea, 108

Yeats, William Butler, 30
Yosemite Park, 127
Young People's Concerts, 87
Yucatán, 64

Zukofsky, Cecilia, 95
Zukofsky, Louis, 33, 93, 95